"Luna" by artist Chiarra Huges-Mba.

"In *Ludic Ubuntu Ethics*, Professor Mechthild Nagel artfully brings together diverse understandings and practices of justice and criminal justice in ways that move us out of the tangle of justifications and denial that underlie and perpetuate the historical and contemporary myth of (criminal) justice and the righteousness of punishment and control and oppression through governmental institutions, uniquely including child protective services. Professor Nagel untangles the threads of power and violations of human dignity embedded in current justice beliefs and surveillance practices built around various conceptions of 'the other'. In doing so, Nagel makes a place for alternative indigenous practices and processes that move our thinking from 'controlling and punishing the other' to 'recognizing and strengthening us', to preventing behaviors traditionally met with punishment (so, no need for the carceral state), and embodying an ethic and view of community built on understanding human existence and experience (behavior and its meaning) and support for human dignity."

Lucien X. Lombardo, *Professor Emeritus,*
Old Dominion University, Norfolk, VA

Ludic Ubuntu Ethics

Ludic Ubuntu Ethics: Decolonizing Justice develops a positive peace vision, taking a bold look at African and Indigenous justice practices and proposes new relational justice models.

'Ubuntu' signifies shared humanity, presenting us a sociocentric perspective of life that is immensely helpful in rethinking the relation of offender and victim. In this book, Nagel introduces a new theoretical liberation model—ludic Ubuntu ethics—to showcase five different justice conceptions through a psychosocial lens, allowing for a contrasting analysis of negative Ubuntu (e.g., through shaming and separation) toward positive Ubuntu (e.g., mediation, healing circles, and practices that no longer rely on punishment). Providing a novel perspective on penal abolitionism, the volume draws on precolonial (pre-carceral) Indigenous justice perspectives and Black feminism, using discourse analysis and a constructivist approach to justice theory. Nagel also introduces readers to a post-secular turn by taking seriously the spiritual dimensions of healing from harm and highlighting the community's response.

Spanning disciplinary boundaries and aimed at readers seeking to understand how to move beyond reintegrative shaming and restorative justice theories, the volume will engage scholars of criminology, philosophy and law, and more specifically penal abolitionism, social ethics, peace studies, African studies, critical legal studies, and human rights. It will also be of great interest to practitioners and activists in restorative justice, mediation, social work, and performance studies.

Mechthild Nagel is Professor of Philosophy & Africana Studies and Director of the Center for Ethics, Peace, and Social Justice at the State University of New York, College at Cortland, USA. Dr. Nagel is also a visiting professor at Fulda University of Applied Sciences, Germany, and Pompeu Fabra University, Barcelona, Spain. She is author of eight books. Her most recent co-edited volume is *Contesting Carceral Logic: Towards Abolitionist Futures* (Routledge, 2022). She writes on ethics of play, critical justice studies, global feminist studies, and African philosophy. Dr. Nagel is founder and editor-in-chief of the online feminist journal *Wagadu: A Journal of Transnational Women's and Gender Studies*.

Routledge Studies in Penal Abolition and Transformative Justice

Michael J. Coyle and David Scott

The *Routledge Studies in Penal Abolition and Transformative Justice* book series provides the leading publishing location for literature that both reflects key abolitionist thought and helps to set the agenda for local and global abolitionist ideas and interventions. It fosters research that works toward the systemic and systematic dismantling of penal structures and processes, and toward social living that is grounded in relationships that consider the needs of all. This international book series seeks contributions from all around the world (east, north, south, and west) that both engages and furthers abolitionist and transformative practice, study, politics and theory. It welcomes work that examines abolition and transformative justice empirically, theoretically, historically, culturally, spatially, or rhetorically, as well as books that are situated within or at the interstices of critiques of ableism, capitalism, hetero-normativity, militarism, patriarchy, state power, racism, settler colonialism, and xenophobia.

https://www.routledge.com/Routledge-Studies-in-Penal-Abolition-and-Transformative-Justice/book-series/PATJ#:~:text=About%20the%20Series,global%20abolitionist%20ideas%20and%20interventions.

Building Abolition: Decarceration and Social Justice
Kelly Struthers Montford and Chloë Taylor

Contesting Carceral Logic: Towards Abolitionist Futures
Michael J Coyle and Mechthild Nagel

Ludic Ubuntu Ethics: Decolonizing Justice
Mechthild Nagel

Ludic Ubuntu Ethics

Decolonizing Justice

Mechthild Nagel

Routledge
Taylor & Francis Group
LONDON AND NEW YORK

First published 2023
by Routledge
4 Park Square, Milton Park, Abingdon, Oxon OX14 4RN

and by Routledge
605 Third Avenue, New York, NY 10158

Routledge is an imprint of the Taylor & Francis Group, an informa business

British Library Cataloguing-in-Publication Data
A catalogue record for this book is available from the British Library

ISBN: 978-0-367-51822-6 (hbk)
ISBN: 978-0-367-51825-7 (pbk)
ISBN: 978-1-003-05532-7 (ebk)

DOI: 10.4324/9781003055327

Typeset in Times New Roman
by Newgen Publishing UK

Contents

List of Figures viii
List of Tables ix
Foreword x
Preface xiii
Acknowledgments xvii

Introduction 1

1 Just-us or Justice as Vengeance 25

2 Policing Families: The Many-Headed Hydra of Surveillance 66

3 The Context of Insurrectionist Justice: Resisting the Looting of Black Bodies 88

4 Between *Ressentiment* and Forgiveness: Transitional Justice in Rwanda and South Africa 110

5 A Transformative Justice Paradigm: A Call for Ludic Ubuntu Justice 130

Bibliography 195
Index 218

Figures

0.0	"Luna" by artist Chiarra Huges-Mba	i
0.1	"Spirit Dancer" by artist R. Patrick Brown	2
0.2	Illustrations of the five levels of ludic Ubuntu	11
1.1	Photo taken after Hurricane Niklas, at TV Station RTL2, Munich, Germany, March 2015	56
1.2	Prison demolition and composting services	63
5.1	"Miklat"	156
5.2	Instruction for "The Scapegoat"	157
5.3	"The Circle of Courage," portrayed by Lakota artist George Bluebird	165
5.4	The Western Box of Punishment	165
5.5	A Ludic Ubuntu Circle of Courage	166

Tables

5.1 Restorative Justice vs. Transformative Ludic Ubuntu Justice 142
5.2 Newtonian physics (RJ) meets quantum physics (TJ) 143

Foreword

Mechthild Nagel, a social philosopher and prison abolitionist activist of long-standing, has written an avant-garde book that deploys the growing transcolonial constructivist approach in African philosophy to open new vistas for Afrotopia and the world, especially, in the sphere of justice, on a transcultural scale.

African philosophy in the past three decades or so has been undergoing changes in response to the circumstances in which it finds itself and out of which it emerges (especially the existential and epistemic concerns of Africanity). It was sufficient in the decades of the anti-colonial independence struggle and its immediate aftermath to expose and affirm traditional African thought as many ethno-philosophers did. However, from the 1990s or so onward, post-independence disappointments, the challenges of development, lingering subalternity, and the alienation-negativity complex of the African posed the deep existential challenge that I have described as the neo-black problem, building on Franz Fanon's notion of the existential challenge of the black problem.

The project of a new, vibrant, vigorous, attractive Africanity, explored in Afrotopia by Felwine Sarr and by others, myself inclusive, requires an approach that is both deeply self-reflexive and creative (constructivist) because it has to build a new transcolonial and transcultural African identity out of the hybridized world of contemporaneous Africa. Modern Africa has been exposed to, and imbued with, ideas and practices from the Euro-American North, and increasingly from Asia, as well as from her insertion into the global economic system within which she must struggle for economic sustenance and prosperity. Consequently, the scholarly approaches of anti-colonialism (and its essentialist self-affirmation) and postcolonialism and its mainly deconstructive critiques of lingering colonialism and production of negative knowledge, as Emmanuel Chukwudi Eze says, are not enough to generate a developmentarian movement with clear objectives and trajectories, capable of bringing positive freedom and self-capacitation. This can only be done by Africans themselves and Africanists like Professor Nagel committed to transcolonial projects, especially constructivist, positive knowledge-generating types.

Nagel's book speaks to specific issues of practical justice, but also in the processes, it shows a good deal of the strong points of transcoloniality as an Afrotopia, namely, interculturality, constructivism, heterosis (hybrid vigor), etc., as well as the promise of the transcolonial perspective, which is born of the realization that the colonial deposit is too deep and embedded to be scrubbed or disentangled entirely (hence the futility of radical decoloniality), and more importantly, the realization that the knowledge power that made colonization possible (and which continues to make coloniality possible) has to be appropriated via rational evaluation, as Kwasi Wiredu says; adapted, transformed, and defanged as much as possible and necessary via Africanist creativity/constructivism and deployed for the greater good of the colonized and humanity in general. And, further, that this process of forging a synthesis out of the opposition of traditional culture and received colonial modernity, and transcending the limitations of the colonial cultural borders and African traditions, is essentially a constructive process involving creativity in all spheres, especially in the spheres of knowledge, aesthetics, values, organization, and technology. In other words, the uplifting, border-transcending power is surging Africanist creativity, expressed in and through Africanists that find inspiration, building blocks, and generative elan in a synthesis of traditional African cultures, the colonial deposit, and global philosophical resources. In this way, and for these reasons, transcoloniality and Afro-constructivism are not limited to Africanists on the African continent, or biological Africans, rather, it is open to Africanists from all over the world—people who study Africa, reflect on her, above all embrace her by owning her cultural and environmental heritages, adding value to these heritages through creativity and constructivism in which the African context serves as inspiration, guide (means), or end in terms of developmentarian transformations for the good of Africans and humanity generally.

This is the process of creating the post-dependence African identity, which depend, principally, not on heritage but on creative self-presentation or self-manifestation, in which agents (especially contemporaneous Africanists in this case) put the stamp of their African life value in the manifest works of their creativity and constructivism, thereby presenting the identity and meaning of Africanity to the world of today. Post-dependence Africanity cannot depend on either the traditional African precolonial heritage or the colonial deposit or heritage—because heritage is but one source of identity, and a rather static, often stultifying aspect if care is not taken, that is, if not leavened by positive creative dynamism.

Further, transcoloniality does not simply have a constructivist developmentarian side, as seen above, it also has its therapeutic aspects. Its power of transcending colonial borders is a positivizing power that brings healing to the negativity complex of the African as well as colonizers of all trips by opening a path to bracketing and quarantining imperialist instincts and intentions in humans through the affirmation of interculturality, and the positive creative and integrative creations of other cultures thereby concretely affirming recognition and dignity of others as well enriching the human culture-scape through heterosis. In this way, transcoloniality brings healing to all in need of it in the colonizer and colonized populations, among jailers and the jailed, brutalizers and victims by transcending cultural borders and limitations and transforming peoples and attitudes.

Fortuitously, Mechthild Nagel is steeped in interculturality, being German in origin, African by marriage, and American by citizenship and residence. In this book, which is a culmination of her research and reflections over many years, she has been able to draw on her intercultural experiences to embark on the transcolonial constructivist venture of opening new vistas of understandings and possibilities in the fields of justice, especially restorative and transformative justice, based on Ubuntu, which envisages a world without jails and its brutalizing, dehumanizing effects on both jailers and the jailed. "Can we imagine an un-policed life," she asks; a world without jails?

Professor Nagel sets out to show how this is possible with her theory of ludic Ubuntu which explores stages of the existence and refinement of the notion of Ubuntu in the thoughts and practices of individuals and collective agents. She identifies five levels in ascending order, beginning with the stage of rage and retribution (vengeful justice); inducement of guilt and shame (shaming justice); expression of moral indignation and outrage (insurrectionist justice); transmutation of rage into forgiveness, to allow space for positive discovery or restoration of the humanity of offenders (restorative justice); and fully ludic levels of loving life as it is, staying interconnected, lightheartedness (transformative justice).

A very important aspect of her approach is its suspicion, indeed rejection, of the coercive modern state and its carceral powers. The state as presently constituted is a vehicle for the expression of negative justice in theory and practice, which is often masked by elaborate theoretical justifications and appeals to reason, she argues. So, ludic Ubuntu, initially, and especially in its higher levels, is to be worked out and developed by individuals and communities as counterpoises to the state and its onslaught of negative practical justices of retribution, incarceration, infliction of physical and psychological pain, and brutalization of society. And success in this is seen as a prelude to the complete abolition of the contemporary penal and carceral system and the arrival of a more human system of restorative and transformative justice. Mechthild Nagel has written a very remarkable book, not simply in terms of the breath of her research and factual details but even more importantly in the boldness of her vision and the challenge it presents to the judicial status quo. It would be a rewarding read for those interested in justice, including in its intersection with psychological and social development of individuals and communities.

Joseph C. A. Agbakoba
Professor of Philosophy
University of Nigeria

Preface

This book brings together several unlikely readers together, specifically play theoreticians and practitioners and critical criminal justice theorists and activists. As a social philosopher and critic of the prison-industrial complex, I want to engage an audience that is ready to engage with abolitionist solutions, and my humble hope is that we are globally ready for a praxis philosophy dedicated to converting walls into bridges. I draw inspiration from imprisoned intellectuals, African philosophers, and from Black feminists writing in the African diaspora who reinforce my view that "much good comes from Africa." Decolonizing social philosophy and critical justice studies are of upmost importance. It means to be in respectful dialogue with those who are rightfully suspicious of increased attention to Ubuntu and other Indigenous virtue ethics and metaphysical principles. The charge of academic tourism still rings true (Zeleza, 1983).

Viviane Saleh-Hanna's critiques Western penal abolitionists who think their critique is just an academic exercise or that harm is a social construction. She charges that they remain silent on the criminalizing system's hidden pillars of violence: racism, imperialism, and patriarchy, in short R.I.P. Furthermore, they have been oblivious to how these systems of oppression have impacted Indigenous and Black communities as the carceral tentacles kidnapped their loved ones (2017, p. 430). As someone who writes as an outsider (white, cisgender) and has not been personally impacted by the penal system, but who has visited loved ones in US jails and prisons and taught philosophy in US and German prisons, I have witnessed the effects of direct harm of the penal system and the specter of colonialism and chattel slavery. As I visited with a Malian former political prisoner and judges, their first words to me were always: "Prisons were a French colonial invention." To them, both the elites and the persecuted, it is crystal clear that colonialism and racism are part and parcel of the penal system. Given these different experiences and encounters, I have been driven to speak with, rather than for the oppressed as local activist, or when I have organized conferences and write on the prison regimes. Here I take my cue from philosopher Linda Martín Alcoff's (1991/1992) important essay "The Problem of Speaking for Others."

We live in difficult times—ecological calamities, threats of nuclear proliferation, and a slow death of the world's oceanic life due to Fukushima's unmitigated nuclear spillage. Never has the world seen such massive refugee movement, totaling over 60 million people at a time, yet Steven Pinker (2011) has declared our species has never been more peaceful in the era of the Anthropocene. However, we can ask with freedom fighters Assata Shakur, Mumia Abu-Jamal, Frederick Douglass, Steve Biko, Harriet Tubman, and Óscar Arnulfo Romero y Galdámez what is the meaning of peace for those who fight the neocolonial state, hetero-patriarchy, chattel slavery, and penal democracy?

The ludic Ubuntu model came to me during the birth of the (global) Black Lives Matter movement in Ferguson, Missouri, 2014. The execution of an unarmed Black teenager, Michael Brown, and his grieving mother looking onto the lifeless body of her beloved son for four and a half hours were too much to bear for the public, and moral outrage turned into insurrectionist rage against the unjust, racist police system. Today, popular books are published on abolishing the police (Vitale, 2017), which would have been considered 'fringe' before August 2014. Even criminology experts, with much less radical tenor, seem to be sensitized to publish books that rein in police power, with suggestive titles: *Policing Encounters with Vulnerability* (Asquith et al., 2017), noting the vulnerability approach as one of the biggest challenges for contemporary policing, and the editors' targeted audience is police academies. Two decades ago, Gabriella Pedicelli, author of *When Police Kill: Police Use of Force in Montreal and Toronto* (1998), faced continuing surveillance, if not harassment, from an irate Montreal police force. Pedicelli wrote as an insider since she underwent training in the police academy before her academic studies. Authors who indict state violence often do so at personal cost from the prison cell to the ivory tower. In the end, Vanessa Thompson (2022) reminds us, we need a postcolonial feminist critique of policing and with decolonial concepts of justice focus on community accountability praxis empowering anti-police and anti-prison groups and alliances across marginalized peoples.

A Note on Method

Taking my cue from philosopher Joseph Agbakoba (2019), I hold that the ludic Ubuntu model is constructivist. Agbakoba explains that such method borrows the Hegelian insight of creating synthetic connections of opposite couples: anti-colonial political impulses oppose the colonial ideological onslaught and produce hybrid constructs within the postcolony. I am also mindful that there is no such thing as a postcolonial condition across the continent. Some nation-states like Kenya went from a colonial to neocolonial governance, where those who violently resisted the colonial oppressors were installed as rulers and immediately began to jail political dissenters—in those prisons built by the British (cf. Asumah, 2007).

I chose the construct ludic Ubuntu to signal a hybrid, constructivist commitment toward African Indigenous ethics and a nod to communal play. Living on unceded territory of the Onondaga Nation, I am not pretending to give an authentic account of Indigenous wisdom traditions, especially given that I am only schooled in various colonial languages. It is noteworthy that every African scholar writes that Ubuntu is immensely difficult to translate into English (cf. Tutu, 1999; Ramose, 2003). By drawing on the metaphor of the tilted maze, a favorite toy of my childhood, I suggest that life and its trickster Other are spiraling between Ma'at and Justitia, creating possibilities for reimagining disorder, dis-ease, chaos, and order, alignment, resonance. The model outlined in five phases gives us a description of human thought, emotion, and action while it makes normative claims about justice. This is presented as perspectivalism, suggesting that some perspectives are better than others.

A Note on Justice

At the World Social Forum at Puerto Alegre, Brazil, the late Nobel Prize Winner, José Saramago, told the following story:

> In a village near Florence, Italy, in 800 A.D., church bells were rung whenever someone died. One day the bells rang and everyone returned from the fields. They looked to see who had died, but all were present. They asked the bell-ringer, "Who has died?" He said: "Justice has died".
>
> (Babbitt, 2017)

During a hurricane, a statute of blind-folded Lady Justice, Justitia, was damaged; precisely put, it was perfectly decapitated by a fallen tree. One might say, with Chinua Achebe, a trickster spirit, an arm of justice delivered an arrow of God. Clearly, justice apparati the world over must be troubled by social philosophers (and others). Ringing the bell to mourn its death is an apt gesture, but it cannot remain there. We urgently need to attend to our urge of melancholia, by organizing against an imperial, arrogant form of injustice and construct something the dispossessed, the subaltern, the giddy multitude truly want. It is here where I turn to the tricksters of history with whom I grew up in West Germany: the mythic Till Eulenspiegel who spooks the church and philistines in medieval Europe, whose name indicates the play with owls (symbol of wisdom) and mirror (mirage). Shapeshifting is part of the divine game, be it the Coyote of the Dineh Nation, Matieng (Botswana), Ogo (Dogon, Mali), and Isis coming to the rescue of her brother Osiris of Egyptian lore. I appeal to the outcasts or Zomnians (with a nod to James Scott, 2010) who cast a die for another moral order that may appear chaotic or unruly yet is born of compassion for vulnerable life. Can we imagine an unpoliced life?

Neo-slave narratives help stir up the human imagination and trigger moral outrage, in a similar vein of "cry freedom" as the 19th-century predecessors, i.e., slave narratives which spoke to the demand of radical abolition of chattel slavery (James, 2005a). I am inspired by neo-slave narratives to provoke all of us (white readers included) to take a leap of faith and embark on the arduous path of transformative justice. It is important to continue to trouble the waters of criminal 'justice.' One of the ways my analysis is different from social theorists such as Angela Y. Davis or Joy James, as I dwell on the abolitionist framework of my ludic Ubuntu model of justice. While I also critique the current system, it is important to engage with Indigenous models which inform transformational justice praxis.

Oddly enough, abolitionist thinking does not arrive naturally to most Western educated people. This book is indebted and dedicated to Tiyo Attallah Salah-El, master teacher, composer, jazz musician, and thought leader. Over 20 years ago, he began to inspire me to adopt the path of abolitionism. Writing from the prison cell, it also took him quite a bit of time and education to understand and to advocate for penal abolition. In his widely cited essay "A Call for the Abolition of Prisons" (2007), he rallies for turning prisons into healing centers and even for retraining guards as social workers. Of course, his guards did not treat him kindly when he started publishing the CAP newsletter (brazenly titled, Coalition for the Abolition of Prisons) and trashed his prize possessions, including his saxophone and typewriter, and they destroyed his archives. They also refused to let him access to his own autobiography (2006), published with the help of his friend Howard Zinn. Such is the list of forbidden books of Pennsylvania. Thanks to the dedication of Lois Ahrens, founder of the organization The Real Cost of Prisons, Tiyo's collected work, including thousands of letters, is archived in the W.E.B. Du Bois Library of my alma mater, the University of Massachusetts at Amherst. Some of the letters are curated by Tiyo's friend Paul Alan Smith in *Pen Pals* (2020). Sentenced to life imprisonment, Tiyo joined the ancestors on my birthday in June 2018. Celebrating his life, Lois worked with saxophonist and composer Felipe Salles to release a collection, titled *Tiyo's Songs of Life* (2022), on the anniversary of his passing. Tiyo, Presente!

Acknowledgments

This project began with an invited talk to an Ethics of Play conference in Prague, Czech Republic, and has come full circle with a research residence in Prague at the Department of Continental Philosophy, Academy of Sciences. My gratitude goes to Alice Kouvoba and Petr Urban for reengaging me with play theory and their kind invitation to a hospitable environment to write drafts of several chapters. I wish to acknowledge that the bulk of this book was written with the support of the Czech Science Foundation Grant No. 16–00994Y "Performativity in Philosophy: Contexts, Methods, Implications" at the Institute of Philosophy, Czech Academy of Sciences in Prague. The ludic aspects of my work were deepened at another keynote of Philosophy at Play at the University of Gloucester. My special thanks go to conference organizers Wendy Russell and Malcolm MacLean. Prior institutional support during a sabbatical leave was provided by Shelly Feldman, Director of Feminist, Gender, and Sexualities Studies, Cornell University, and Peter van der Veer, Director of the Max Planck Institute for the Study of Religious and Ethnic Diversity, Göttingen, Germany.

Over the years, my work has greatly benefited from weekly seminar series participations as senior fellow at the Institute for African Development, Cornell University, at the invitation of Director Muna Ndulo. SUNY Cortland has been very supportive granting research leaves, and I am especially grateful to colleagues in the Philosophy and Africana Studies Departments.

My work has benefited from comments from seminar participants at the Institute of Philosophy, specifically from Alice Koubová, Petr Urban, Zuzana Uhde, and Marek Hrubec, as well as from commentator Drucilla Cornell at the African Studies Association, Chicago, participants at the New York African Studies Association, Buffalo, and at the African Philosophy Conference, University of Vienna. Many ICOPA conferences have provided an intellectual home for penal abolitionist inspiration as well as Radical Philosophy Conferences. I want to highlight some of the groups and organizations and their members who have engaged with my work.

Sofphia group: Margaret McLaren (respondent), Ann Ferguson, Richard Schmitt, Karsten Struhl, Nanette Funk, Kathy Russell, and Don Hanover.

MPI Göttingen: Peter Kankonde, Sabine Mohamed, Mark Geraghty, and Nathaniel Roberts.

Lichtenberg-Kolleg in Göttingen: Franziska Dübgen, Demetrius Eudell, and Sheela Saravanan.

Dignity and Humiliation Studies group: Tony Gaskew, Janet Gerson, Evelin Lindner, Linda Hartling, Michael Britton, Martha Eddy, Michael Perlin, Brian D'Agostino, Michelle Brenner, Candace Mama, and Sultan Somjee.

Central New York prison research group: David Connelly, Lucien Lombardo, Herbert Thomas, and Ruth Thomas Suh.

NYS Jail Justice collective: William G. Martin, Sue Ruoff, Mardi Crawford, Naomi Jaffe, Thomas Kerney, Tarik Grand, Rozann Greco, Jim Murphy, Joshua Price, and Nick Malinowski.

United Voices of Cortland: Kathie Arnold, Lee Miller, Pam Jenkins, Joaquin Santana Lira, Patricia Roiger, Andrew Pragacz, Brendan McQuade, Brendan McGovern, John Howard, John Bondi, and Vera partners Insha Rahman and Sandra van den Heuvel.

Sophia's Garden Institute teaching and research colleagues: Chea Snyder, Margaret Gichuru, Lin Lin, Rhiannon Maton, Katarina Silvestri, Lisa Czirr, Michelle LoGerfo, Shufang Shi, Joseph Rayle, Susan Kilonzo, Ross Borden, and John Suarez.

Andrew Fitz-Gibbon read this entire book and provided valuable feedback. Lesley Teitelbaum's probing questions and analysis inspired a rethinking of the ludic Ubuntu model. S.M. Rodriguez guided me carefully through a reevaluation of the restorative and transformative justice frameworks. Joseph C.A. Agbakoba's encouragement and methodological guidance has been extremely helpful. I benefited greatly from Lucien Lombardo's and Michael Coyle's careful reading of several chapters. Alliyah Dookie, Jacob Wright, Hal Pepinsky, and Bernhard Rohrbacher provided helpful feedback on a chapter. I am grateful to Kassim Kone for providing translation assistance with interviews conducted in Mali (2002).

Research and travel were funded by a grant from SUNY Cortland (2002–2003). Dean Mattingly provided generous funding for the artwork by R. Patrick Brown and Chiarra Hughes-Mba.

Alba Katherine Nagel Gonzàlez sketched some of the original models, which were expanded upon by SUNY Cortland Graphic Design student Virginia Alvisi with the assistance of Prof. Szilvia Kadas.

The following friends, students, and colleagues have provided inspiration and support on my own meandering journey to transformative justice: Thomas Adajian, Brendon Absher, Bakhtiar Ahmed, Eric Agee, Lois Ahrens, Anatole Anton, Erika Arthur, Seth N. Asumah, Muriel Bell, Liat Ben-Moshe, Doug Bentley, Erik Bitterbaum, Keri Blakinger, Patrick Brown, Susan Buechler, Antonio Cabrales, Peter Castro, Helen Codd, Sheila Cohen, Andrew Cutrofello, J. Soffiyah Elijah, Rona Epstein, Emmanuel Chukwudi Eze, Candice Delmas, Nikita Dhawan, Aminata Diabate, Torry Dickerson, Joe Donnermeyer, Kathryn Faso, Chris Garces, Ruth Gilmore, Anke Graness, Sabine Groote, Cristina Güerri Ferrández, Paz Frances,

Thomas Galli, Lisa Guenther, Herbert Haines, Devonya Havis, Gudrun Hentges, Volker Hinnenkamp, Patricia Huntington, Joy A. James, Phillip Johnson, Ibipo Johnston-Anumonwo, Richard Jones, Klaus Jünschke, Albert Kasanda, Kamala Kempadoo, James Kilgore, Marcel Kitissou, Vikki Law, Lin Lin, Daniel Loick, Miriam Mack, Jason Mallory, Candice Mama, James Manos, Cathy Marston, Tiffany McFadden, Patricia McFadden, Eduardo Mendieta, Thaddeus Metz, Erin Miles Cloud, Lee Miller, Maryfaith Miller, Charles Mills, Lehlohonolo Moagi, Greg Moses, Mmatshilo Motsei, Micere Mugo, Parvati Nair, Monty Neill, Anthony Nocella, Chinyere Oparah, Richard Peterson, Justin Piché, Gayle Presbey, Ute Ritz-Deutch, Ron Rocco, Viviane Saleh-Hanna, Barry Schecter, Rashad Shabazz, Joel Shatzky, Nancy Smithner, Elizabeth V. Spelman, Robert Spitzer, Justyna Staszczak, Shari Stone-Mediatore, Henry Steck, Pedro Tabernsky, John Marc Taylor, Lisa Tessman, Vanessa Thompson, My'Shell Titus, Roser Tresserras, Clivia von Devitz, Thomas Wartenberg, Alexei Waters, Cynthia Willett, Jacob Wright, Emmanuel X, Adiam Zerisenai, Tiantian Zheng, and Howard Zinn. And I also wish to honor all my students in adult and youth prisons in the United States and Germany who inspired me to stay the course.

Finally, I wish to thank the series editors Michael J. Coyle and David Scott for their enthusiastic support of the project and Routledge for their editorial guidance.

My global family has been supportive in many ways, including my sister Rosemarie Nagel who secured a teaching and research position at Pompeu Fabra University, Barcelona, where I exchanged ideas with many economists. Specifically, I thank Gert Cornelissen, Antoni Bosch-Domènech, Andreu Mas-Colell, Luigi Pascali, Robin M. Hogardt, Ralph Meisenzahl, law professor Elena Larrauri Pijoan, and Helena Rosa Trias.

This long-term project flourished with the loving encouragement of Loni and David Saunders and my partner Philip R. Otieno.

Introduction

The White Mountain Apache Spirit Dancer

Spirit Dancer is the depiction of a ceremony performed by the White Mountain Apache that I had the honor to attend. The lessons and takeaways from that experience were so profound that I was driven to illustrate what I had witnessed.

In this ceremony as in life, there are many things that can "swallow" an unwary soul. Demons of greed, hatred, jealousy, envy, deceit, fear, doubt, and indecision. These are dark energies and not what we want to allow to take root in our lives. They will stop success in its tracks and derail happiness.

When the hood was placed over the dancer's head and a blindfold placed over his eyes, it was clear that physical eyesight was not needed in this ceremony just as physical eyes aren't used to see and identify the demons. When we live in the light, it holds back the darkness and renders it helpless. A thousand candles can illuminate a room and cause the darkness to retreat, but a thousand miles of surrounding darkness cannot cause a single candle to be extinguished, such is the power of light.

Spirit Dancer is about the light! It is also about trust. Trust that when you do the right thing at the right time for the right reason you can always be confident in your journey. You know the way intuitively and you can trust the knowledge of right and wrong inherent within, but more importantly, you can rely on guidance from the Creator to move you through life to a rich and abundant end.

My ancestors say, "Be careful where you place your feet because the faces of Seven Generations are looking up at you." This speaks to the fact that everything we do has an effect on seven generations that follow. Walk in a good way upon the Earth and be aware that you walk in the light!

R. Patrick Brown, Mohawk Artist, is known as Tawennihake (pronounced Dahwanehage, which means in English, "Making Path") (Figure 0.1). Brown is a tribal member of the St. Regis band of Mohawks. He specializes in drawing Indian people and nature in his artwork. He is a traditional storyteller, author, pipe carrier, and ceremony leader.

DOI: 10.4324/9781003055327-1

Figure 0.1 "Spirit Dancer" by artist R. Patrick Brown.
Source: Printed with permission.

Introduction: Troubling Western Justice[1]

> The artistry of ethics is in the last analysis unanalyzable—it is a gift. This gift in its regenerative force offers an alternative to J.S. Mill's pity for the lower pleasures of the pig and the common fool who would never know the higher life of reason. Logos can only judge. Eros is a festival.
>
> (*Interspecies Ethics*, Cynthia Willett)

> Everything is sacred. [...] And at the seed of everything is relations. That anyone is really separate from anyone else or anything that is happening in the world is an illusion. [...] This is true for all the kingdoms of nature, as well as for humanity. Every time a tree is felled in the Amazon, a tree in Africa responds.
>
> (The International Council of Thirteen Indigenous Grandmothers)

> Ubuntu is very difficult to render into a Western language. It speaks to the very essence of being human. When you want to give high praise to someone we say, "*Yu, u Nobuntu*"; he or she has Ubuntu. This means that they are generous, hospitable, friendly, caring and compassionate.

> They share what they have. It also means that my humanity is caught up, is inextricably bound up, in theirs. We belong in a bundle of life. We say, "a person is a person through other people" (in Xhosa *Ubuntu ungamntu ngabanye abantu* and in Zulu *Umuntu ngumuntu ngabanye*). I am human because I belong, I participate, and I share.
>
> (*No Future without Forgiveness*, Desmond Tutu)

During the constitutional deliberations envisioning a democratic New South Africa, the concept Ubuntu emerged in order to celebrate a relational justice ideal. While short-lived as a constitutional promise—it disappeared from the final constitutional document—it has enjoyed a growing popularity thanks to Archbishop Desmond Tutu's prophetic appeal to Ubuntu during the Truth and Reconciliation Commission (TRC) and is even used as justification for the abolition of the death penalty. An Ubuntu ethics refers to a Southern African concept of intersubjectivity: one is interpellated into the human community by recognizing others as human (Tutu, 1999). As such, it invites the acknowledgment that we are all interconnected. In the context of apartheid on trial, it means that perpetrators and victims' lives and fates are inextricably intertwined. It encourages us to move from vindictiveness to forgiveness. I want to add the element of play into this pan-African ethics, as I have come to realize that through playfulness (e.g., therapeutic play, child's play, playing across cultures, cooperative play, and trickster play), we develop an ethical capability toward a transformational relational justice mode. With a cooperative playful attitude, I trouble an agonistic justice paradigm.

A ludic Ubuntu ethics encompasses the variations of justice at play, a dance of interdependence and recognition and its others. Ludically speaking, we move from conflict-laden, competitive encounters of agonism to those displaying a non-agonistic, cooperative spirit of social justice. In the field of legal justice, the question is how we move from win–lose propositions to cooperative win–win 'verdicts'? Ubuntu stands in as a signifier for relational justice that is prevalent in many peaceful, Indigenous societies. The 'we' whom I appeal to are those interested in troubling criminal justice administration as we know it—at least, troubling the system which has been based on the Western carceral regime for over 200 years. Ludic Ubuntu also challenges the ideological underpinnings of the possessive individualist, autonomous subject wedded to a settler colonial paradigm.

Agonist Play in the Western Punishment Theater

Vengefulness, disguised as retributive punishment, pervades the current criminal legal system. In fact, its warlike ethos has found legitimation by Western philosophers who have also created other masks such as deterrence, reform, and incapacitation to deflect from the 'eye for an eye' maxim of retribution. More recently, during the era of mass incarceration, some have gone as far as defending torture (Kershner, 2012; Steinhoff; 2013). Less controversially, ethicists and political theorists have endorsed shame (Deonna, Rodogno, & Teroni, 2012). I argue that none of these theories hold much promise, except in justifying a logic of revenge. One might also suggest that they are the workings of "decorative justice" (Cheliotis, 2014); those who take on the mantle of justice hide behind 'just us.' Zarathustra mocks the virtuous who boast that they are "just" (*gerecht*) when they actually mean they are "revenged" (*gerächt*) (Nietzsche, 1993, p. 117). The Western procedural justice system is also implicated in a colonial settler ideology as a deadly dance of victor's justice (Agozino, 2003; Saleh-Hanna, 2008). How else does one comprehend the fact that people of color tend to be preselected for carceral punishment in the United States (or other settler colonial regimes) at disproportional rates?

Even the theory of incapacitation of a wrongdoer demands a prison cell, which becomes the focal point of violence foisted upon the indolent body condemned to 'do time.' Prisons are hardly equipped to restore humanity. Imprisoned intellectuals give us a timeless glimpse into the gross inhumanity of jail, fostering more mental illness in the vast majority of prisoners. Such are the collateral effects of incarceration, which has faced opposition by a growing multitude of people (from prison reformers to restorative justice advocates and penal abolitionists) to mount a strong critique against the behemoth of the Prison Industrial Complex worldwide. What I argue for is that it is time to bring a playful element into the abolitionist movement that is 'working hard' to overthrow the shackles of the carceral system.

So here I take exception with the Western philosophical tradition that assumes that a playful attitude is mostly agonistic and is to be celebrated as authentic play (Nagel, 1998; 2002). The traditional criminal law system rides on agonism and hierarchical order. In the courtyard of Lady Justice, lawyers for the perpetrator (the defense) face off with the lawyers for the victims (the prosecution, standing in for 'the people' or 'the crown'). Their fencing game is performed in front of a decorated judge (in robes, seated upon an elevated 'throne'), who, like Plato's charioteer, manages the game. Meanwhile, both parties who really need to talk with each other, i.e., the accused and the aggrieved and their families, get silenced in this showdown of rhetorical bravado between legal experts.

Rather than tarrying with the negative, I suggest another way out of agonism by taking us to Indigenous justice practices of the Global South. I am joining a growing group of philosophers and others who are inspired by an Ubuntu ethics (Ramose, 2002; Bhengu, 2006; Eze, 2010; Cornell & Muvangua, 2012; Cornell, 2014; Gade, 2017; Metz, 2022). While some of them look at its promises in the field of jurisprudence and criminal justice, they do not engage with Ubuntu from a penal abolitionist stance. Specifically, I argue for a complete re-evaluation of the judgmental gaze: what colonial juridical discourses consider backwards and uncivilized is in fact highly advanced and demonstrates a social intelligence that may in the end bury the Western carceral box altogether.

Ubuntu—A Forward-Looking Relational Ethics

The most promising aspect of Ubuntu is that it can serve as a powerful antidote to Western punishment theories. Metz outlines that Africans tend to resort to forward-looking rationales for punishment, for spiritual and practical reasons (Metz, 2007, p. 325). As part of the forward-looking justification, an Ubuntu ethics favors restitution over revenge. Arguably, restorative justice as reparative justice is actually both forward and backward looking, focusing on the victim's harm in moral and material terms (Roth-Arriaza, 2004). This is what Desmond Tutu strategically deployed in the TRC. He admonished victims and survivors of apartheid violence to forgive as well as encouraged offenders to deliver genuine, credible apologies for their atrocities and crimes against humanity. It is worth quoting Archbishop Tutu's explanation of Ubuntu at length because it shows how he conveys the concept to a global audience who may not understand ancestor reverence or the interrelatedness of all living beings. He makes the connection with Christian morality by appealing to *agape*, reciprocity, and resilience in this famous passage:

> [Ubuntu] is the essence of being human. It speaks of the fact that my humanity is caught up and is inextricably bound up in yours. I am human because I belong. It speaks about wholeness, it speaks about compassion. A person with ubuntu is welcoming, hospitable, warm and generous, willing to share. Such people are open and available to others, willing to be vulnerable, affirming of others, do not feel threatened that others are able and good, for they have a proper self-assurance that comes from knowing that they belong in a greater whole. They know that they are diminished when others are humiliated, diminished when others are oppressed, diminished when others are treated as if they were less than who they are. The quality of ubuntu gives people resilience, enabling them to survive and emerge still human despite all efforts to dehumanise them.
>
> (Tutu, 1999, pp. 34–5)

During the TRC hearings, Tutu forcefully guided victims toward a forgiving stance, which, according to some critics, was perhaps a bit too forceful. What I want to add is the following perspective: if it is the case that my humanity is connected to another person (for example, an offender), then I have a bit of cruelty, sadism, and lack of love in me as well, and, as such, I can relate to the action of the offender/oppressor. Tutu's description of the importance of Ubuntu also powerfully speaks to the resilience of African peoples having suffered through hundreds of years of systematic dehumanization (Maafa, imperialism, and (neo)colonialism).

Yvonne Mokgoro defines Ubuntu as "one of those things that you recognize when you see it" (1998, p. 15). In a way it is similar to the Yiddish commendation of someone as a *mensch*, as someone who is generous and compassionate toward others. Mokgoro, however, warns that Ubuntu should not be deployed as a personal defense tool, say, in a criminal case.

> [It serves as] an opportunity given to all to survive under the protection of the order of the communal entity; communalism which emphasises group solidarity and interests generally, and all rules which sustain it, as opposed to individual interests, with its likely utility in building a sense of national unity among South Africans; the conciliatory character of the adjudication process which aims to restore peace and harmony between members rather than the adversarial approach which emphasises retribution and seems repressive.
>
> (Mokgoro 1998, p. 20)

An Ubuntu ethics serves as a general guiding principle for the pursuit of restorative justice. Another framing concept is the witnessing dance.

Psychologist Pumla Gobodo-Madikizela describes the careful process she chose to bring together victims' families, meeting with them an entire week prior to their scheduled meeting with a Black policeman who acknowledged killing their beloved kin. She also counseled the policeman for a few hours. She calls this encounter "making public spaces intimate" and supports research claiming that remorse paradoxically triggers woundedness (feelings of pain) in the perpetrator, which leads toward ethical recognition of the other (the victim) in a "witnessing dance":

> This responsibility towards the other invites victims and villains to share in the common idiom of humanity. It also provides an opportunity for reflection on the historical circumstances which dangle like the sword of Damocles, threatening to divide groups and individuals within the larger society in its efforts to heal after a violent and hateful past.
>
> This woundedness, and the remorse that animates it, draws the perpetrator into a relationship with the victim. It is the recognition of the victim's pain that awakens remorse in the perpetrator, and it is remorse that lays the ground for the emergence of empathic sensibilities expressed on the part of the victim towards the perpetrator.
>
> (Gobodo-Madikizela, 2008, p. 177)

There is no command here given to the perpetrator ('you must become accountable') or to the victim: ('you must forgive'). A witnessing dance follows its own dynamics rather than being scripted from outside experts or a community that demands certain behavior.

By contrast, restorative justice expert John Braithwaite notes that asking victims to forgive or offenders to apologize is wrong, if not cruel. Forgiveness and apology "are gifts that have no power as gifts when they are demanded" and they only play a role in restorative justice as "emerging values" that might arise out of the process (2011, p. 349). Tutu's overreach then consists in making these values into "constraining values" that have to be part of any successful restorative process. Braithwaite clarifies that constraining values deal with respectful listening, non-domination, empowerment, equal concern for all stakeholders, and freedom from racist and sexist oppression, appealability, and accountability (p. 348). Yet, what does "accountability" mean and who gets to appeal a verdict? My concern is that this traditional (Western) practice of taking stock of debt is still steeped in practices of shaming. In an earlier work, Braithwaite quite forcefully argues for the "reintegrative power of shaming" (1989). The neutral language of "stakeholders" masks that restorative justice ideology carries the torch for victims' rights. I wonder what happens to those who do not appreciate the stern guidance of reintegrative shaming? Odera Oruka takes a different approach, reviewing themes of securitization and harmony from a macroscopic perspective akin to one of Ubuntu.

> Social harmony is brought about in a society when one group is not made to feel too superior or inferior to another; when the gap between the rich and the poor is insignificant or felt by the citizens to be so; when society is free of hatred (racial, tribal, communal, etc.); when moral fanaticism is discouraged and both men and women feel free to solve their moral problems; and when the government in such a society aims at eradicating the criminal forces rather than sending the criminals to prison. Such a society is one in which there is little or nothing at all of class conflict. It is a society in which the law aims not only at social security but also, and this is more important, at social harmony. It should be noticed that social harmony implies social security but not vice-versa.
>
> (Oruka, 1976, p. 29)

Seeking security without social harmony is precarious, while social harmony already guarantees safety for all.

South African philosopher Mogobe Ramose claims that the Zulu concept of Ubuntu pulsates through all of African philosophy. It is based on a proverb "*umuntu ngumuntu ngabantu.*" The translation is only approximate: One is only human through other humans. According to Ramose,

> [T]he English language does not exhaust the meaning of this maxim or aphorism, it may nonetheless be construed to mean that to be a human be-ing is to affirm one's humanity by recognizing the humanity of others and, on that basis, establish humane relations with them. *Ubuntu* understood as be-ing human (human-ness): a humane respectful, and polite attitude towards others constitutes the core meaning of this aphorism.
>
> (2003, p. 231)

The witnessing dance of recognition, of relational obligations, showcases the sociocentric and community-centric characteristics of Ubuntu. "We come into a world obligated to others and these others are obligated to us, to support us in finding our way to becoming a unique and singular person" (Cornell, 2014, p. 135). Such generous feelings and ethical comportment benefit from a lived experience of nested care. An innate knowledge of belonging to family, clan, village, and community creates a sense of freedom and autonomy that is quite different from the Western social ontology, which prizes individuation as freedom *from* the community.

Where does the prison experiment in an Ubuntu ethics fit in? Well, very badly, indeed. How does one become human inside a total institution? Prison is precisely the location where one ruptures interrelatedness. Stripped of personal goods and personhood, a prisoner becomes a number and loses bodily integrity. His hair may be cut against his wishes. Her body is violated through strip searches; she may endure forced sterilization; forced abortion; and, if allowed to continue the pregnancy, she will have her newborn child ripped away from her, suffering natal alienation. And everybody is issued uniforms, which include ill-fitting bras for women and losing the right to religious dress. Trans women are put in male prisons and lose their right to hormone therapy. Shackles on joints (hands and feet) hamper movement, which is especially dangerous for pregnant prisoners and those with disabilities—one has become chattel, a good to be moved around at will, tampered with; a human has been reduced to being property of the state. Even those prison regimes that treat the incarcerated humanely are unable to reconstitute an Ubuntu ethics. Once a person is cordoned off, put into a uniform, etc., she loses the right to dignity. Philip Zimbardo's study, the Stanford prison experiment (1971), makes it very clear that the guarantors of dignity, the guards, assume an authoritarian stance that becomes sadistic. Putting a person into a uniform almost automatically transforms the 'guard' into a monster. A Malian prison warden proudly shared that visitors would not be able to distinguish prisoners from guards because nobody wears a uniform. He explained that it is his way on humanizing the prison. The prison was built by the French colonial power in the center of the capital Bamako, as a sign of terror and keeping the population in check (Nagel, 2007).

African critics of the prison understand very well that the prison was an invention of colonial powers. It had nothing to do with a benign ideology of reforming the wayward people. As Ngũgĩ wa Thiong'o writes in his novel *Petals of Blood*, the white man came to the village to build a church and a police station. Decolonizing the mind means to understand the ideological connections between the colonial religion and the jailhouse. Christian religion obfuscated the colonial project of land grabbing and social control by preaching love and acceptance of the *Osu*, as portrayed in Achebe's novels about Igbo culture. However, Joseph Agbakoba (2019) presents another productive reading of *Things Fall Apart* (Achebe, 1959): Christian missionaries preach not only an alternative divinity that troubles the oracle and malediction of the Osu, i.e., outcast people, but gives critics of the oracle a rationalistic alternative. This is to recognize that not all (local) cultural values are life affirming; living in the postcolony also creates opportunities to create transcolonial, transcultural values, while still validating the Igbo sociocentric model of justice (Agbakoba, 2019, pp. 356–9).

Musings about a Ludic Ubuntu or: What Does Play Have to Do with It?

What if the virtuous were indeed motivated by relational, sociocentric justice or just compassion, according to an Ubuntu ethics? Indeed, in my model, I argue for a normative perspective, encouraging us to move from the lowest level of seeking vengeance to the highest level of child's play that we may listen to the play of the wave that moves beyond base, exacting, rationalist games of shaming to the life-affirming interplay of care and comforting the wounded child in us.

This book brings together my earlier interest in philosophical play theory with my recent investigations in criminal justice ethics. My term 'ludic Ubuntu' expresses this convergence: humans are playful beings, and the Southern Africa ethics of *Ubuntu* reminds us that the principle of shared humanity critical to forgiveness and reconciliation. Humans are essentially playful. Furthermore, as ethical players, we recognize our interrelatedness and shared purpose—in other words, Ubuntu. Human play represents a shift from the weightiness of overcoming tragic conflict through punishment, and we are called to express our shared humanity with compassion.

I propose the term 'ludic Ubuntu' to develop further an aesthetic and perspectival ethics which makes coherent and legible the level of engagement with conflict (or resolution) at each of the five phases. It is a dynamic model which is inspired by Elizabeth Kübler-Ross's (1969) five stages of grieving: denial, anger, bargaining, depression, and acceptance. My ludic Ubuntu model reorders Kübler-Ross's descriptive stage theory. In my version, I draw on Indigenous and Western justice models for the five phases in the following descriptive and normative schema:

1 Rage and retribution; feeling of separation from the community (vengeful justice)
2 Facing shame, *ressentiment*, guilt (shaming justice)
3 Expressing moral outrage (insurrectionist justice)
4 Transforming rage into forgiveness (restorative justice)
5 Loving what is; laughter, comic relief; being interconnected (transformative justice)

The five phases/faces of ludic Ubuntu also approximate Nietzsche's (1993) metamorphoses of spirit, from the spirit of gravity, the camel, burdened with the ghosts of the past, of the graveness of the crime and its thirst for revenge. The second transformation is the emergence of the free-spirited lion: one questions tradition and customs and is ready to break out of the cage of convention. Finally, the third is that of the child, content with playing at draughts, blissfully forgetting the burden of the past and letting go of any judgment. There are no villains or heroes in the play-space (*Spielraum*) of child's play except for those who emerge as imaginary ones. Hans-Georg Gadamer famously states: "The player belongs to the play" (1986, p. 26). However, I argue that such play is not a solitary endeavor: one is embedded in community, in nested care, in knowing that one does belong. One's fate and fortunes are interwoven with the ancestors and the not-yet-born.

An Ubuntu ethics is concerned with transformative justice. (1) It is about making amends and making whole; having compassion and focusing on healing forces; prizing harmony by participating in goodwill practices in the community, especially working with those who are socially displaced. As a dignitarian ethics, it also is concerned with (2) a politics of recognition and solidarity, that is, challenging racism, sexism, and state violence (neoliberalism, settler colonialism, etc.). Simply put, it draws our collective attention to certain harmful practices, which deny dignity and bodily, emotional, and spiritual integrity. An ethic of solidarity bolsters a being-in-harmony, which promotes and is supported by "transparency, voluntariness, trust, and mutual aid" (Metz, 2010, p. 268). In a ludic Ubuntu ethics, belonging is a key constitutive part. To recognize the other as human is to say 'you belong to us, and we will have no part in excluding you from our ways.' It is a constitutive part of the healing circle or Medicine Wheel of the Lakota nation (Brendtro, Brokenleg, & Van Bockern, 2019). I argue that belonging is actually more foundational than the other three values (mastery, independence, and generosity). Another way of putting it is that attachment is only engendered through a sense of belonging, which is critical to the self's well-being. Thus, saying 'you no longer belong to our group'—sending someone into exile, which brought certain biological death due to the unimaginable experience of social exclusion—used to be regarded the ultimate (extreme) form of punishment. Social death normalized by the carceral regime must be troubled.

A post-humanistic Ubuntu ethic encompasses an ecological horizon—the Web of Life. As the Cherokee note that animals and humans are part of one family and thus part of one ecosystem (Mooney, 1902/2014). Ramose (2003) argues that Ubuntu is really a "be-ing becoming." Being and change are enfolded into one, not representing a contradiction or "chaos" (p. 231). On the contrary, it symbolizes harmony (of all relations including with one's environment) and thus represents an ecological ethics or interspecies ethics (Willett, 2014). This Ubuntu dance of interrelatedness Ramose calls a rheomode (from the Greek rheo = to flow) (p. 233). It is illustrated in the model of ludic Ubuntu (Figure 0.2). The image showcases a tilted maze to show the trials and tribulations of staying on course at the highest level (5) while the temptation is always there to be pulled into the depths of despair at any given moment, depicted by a path or line that becomes a snake. It is not the case that one can simply play in the realms of positive peace-making and forego feelings of rage, revenge, justified anger, or resentment, especially,

Figure 0.2 Illustrations of the five levels of ludic Ubuntu.
Source: Designed by Virginia Alvisi.

when triggered by shame. Shame is a powerful motivator to propel us into self-harming or lashing out at others (Thomas, 2006).

The maze is flanked by two figures of justice, Egyptian goddess Ma'at and Roman persona of Justitia. Ma'at, birthed from chaos and breath, also embodies abstract principles such as truth, justice, integrity, and holding an ankh, signifying life. Later depictions include scales weighing a human soul (heart) against a feather leading to the mortal's judgment in the afterlife. The hieroglyphs of goddess and snake are the same. Ma'at is also depicted in kneeling position spreading her winged arms. Doing right by Ma'at is to enjoy her divine substance (bread) and to be in harmony with the human community (Sjöö & Mor, 1987; Naydler, 1996). By contrast, Lady Justice towers over her subjects facing their verdict in front of courthouses. In later renderings, her eyes bound, she holds a sword in her right hand and balances empty scales in her left. She stands her ground, feet firmly planted on top of a snake, a symbol not of wisdom but of sin or transgression. Ma'at represents the divine sage, the cosmic ur-mother, while Lady Justice's depiction exudes a stance ready for civic warfare in the courtroom, executing swift verdicts, while crushing the sacred serpent, demoted to a representation of sin. Ma'at presents us the opportunity to envision a heart-based justice which reverberates through all kinship and communal relations and beyond. Justitia might as well be weighing the human's brain, as it represents the mind's ego-centric worldview without regard of relations and the social environment. A just-desert mindset's major flaws are unforgiveness and lack of compassion.

My main interest here is to show individual or organized-group interaction with state power. At most of the levels, the focus is on addressing the state's impunity. At level 5, it will be difficult to give examples of notable state actions. Perhaps, former President Nelson Mandela stands out for assuming a quasi-messianic stature being credited for averting civil war in South Africa and also for giving blanket amnesty to women prisoners who are mothers. But there are other ludic moments of disarming state actors and others, such as Pumla Gobodo-Madikizela's evocative "witnessing dance" between those responsible for harm or violence and those victimized by such actions.

Among the Apache, the Ga'an Dance is of great significance for major ceremonies and healing conflict. It is a spiritual masked ritual performed by five men. Patrick Brown's artistic rendition (cf. Figure 0.1), included in the beginning of this introductory chapter, showcases what is at stake. Masked dancers carry wooden swords and move to the beat of the drums and songs without ever touching each other. They develop a second sight to perform this powerful dance and purify the community of evil spirits, powerfully depicted as fanged entities in Brown's artwork. Their head mask is not to be confused with the blindfold of Lady Justice. The Apache Ga'an Dance is a cooperative play of humans communing with the spirit world. One of them assumes the role of a messenger who usually wears a white mask and has the dual function of a trickster, bringing healing through comic relief and laughter as well as scaring the evil spirits away (Second Face, n.d.).

Each of the levels of the ludic Ubuntu model will be discussed separately in the following chapters and in what follows, I will provide a synopsis.

At **level 1**, cruel games of coercion and social control are typical but often disguised in moral persuasion. From the bench, the judge bellows at the defendant that they ought to show remorse, or else. Condemnation is certain, and harsh judgment is assured. As the German Supreme Court presiding judge, Thomas Fischer, reveals in an interview: "criminal law is always meant to target the underclass" (Sack, 2018). Whether the judgment is politically motivated but 'legal' or extra-legal as were lynchings of Black people during the brutal Jim Crow era, revenge is the state-sanctioned *modus operandi*. Jim Crow, the American version of apartheid law, had its sinister roots in a Jim Crow dance in the 1820s, originally performed by a white Irish man imitating a disabled Black enslaved man dancing. This 'blackface' dance routine became wildly popular even across the northern states of the union to justify the brutal subjugation of African descending people on the plantation (Riggs, 1986). Today's death-dance in the era of the New Jim Crow (Alexander, 2010) is the ongoing American fascination with the racist (and capitalist) death penalty. As imprisoned intellectuals on death row point out, 'You ain't got the capital, you do the punishment!' The elites are not condemned to the ultimate penalty. European pharmaceutical companies have been shamed into refusing to sell drug combinations used as 'cocktail' in American death chambers.

Here, we see a 'productive' use of shame tactics which seems to be effective when targeting multinational pharmaceutical corporations (Culp-Ressler, 2015). However, retentionist states such as South Carolina are returning to electrocution and the execution squad (DPIC, 2022).

The **second level** is concerned with invisible prisons, targeting the family regulatory system and the family court institution. An astounding 50% of Black children will face this system in their youth and see themselves becoming the invisible prisoners of the state. Activists have labeled this the foster-to-prison system. Its roots go back to Maafa, the violence of trafficking humans from Africa and separating enslaved children from their parents on the auction block. Its twin monster is the systematic assault on Indigenous family structures and long-term separation of children sent to so-called residential schools run by all the mainline churches in Canada, the United States, and Australia for over a century. The system's modern face is draped in humanitarian ideology seeking to do what is in the "best interest of the child." In 2022, the Canadian government has settled with Indigenous nations for over 31 billion dollars. The settlement covers only the period between 1991 and 2022 and affecting over 200,000 children, who faced removal from their families and kin because of poverty, not abuse, according to activist family defenders. Seven percent of children in Canada are Indigenous while they represent a shocking 52% of all children in the family regulation system. It is compelling to see such child welfare policy as a legacy of the residential school system (Coletta, 2022). It should not come as a surprise that this long-standing class-action suit has propelled the national government into action, given the unearthing of unmarked children's mass graves at several residential 'schools.' As it stands currently, about 50% of the reparations sum will be put into reforming the family regulation system. Abolitionists need to pay close attention to this settlement as such reforms are rarely benefiting marginalized families and tend to contribute to net widening of social controls, again, using language of carceral humanism.

At the **third level**, we see the violent punishment game played out in policing. In the 2015 Justice Department report on Ferguson, Missouri's police department's racist practices might very well implicate cities across the country which not only engaging in racial profiling but also in containing poor people of color with endless fines for trivial offenses, aptly labeled new black codes. In North Charleston, South Carolina, Black bicyclists were jailed for failing to have a horn, according to the bondswoman who secured bond for them. Under this 'fine-and-fee' system, a defendant pays a debt to society and is shamed publicly. It is a fear-based penal system which in the United States is deeply embedded in anti-Black racism and settler colonialism. African descending and American Indian people are criminalized and stigmatized at levels that are even beyond incarceration rates in South Africa under apartheid. One in three Black males will face arrest in his lifetime. There are more Black men in prison than in the university system nationwide (Sentencing Project, 2017). The psychic effects of power wielded against marked subjects embroiled in the imprisonment game also weighs heavily on their families, e.g., on children who get limited weekend or holiday visits in America's dungeons. Furthermore, this agonism is intrinsic to the military/militarized and carceral regimes and their puppeteers who demand crushing penalties from those who "lose the lottery" (García, 2007). Extra-legal agonistic practices are exemplified in the popular pursuit of shamed justice-impacted people. Vigilante neighbors publicize widely those marked as sex offenders, sometimes they are driven out of town or have their windows broken. Some even meet violent death or commit suicide. These stigmatized people have served 'time,' yet they lack privacy and continue to be under lifelong surveillance. Another example comes from *causes célèbres* such as former Black Panther Mumia Abu-Jamal, award-winning journalist and author of several books from death row, is fighting for his release. He was tried for the crime of killing a white police officer, even though another prisoner confessed already for shooting the victim. At a concert in Pennsylvania by the rock musician Sting, a phalanx of uniformed white police officers showed up to signal their protest over the rock star's unflinching support for Abu-Jamal (BBC, 1999). The state never forgets the crimes of those who are committed anti-racist freedom fighters. While the kangaroo trial outcome was vacated, Abu-Jamal is unable to receive a new trial; he remains in a Pennsylvania prison, bearing the marks of a political prisoner.

Since the Ferguson, Missouri uprising during August 2014, there have been many illustrations of the public's expression of symbolic outrage, which characterizes ludic Ubuntu at the third level. It tends to spike with high-profile cases absolving white police officers of any criminal responsibility for killing unarmed Black men. Thus, witness an explosion in major US cities of creative protests that defy helicopters and other conventional surveillance tactics by generating a nonviolent wave of protesters who pop up in different critical arteries around the city. Some of the protest at times can no longer be 'managed.' It is guerilla warfare without weapons of destruction. (Of course, the state gets very nervous about its failure to appear in charge.)

Another contemporary example of ludic Ubuntu is drawn from a contemporary example and growing movement against legally sanctioned Afrophobia. During the first week of uprising in Ferguson, Missouri, and across Black America in August 2014, social media images: "Hands up, Don't Shoot!"—twitter photos from the incoming class of Howard University, echoed by another photo of somber looking women from the first-year class of Spelman College: reminding police across America, whites across the nation, that Black life matters. As demonstrated by the murders of countless Black men and women, Black people marooned in the United States, live beyond the pale, are not (yet) citizens whom codified racist law and its enforcers need to respect (Nagel, 2014). The videotaped lynching of George Floyd in May 2020 again became a lightning rod for sustained street protests, not only in the United States but globally.

It remains to be seen whether the Movement for Black Lives will inspire a new approach to justice. Calls for defunding the police have already been quietly circumvented in California, where cities used millions of federal Covid funding for policing budgets, not for housing, healthcare, childcare, etc. (Levin, 2022). Perhaps, the movement will find inspiration from former federal prosecutor Paul Butler who suggests a protest Hip-Hop theory of justice. After all, while mostly white police officers and other law enforcement agents get the benefit of absolution with the tag of 'justifiable homicide,' most Black civilians plead guilty to bogus charges even when they 'stand their ground.' Butler's solution to the racist deployment of the war on drugs includes the refusal of Black defendants to take a plea (in return for a lighter punishment), instead forcing a trial, which rarely occurs anymore. Juries need to be instructed of their right to speak back against an unjust law and engage in jury nullification. Such concerted protest has indeed occurred in cities such as Washington, DC, to the dismay of prosecutors who respond by declining nonviolent drug cases. Butler calls on other prosecutors to drop out of the agonist game:

> My conclusion is that prosecutors are more part of the problem than the solution. The adversarial nature of the justice system, the culture of the prosecutor's office, and the politics of crime pose insurmountable obstacles for prosecutors who are concerned with economic and racial justice. […]. [I]t seems an odd job for a humanitarian.
>
> (2009, pp. 101–2)

The main theoretical inspiration for this level that contests the 'looting of Black bodies' comes from philosopher Leonard Harris (2002) who invokes insurrectionist justice. This strikes me as a productive agonist approach to deal with the outlaw character of the settler colonial state, which deploys carceral structures the world over, which can only be called "profoundly immoral spaces" (Scott, 2018, p. 41) as they serve to incarcerate only those opposing state power but never those who propagate monstrous transgressions in the name of 'law and order.'

At the next level (**four**), we see a conceptual shift from expressing righteous rage to reflective, more holistic ways of understanding violence in a larger context, which begins to respond to an 'us versus them' approach. Some theorists of restorative justice consider reintegrative shaming as a productive, nonviolent approach. However, shame triggers feelings of rejection, which often leads to a pain response in the body (Thomas, 2006). How then is it possible to label shaming ever as reintegrative or healing? Such philosophy endorses the Rwanda's Gacaca village court system heralded as a peaceful way to harmonize relationships in the aftermath of a genocidal conflict. Its detractors claim that it has led to vigilante justice against innocent Hutu and has also been used for political retaliation. By contrast, South

Africa's TRC has been described as issuing symbolic judgment without punishment (Loick, 2012). The TRC did not require amnesty applicants to be remorseful. Neither were they required to pay restitution. I argue that the TRC's philosophy was committed to an Ubuntu ethics in the positive, whereas the Gacaca system was bound up in a negative Ubuntu ethics, violating basic principles of restorative justice. This critique is contrary to most Western analyses which suggest that Gacaca served as an ingenious way to recuperate precolonial practices for a transitional justice purpose, as the (Western) courts would have been overwhelmed with carrying out punishment for those who were accused of crimes against humanity during the 1994 genocide, affecting primarily Tutsi. However, the local courts soon were overcome by corruption charges or pressure by the central government and handed out long-term prison sentences even against those who harbored and saved Tutsi. Penal abolitionists must take care not to romanticize Indigenous restorative practices when they are all-but restorative.

Among American Indians and First Peoples, healing circles have been noted as successful alternatives to incarceration. However, there is a catch. In North America, especially in Canada, labeled as sentencing circles, there is still a possibility to appeal a community sentence if the state believes the verdict is considered too lenient. Arguably, a non-agonistic way of pursuing such justice may still be possible through Indigenous healing or peacemakers' circles, even if they are not yet decoupled from neocolonial oversight (Ross, 1996). Alternatives to Violence Programs (AVP) in United States prisons, established by Quakers, also focus on those who have harmed. Thus, the focus of these practices is still on the transgressive ways of the individual, rather than on a holistic approach that shows how all, including those affected and harmed, contribute to repairing relationships and the community at large. At this level, peacemakers may use creative means to stop the violence and bring warring parties to a peace table as shown in *Pray the Devil back to Hell* (Reticker, 2008). Nobel laureate Leymah Gbowee began organizing resistance by first heeding God's command in her dream "Gather the women and pray for peace!" Her daring, peaceful actions uniting Muslim and Christian women eventually brought down the regime of Charles Taylor and earned her the Nobel Peace prize (Gbowee, 2013). Naminata Diabate (2020) describes Gbowee's ludic Ubuntu expression as naked agency. As a shaming practice or, worse, as cursing, it is intended to inflict serious harm on those who face the insurgent women opposing oppressive governments, market conditions or multinational corporations.

Transformative justice invites a postsecular or spiritual turn where the ancestors and spirit world are involved in transmutation of conflict; they are not wrathful, revenging Erinyes—then again, they may be taunting the hapless soul in nightmares, visiting those who commit violent transgressions. Fanon famously treated torture victims *and* torturers in his clinic in Algiers during the revolution against the oppressive French colonial regime, depicted hauntingly in a biopic film *Frantz Fanon: Black Skin, White Masks* (Julien,

1995). Goddess Ma'at sits in judgment of human souls in the afterlife. But does she really do the judging, or is it that the ego sits on one side of the scale while the soul or heart rests on the other side? In other depictions, it is Ma'at's feather placed against the vessel which harbors the heart. The ego may wail in guilt and sorrow over earthly transgressions and offer itself up to the personal realm of hell, internalizing punishment. Justitia reigns over earthly conditions (levels 1-4) and externalizes swift justice, depicted by the sword, which is feared in the ultimate punishment of execution. There is an excessive focus on individual acts taken out of context and magnified for certain populations and minimized for others, contrary to the myth or mask of objectivity. Ma'at inspires heart-based, right-brain justice while Justitia's purview is left-brain, analytical, iron-clad fist retributive justice.

A Ghanaian proverb says: "When two people fight, the third one is the peacemaker" (Mbiti, 2010). By contrast, a German proverb says: "When two people fight, the third one rejoices." The latter signifies the vengeful emotion hovering over the first four levels, marked by the term *Schadenfreude*. Even judges are not immune to such base feelings, relishing over vindictive verdicts, whether in Rwanda's village courts or in a US court condemning Larry Nasser to hundreds of years of penal servitude (Stelloh, 2017). It is also the colonial attitude of divide-and-conquer, which the British perfected. By contrast, the Ghanaian proverb signals, as John Mbiti (2010) notes, peacemaking being constitutive of African religion, as it "does not preach, foster, or justify war between communities or nations." It is an ethical call to respond to the demands of the spirits of family members who have transitioned and are called the living dead (*Ibid.*). Ubuntu ethics and Buen Vivir philosophy of South America's Indigenous communities prize nested care, being embedded in a webbed network, where an individual's well-being or ability to live well is constituted by living harmoniously (cf. Graness, 2016). Many Africans have *harambe* obligations, 'pulling together' for funerary offerings. To a Western observer, such generous giving looks like political, rather than moral duties; however, they are done as a demonstration of one's humanness, as spiritual obligations, to do right by the living dead. Ma'at's watchful gaze takes note of each thought and act of kindness and generosity. However, there are times when major conflicts break out and everyone is badly affected by the violence—except the elite: "When elephants fight, it is the grass that suffers most" (Mbiti, *Ibid.*). We now turn to peacemaking at individual and at communities' level to give real utopian examples of abolition.

At **level five**, the highest level so far conceived (there could be other levels), the necessity for punishment fades away and the focus on healing becomes all important, as a non-aboriginal Crown prosecutor was told by an elder who dismisses the Western procedural way as meting out "terror" (Ross, 2014). While the example of a nonviolent revolution may not fit, especially given the usual aftermath (consolidation of power, state repression, take-over of industries, mass unemployment, xenophobia, etc.), the in-the-moment ludic street encounters of the Velvet Revolution gave us the illusion of harmony.

With respect to criminal justice concerns, the short-lived Paris Commune (1871) experiment may be a case of ludic Ubuntu at level five. Prisoners were released and policing was suspended during the popular occupation of the city and crime apparently disappeared, at least according to the popular anarchist imagination (Abidor, 2010).

Peacemaking criminology also endorses transformative justice and goes beyond the individualist focus of restorative justice approaches between offender and victim (Pepinsky & Quinney, 1991). Such a transformative model provides a macroscopic analysis of injustice and how it contributes to further harm at the community and family level. Organizations for and by Black queer penal abolitionists such as Safe OUTside the System of the Audre Lorde Project provide innovative strategies for sustained community support and guidelines for trained peacemakers who also set up emergency phone numbers to avoid interaction with police and other state agencies which are considered a threat to trans individuals and community safety (Rodriguez, 2021).

It is still difficult to divest from punitive justice, as penal abolitionists still argue for making things right through some form of shaming, forgiveness prescriptions, which all activate the principle of accountability. It is therefore not surprising that state-run Alternatives to Incarceration programs attach to probation departments, which means that any slip-up in community work, illicit drug use, etc. or other conditions placed on the probationer, bears the threat of jail, including youth jails. At level five, such schemes are not considered abolitionist practices in a robust sense.

South Africa's high court judge Albie Sachs, who survived a bomb planted by the apartheid regime, alludes to an aesthetic ludic Ubuntu in this way:

> Hopefully, we will one day see the word "ubuntu" also taken up by the international community, the term in our new Constitution that represents respect for the intrinsic dignity that each individual possesses simply by virtue of living with other persons in a community; trying to explain the concept to non-South Africans, I always suggest that if one could harmonize faith, hope, and charity with liberty, equality, and fraternity, and give it to an African choir or a mixed African-Afrikaner choir to hum, then you would have ubuntu.
>
> (2014, p. 242)

Sachs, a former political prisoner, not only refers to the metaphorical healing power of shared musical performance for a post-racial South African society, but also suggests that democratic individualist values could easily be folded into a communitarian ethos, even or especially granted through the rule of law. Sachs' example gestures at a post-moral aesthetics in the way Willett frames it as "unbound experiences where ethical valences occur as acts of moral beauty in generosity toward loved ones or as sublime compassion toward an orphan or stranger" (2014, p. 133). What if that stranger is demonized? Are they still deserving of compassion? Candice Mama's autobiography *Forgiveness Reconsidered* (2019) gives us a glimpse of extraordinary possibility of compassion with someone who was an assassin of the apartheid regime, killing her father.

Relational justice is a complex idea. Ludic Ubuntu at level five (or higher) does dispense with "desert" and "punishment" altogether. If justice is indeed transformative (and nonjudgmental), it no longer makes sense to talk about positive aspects of shaming practices, even if playful ceremonies are tempering the coercive aspects of demanding appropriate apologies and gestures of remorse from those who have harmed others. Friends of transformative ludic Ubuntu justice would rather see the spirit of gravity, the camel, transform into playful children, freed from the trauma of history and memory that chains us to a past that no longer serves us in its weightiness. Forgiveness rituals that focus on healing from generational trauma and bloodshed such as drinking from the bitter tree, the Acholi way, involves all parties in the conflict. Among the Bamana of West Africa, a tight-knit social connections model such as joking relations among extended family constellations ensures that the community focuses on healing, not punishment so that people can forgive and forget bygone transgressions and practice friendship, intermarriage in future generations.[2] Intersubjective, affective attunement are powerful reminders that great tragedy can be transmuted into playful laughter—a hopeful interplay where the boundaries between victim and offender have vanished.

In what follows, I present a sketch of the five levels in an individualized way using insights from child development psychology as well as dignity and humiliation studies. It is a dance and interplay of the individual with her community.

Several years ago, a video circulated social media. A couple had a verbal disagreement in the doctor's office where an ultrasound was administered on the pregnant person. As screams circulated, it showed the fetus taking a leap in what seemed to be a reaction to the heated exchange. A pregnancy can be affected by so many external stressors and life circumstances. The fact that the fetus acts with stress is an indication that our environments are reactive. Being pregnant *and* imprisoned leads to a heightened stress level, exposing prisoners to increased complications, miscarriages, and premature death. A prison environment is de facto one of the worst places to bring a fetus to term. In her autobiography, Assata Shakur (1987) describes her relentless fight against the system to gain access to healthy food. Even the birthing process can be dangerously delayed when guards fail to unshackle birthing persons in prison hospitals. Trauma accumulates for both parent and child when they are forcibly separated by the prison and family regulation system. All these examples illustrate a lack of understanding of a nested care world view, which is part and parcel of many Indigenous traditions. In East Asian cultures, at birth one is considered one year old, not zero, as breathing on one's own is not an exclusive fact of individuated existence. The Western perspective on policing pregnancy is marked by contradictions. In the 'progressive' city of Ithaca, New York, a judge told me that he sent a pregnant woman to jail for her "own good," to interdict illicit drug use (as if one could not get them in prison). Apparently, he had no concern that imprisonment would impede prenatal care and increase the mother's stress level; in addition, she was not offered any medication assisted treatment. Pregnant drug users are deemed a threat to their fetus, but the prison system seems not to be considered a threat to pregnant people and the unborn.

An example of a community operating at level five is a justice system that recognizes the needs of the unborn. At this level, community members experience being one with "all my relations," a deep understanding that we are interconnected and experience unity consciousness beyond the duality of the seesaw movement of life. It makes no sense to harm another with punishment, as it would be akin to harming oneself. The transformative strategy then is to focus on self-healing, acceptance, loving what is and exploring truly nested-care approaches that reduces all violence at the community level. What would education look like, how would we all live together in harmony on earth? At its highest expression, it means to let go of a traumatic past, even intergenerational trauma, and learn to play and laugh like children, forgetting grudges and learn the compassionate way as one of gifting oneself: the art of fore-gifting. One has a reverence for all life, for the not-yet-born and the living dead, the ancestors, as well as the elements representing the four directions, being embedded in the circle of life. Such reverence comes from a deep understanding and appreciation of growing up with a visceral sense of belonging, being loved: it comes with the lived experience of nested care, of bonding with parents, relatives, and all who are in kin relations. Becoming human and understanding one's own humanness means that I have sensed belonging—not in an abstract sense of imagined community—but in a visceral sense of being, whether as a newborn, as infant, or as an older child, the center of the family and society. At this level, the Lakota Circle of Courage exemplifies the nested care philosophy that is so similar across cultures who reject the Western individuated, alienated approach to un-nested caring of infants and children. Separated from their mother at birth, children get punished for crying, withheld good touch, co-sleeping with the newborn and older child is forbidden if one is under the public eye of the state, the family regulation system. Children are considered a burden, a nuisance, and are clearly not the center of social policy and regard in Western societies. In Indigenous cultures and marooned communities which are suspicious of state institutions, children are supported to freely explore, master their skills, and willingly share their toys, generously, as property is circulated rather than hoarded. The well-being of the individual is directly connected to the well-being of the community.

Level four is still connected to a caring approach, but it already has a weightiness to it. The community displays an element of perceived separateness, both for those accused and the group of accusers of the greater community. There is judgment instead of compassion and understanding. A tinge of shame pervades the accountability justice game and creates feelings of perceived separation. If I am hurt, I will demand apologies and I may relent and forgive based on conditions placed on the other. In that instance, I may forget that I have also harmed others in the past but now it is my turn to insist on getting my due. Thus, to observers, this justice game will feel like retribution lite because somebody will need to be shamed and held responsible. But since the focus is on restoring or reparation, it does not carry the intense charge of indignation, revenging for past ills. Still, there is a remnant of such emotion at play. As the saying goes in African proverbs and elsewhere, when I point my finger at the other, there are three fingers pointing back at me. Furthermore, at this level, compassion is replaced by the sense of empathy. While compassion is bi-directional, which means that I have this feeling for myself and for the entire situation, empathy is uni-directional. I could be you, but I am not you. And what can I offer you is what would assist you without doing it for you. I will create conditions for possibility of taking responsibility so that you can become accountable for your own actions. At this level, there are opportunities to look at the effect of harm from multiple perspectives. For the most part, people who are mediating or pronouncing judgments appear calm and stern community stakeholders. At level four, the community attempts to find ways to repair and teach in a way that it prevents harmfulness in the future. They will ponder how to teach children the restorative ways and may even appreciate learning from children's wisdom about fairness and reciprocity relations.

At level three, we are very much involved in the emotional game of the seesaw. Charges and accusations are met by countercharges such that I assert my humanity and deny yours in this game of winners and losers; a polarized, highly emotionally charged game of us versus them. There will be sparks of sympathy accompanied with expressing moral outrage, and I side with the party who appears as the proper victim in the conflict. Even if they harmed somebody, I should give them a pass because they have not felt nurtured. One should excuse the behavior because they are a victim. Furthermore, my righteous anger and wagging finger are channeled in ludic ways, such as street performances, rallies, blocking highways to express rage against the system, speaking truth to power in front of court houses and legislative institutions. It is a serious game where much energy is spent on shining a light on injustice or perceived injustice, on systemic injustice. There is much focus on expending negative emotions, which means that everyone strongly perceives the stage of separation from those who need to be shunned and shamed. One's judgment is governed by perceived morals of superiority. And it is messianic, savior-like as it propels one to side with the victims who are in need to be rescued. Such expression of toxic shaming will lead me to celebrate when police officers or a "wolf pack" of sexual aggressors are sentenced to long prison terms.

I internalize the pain of the victim, feeling triggered due to past trauma and externalize such sympathetic emotions as indignation in speech and deeds such as setting structures on fire or liberating goods from a department store. My actions and those of others may result in (short-lived) reforms of the oppressive system, and I forget that a backlash is certain. Life on the seesaw; when I am up, I relish in the excitement of the giddy multitude, raising our fists and forcing change.

Level two and one seem at first difficult to separate conceptually. The predominant feeling is one of fear. It expresses as hatred and contempt for the other. Level two simulates intense constriction, living a prison life on the outside. I do not know what freedom tastes like, because I have never experienced the intensity of belonging. My children are all taken away at birth because I do not fit the ideological framing of a proper middle class white motherhood. My resentment against the system of policing, social workers or clergy is intense, and my rage is directed against other family members and associates. I do not trust anyone, including those who should be my advocates. I do not feel my own power and do not know what it is like to organize for change. I have internalized shame and cannot access my self-worth. When somebody criticizes me, even in a benign way, it is felt as rejection and I over-react in emotionally abusive or aggressive ways. I may develop an inner and outer life; internally, torn apart, while externally, playing the part of an emotionally adjusted personality. I don the mask of someone who is well equipped of hiding raw emotions. At this level of perceived separation, we long for community and participate in toxic games perfected by Mafia-type organizations. In the beginning of this authority-obedience entanglement, it is a slow game of separation: I may be tested to do a tiny bit of harm to another and receive a reward for it. It is similar in a toxic relationship: how do I react to the request by the partner forgoing family visits? Do I protest, leave the partner or acquiesce and then learn to heap criticism and abuse onto my family, too? This is also the level where we internalize cultural shame brought on by the violent assimilation game and terror of the boarding school system. Such residential schools were run by nuns and priests who want to possess the soul of the child and beat the Indigenous traditions out of the children. Feeling ashamed for speaking one's mother tongue, a trauma is carried into the next generations of the survivors of such genocidal practices.

At level one, I feel all alone in the world, socially dead physically, emotionally, spiritually. The feeling of separation is so great that I do not feel accountable for any destructive transgressions. I feel utter abandon, unloved, humiliated. Even when facing a judge in criminal court, I have nobody who is supporting me. I do not feel responsible for my actions, because the world has been against me all along, all my life. It is the ultimate expression of not being one, i.e., an intense perception of separation from those whom I victimize or torment. All is stacked up against me, and all I can do is lash out to preserve a shred of dignity, of believing that I still have a right to exist. My cry for belonging and lashing out is misunderstood by all authority figures as acting out and becoming the bully that they all get to fear. Their fear of me fuels my hatred and strength: even in a solitary cell, I know of my superpowers: I have become invincible. Years and decades in prison leave their mark on my body (and soul) and I develop persistent, repetitive traumatic stress disorder. When I leave the prison, my soul returns and can no longer exist in the 'free world.' I have truly become a prisoner of the system. The agonism of the seesaw eventually tears me apart, as I can only feel a sense of respect when I am lashing out emotionally and physically at guards or informants. Making myself vulnerable would be akin to a death sentence.

Conclusion

In the past two decades, we have seen a proliferation of publications using a penal abolitionist, anti-imperialist lens.[3] Ruth Morris (2000) created the term transformative justice. What has been less clear is whether defenders of transformative justice, use a statist lens, demanding stronger, egalitarian state institutions or whether they defend mutual aid, anarchist, anti-statist programmatic changes (cf. Dübgen, 2020, pp. 160–1). My sympathies are with the latter. With Scott (2018; 2020) and Coyle (2018), I am arguing for real (existing) utopian solutions. Biko Agozino's call for action adds that it is not sufficient to indigenize criminology in the Global South but instead Western criminologists should humble themselves and "remain open to opportunities to learn from the experiences and struggles of others as well through an exchange of knowledge" (2003, p. 246). I argue that the prison devolution or decarceration movement will arise most urgently from the African continent. Africans can still remember the power of precolonial reconciliation practices, which did not rely on social death. Exile was an extreme form of punishment as was the death penalty. In the postcolony, prisons are pervasive across African nations-states which invest in securitization and anti-terrorism measures, thereby neglecting traditional restorative measures to solve conflicts. South Africa's embrace of neoliberalism under Thabo Mbeki has also had nefarious consequences for prison policies. Multinational corporations set up private prisons, including massive youth prisons (Martin, 2007). One of the ongoing faces of colonial terror is the continuation of colonial law and punishment (Saleh-Hanna, 2008). Chapter 1 showcases the need for prison abolition and highlights voices from people in prison from the African diaspora to the Continent.

Notes

1 Another version of this chapter is published in *African Philosophy in an Intercultural Perspective* (A. Graness, E. Etieyibo, & F. Gmainer-Pranzl, eds.), Springer Press, 2022.

2 Kassim Koné, personal communication, 2002.

3 The following are just some of the increasing number of treatises and toolkits on penal abolition: Davis, 2003; 2005; James, 2005a; Sudbury, 2005; INCITE!, 2006; Pepinsky, 2006; Saleh-Hanna, 2008a; Nagel & Nocella, 2013; Coyle, 2013; Brazell, 2018; Loick, 2019; Ben-Moshe, 2020; Dixon & Piepzna-Samarasinha, 2020; Coyle & Scott, 2021; Education for Liberation Network & Critical Resistance Editorial Collective, 2021; Gilmore, 2021; Kaba, 2021; Law, 2021; Whitlock & Heitzeg, 2021; Coyle & Nagel, 2022; Davis, Meiners, Dent, & Richie, 2022; Struthers Montford & Taylor, 2022.

1 Just-us or Justice as Vengeance

La prison doit se proposer de transformer un être en rupture en citoyen utile diminuant ainsi le nombre de recidives. Il n s'agit plus uniquement d'élever les murs et de fortifier.

Les serrures des prisons mais d'y foire penètrer des commissions de surveillance des travailleurs sociaux des associations et organismes d'aide aux détenus, de favoriser tous les efforts qui peuvent contribuer à la reinsertion socioprofessionelle due condamné.

(Prison wall, Mali, Bamako, 2002)

Why Punish?

A popular refrain throughout most of moral psychology and political philosophy literature is the following: 'of course, we need to punish.' Humans seem to be hardwired for revenge, for repairing the loss of status for victims. Paul Bloom's (2013) popular book *Just Babies: The Origins of Good and Evil* makes an empirical case for the human need of punishment, even in babies, which finds its philosophical endorsement in *Why Punish? How Much?* (Tonry, 2011). One's desire is fueled by a need to punish the errant ones out of sympathy for the victim. While five-month-old babies simply prefer nice puppets and reach for them, at eight-months, babies start to "become more sophisticated: they preferred the puppet who was mean to the bad guy over the one who was nice to it. So, at some point after five months, babies begin to prefer punishers—when the punishment is just" (Bloom, 2013, pp. 98–9). This observational evaluation, if true, prompts two sets of questions. First, does it not upset the Kohlbergian order of things, a progression of moral sentiments, of lower-order capacity in children to engage in moral judgments than most adults? Bloom rather playfully suggests that such reasoning gives adults too much credit and children, even toddlers too little credit (p. 100). Second, turning a critical gaze onto Bloom, why is it a sign of more sophistication, to seek revenge and discipline from a status of domination? Perhaps, it would be better to think of the path to adulthood as 'moral degradation' and growing empathy deficit. It is not thought so as such because of adultism

DOI: 10.4324/9781003055327-2

and un-nested-care pedagogy: the adults produce the rules and regulations for the social sphere in a world that is not centered around children. Why not be open to other possibilities, especially, of letting go of judgment altogether, as five-month-old babies still seem to be able to do? Philosophers still find it difficult to part with such ideas, even those who endorse abolitionist principles (Boonin, 2008; Zimmerman, 2011).

Social scientists use experiments such as the Dictator Game and Ultimatum Game to test for a fairness instinct. Such agonistic decision games have been played with children around the world, and yet I wonder about a danger of confirmation bias. To what extent do Western researchers consider childrearing practices, especially where parents and communities adopt a nested-care worldview? Such philosophy thinks of children not as property of parents but as what is owed to them. Nested carers are responsive to children's needs, tuning in to their verbal and nonverbal expressions rather than relishing in breaking a child's willfulness and letting babies sleep in separate beds and in separate rooms. The Western non-nested-care standard of weaning a baby from breast milk is adult centered, and it is considered 'civilized' to wean a baby after five months (Narvaez, 2021). So, what if the date of weaning were the new yardstick in the 'fairness game'? I will leave aside the 'civilized' decision of selling Nestlé baby milk formula to nursing parents as a 'superior' substitute for breast milk. By way of analogy, Western forestry was wedded to the Hobbesian scarcity model: Trees compete for sunlight. Or so it seemed. When biologists averted their gaze from the sky and focused on roots, they found cooperation, instead of competition, even across species. The settler colonial practice of clear-cutting destroys the delicate infrastructure and regrowth, especially concerning old-growth forests, is a sheer impossibility (van Schilfgaarde & Shelton, 2021). Weaning a child prematurely, i.e., before the child determines their preference, is then detrimental from an Indigenous, relational, Ubuntu ethics. Such adultist decision fosters the 'fairness' gene, in other words, encouraging anxiety, anger, resentment, and grudges. Longevity research shows that centenaries' secret for endurance is often this simple skill: giving up grudges. So, what counts as just or appropriate punishment for those who violate pro-social comportment?

Considering retributive thinking 'sophisticated' and believing in the proportionality of punishment will be challenged in this book, and especially in this chapter, including a reformist credo in 'corrections.' The penitentiary has lost its luster for 'penitence' as many prisons are now called correctional facilities. The prison system has never been successfully reformed over the centuries; what has remained constant is that the pendulum tends to swing in favor of vindictiveness and resounding failure (cf. Lombardo, 1995). In fact, correctional ethics amounts to an oxymoron. Such critical insight is reflected in a report by the National Advisory Commission on Criminal Justice Standards and Goals (1973), which crystallized a 'verdict' of previous reform attempts: "The American correctional system today appears to offer minimum protection for the public and maximum harm to the offender." In fact, given that the commission was empaneled to establish national standards, their report comes to abolitionist conclusions: "The prison, the reformatory, and the jail have achieved only a shocking record of failure. There is overwhelming evidence that these institutions create crime rather than prevent it" (cf. Pager, 2007). These damning observations reiterate previous decades of commission reports dating back to the 1870s (ACA, n.d.).

Punishment as Revenge

Others have not been so polite in describing a system that has never worked. In *Punishment and Terrorism in Africa*, Kenyan philosopher H. Odera Oruka (1976) lays out a vision for Africa free from colonial violence. He was ahead of his time. He argues that not only abolition of concept of punishment is necessary but also of the practice of punishment (p. xi):

> [W]e in Africa [...] must first concentrate on abolishing terrorism. When this is done, we shall find it compelling to abolish punishment as well, or, in other words, to abolish the conditions that create crime and criminals and occasion us to punish.
>
> (*Ibid.*, pp. 82–3)

This chapter develops Oruka's call for abolitionist action. The legal instruments for punishing excessively and the innocent, he calls "legal terrorism." He further divides such terrorism into judicial and legislative (p. 108). Oruka was also ahead of his time in laying the conceptual groundwork for law abolition. It is an uncontroversial fact that the world over, those who make the law and execute it focus on penalizing dispossessed and disposable residents and migrants in any (settler colonial) nation-state. In the European conquest of Africa, the prison served as a central organizing function. It was set up to inspire fear and terror, where the prisoner is cut off spatially and psychologically from their kin. In the postcolonial era, no African country has abolished prisons, and political prisoners write with clarity about the afterlife of colonialism and the psychic effects of such punishment. Reflecting on Kenyan writer Ngũgĩ wa Thiong'o's anti-colonial critique in *Devil on the Cross* (1982), written while he was imprisoned, Viviane Saleh-Hanna (2008) disputes the concept of postcolonialism in practice and describes the continuation and expansion of colonial status quo as penal colonialism (p. 21). In *The Man Died*, fellow imprisoned intellectual Nigerian playwright Wole Soyinka prophesizes that prison is a new stage from which the struggle must be waged (1972, pp. 69–70).[1] After a failed attempt at inciting an insurrection and escape, Soyinka was sent to solitary confinement where he reflects on the torture of sensory deprivation: "time vanished. I turned to stone. The world retreated into fumes of swamp land" (p. 86).

In this chapter, I argue that most, if not all, of what is labeled justice administration subscribes to a logic of violence and terror (cf. Cover, 1986;

Roberts, 2022). I question the *correctional ethos*, critiquing both the correctional institutions (prisons in all their forms) and the *judicial ethos* that uses imprisonment as its normative sanction. This juridical system is ensconced in a spirit of gravity, using Nietzsche's metaphor. This spirit is one of revenge, and that is why I speak of justice as vengeance. Rather than stopping harmful behavior, as its logic of 'correction' aims at, I argue that it reproduces harm, not only against the convicted wrong doer but also against their families. This collateral effect is rarely seen because sanctions are individualized. Over 800,000 parents are incarcerated, leaving millions of children who are rendered invisible behind (Bernstein, 2010). In Boston, it affects one in 20 children (HIP, 2017). With the advent of mass incarceration, the scandal of 'orphaned' children has become statistically 'visible' through Adverse Childhood Experiences (ACE) scoring, and these children have a greater likelihood to grow up joining their parent behind bars.[2] To be sure, equating justice with vengeance looks like a poor philosophical claim, opening my argument up to objections of sweeping generalization. Critics will charge that I conflate emotions with procedural malfunctions in individual cases, and after all, the appeal's process allows a defendant to right a wrong. Drawing on Nietzsche's punditry of equating "gerecht" (just) with "gerächt" (revenged), I will show that the ennobling version of juridical retribution is not substantively better than if we had an informal way of halting the actions of wrong doers.[3] Hence, I locate this primitive form of vengeful justice that is mired in the prison-industrial complex in the lowest rung of the five-phase spiral model of a ludic Ubuntu ethics mentioned in the Introduction chapter. It is this logic of vengeance that makes possible gross human rights violations at Abu Ghraib prison and the Guantánomo carceral complex, let alone secret Central Intelligence (CIA) prisons littered around the world. It is the logic of the chokehold (Butler, 2017) which means that officers of the law suspend the rule of law in favor of brutalization.

In protesting his capture by the Canadian police and later his imprisonment in the United States, American Indian freedom fighter Leonard Peltier sums up the indignity of the carceral:

> [Prisons] don't just take your freedom from you—which you'd think would be enough—but they demean and humiliate you, it seems, whenever and wherever possible. They create vastly more crime and injustice and inhumanity than they ever prevent. All prisons, without exception, are cruel and unusual punishment. Every one of them should be declared unconstitutional.
>
> (Peltier, 2000, p. 143)

The US Supreme Court has yet to declare the death penalty as "cruel and unusual." Inexplicably, mainstream media struggles with calling the execution process torture (Cooper, 2018). As drug cocktails are more difficult to obtain, states now turn to legalizing execution by a firing squad.

Even Michelle Alexander's (2010) indictment of the war on drugs leads her only to the conclusion that we should not incarcerate people who have drug addiction. Her critics such as Marie Gottschalk (2015a; 2015b) have charged that that narrow focus would not lead to the end of mass incarceration. Prisons have become so normalized that most do not even think twice that this peculiar space of social death triggers traumatic responses (Lombardo, 2018). We have learned to appreciate the toll of 'war theater' on veterans' mental health which has resulted in some leniency measures as well as a modicum of therapy ordered by Veteran Court judges. But this kind of thinking has not scratched the surface regarding imprisonment of nonveterans of war. Prisons are there to remove 'problem populations'—a convenient operation for the elites who have a juridically justifiable monopoly on vengeance. What happens to the person in that cell does not matter to the sentencing judge or the all-powerful prosecutor. Prisons would disappear overnight if those who prosecute and judge were treating themselves to the same 'medicine' they prescribe. Two examples showcase that personal or policy changes are possible: (1) A Colorado man who had spent seven years in solitary confinement was directly released to the streets, found the home of the prison warden, and killed him. The warden's successor decided to try out solitary for a night and was instantly 'cured.' His psyche could not bear the noise of the 'screamers.' He greatly minimized the use of solitary and adopted the United Nations (UN) Nelson Mandela rules, i.e., sparingly using this punitive practice and for less than 15 days (Raemisch, 2014). (2) In Germany, a long-term warden wrote a memoir of sorts by focusing on a typology of imprisoned men, including a former guard convicted of corruption. Thomas Galli's bestseller (2016) turned into a sequel (2017). By then, the warden who outed himself as a prison abolitionist left the profession and now works as attorney in private practice.

Post-traumatic Stress Disorder of Prisoners—The Psychological Effects of Institutionalization

While post-traumatic stress disorder (PTSD) is recognized as a disease when it presents in veterans of war, there is no such thing as a post-carceral stress disorder label for those leaving the prison. However, there is a stigmatizing 'felon' label. Occasionally, a spotlight shines on sympathetic victims of the injustice apparatus such as Kalief Browder, who spent three years in notorious Rikers Island jail (New York City), two of them in solitary confinement. After charges were dropped, he returned to his studies but could not cope with the depression and anxiety. His mother found his lifeless body at home. Browder's untreated PTSD symptoms and his suicide have been used as rallying cry to stop the use of solitary confinement for teens, an important reform measure, but what is still lacking is an awareness that all jail is bad for teenagers. New York has raised the age of criminal responsibility to 18, but it remains to be seen, if loopholes will continue to be used for teens who are accused of committing violent offenses. Browder also complained about the beatings by other prisoners and guards (corroborated by videos that appeared after his death), about starvation punishment; these and other forms of torture are daily occurrences in most jails and prisons around the world. Premature death "by natural causes," suicides, or murder are collateral experiences behind walls—literally, prison is a war zone. Unfortunately, Kalief's Law set in motion more youth prisons, replete with isolation cells, the opposite of what justice advocates had demanded.

Criminal justice defenders discuss recidivism, a practice of the infamous revolving door, as haunting the prison project since its inception in Philadelphia. But oddly, they rarely discuss it in context of the traumatic effects of incarceration, which in turn induce non-coping antisocial behavior in civil society. Once declared civilly dead (as prisoner) without immense social supportive practices in place, how does one get 'resurrected' or 'rehabilitated' [*sic*]? It is only the heroic or stoic prisoner such as Nelson Mandela, who can leave the prison behind them. Prisoners, of course, teach us, urge those of us in the "free world" to press on, to demand more, first decarceration, and then, in true abolitionist spirit, excarceration for all. Tiyo Salah-El was caged for some 50 years in Pennsylvania and turned penal abolitionist and imprisoned intellectual. He calls for refurnishing the ghosted abandoned prisons into "Healing and Caring Centers for the homeless, shelters for abused and battered women and children, meaningful and productive drug and alcohol treatment centers, meaningful education and vocation programs for families living in abject poverty" (Salah-El, 2007, p. 205). Salah-El was very aware of the institutionalization effect of the post-incarceration syndrome and worked hard to help young men get literacy skills, running clandestine schools, which had a higher graduation rate than the legitimate classes offered by civilian teachers. Attaining the high school equivalent diploma (GED) is the ticket to freedom for many of the men who apply for parole. While being committed to prison abolition, Salah-El was committed to turning the carceral into a place of learning and theorizing. Similarly, Robben Island was known as a premier university of resistance once Black Consciousness activists were imprisoned.

Two Senses of Justice: Roman vs. Egyptian

We must trouble justice in two senses of the word: one has to do with real-world justice administration (*justitia* or *Justiz*), the other has to do with righteousness, a heart-based worldview of social solidarity (conformity to Ma'at, cf. Hare, 1999, pp. 29–31). *Justitia*, Lady Justice, is derived from its Greek counterpart, *Dike*, but, ultimately, from the Goddess Ma'at, prominently featured in sculptures of the Ancient Kingdom, Egypt. At death, a soul's right action is carefully measured: the heart lies on the scale, opposite a feather (of truth); if the human heart is heavier, full of mischievous acts, the hell hound stands by and devours. Where things go awry is when Ma'at is 'translated' into Roman law, and, even worse, into contemporary penal codification. Lady

Justice, eyes bound, holding a sword in her right hand and balancing with the left a scale, stands on a serpent in front of many Western court houses. The scale dangles, an empty symbol bereft of compassion and love. Ma'at, goddess of justice, truth, and the kosmos, by contrast, sees everything, has rows of feathers attached to her arms, simulating wings, and carries an *ankh*; a large feather serves as crown. Ma'at is often depicted in a kneeling, devotional position. There is nothing to avenge as judgment comes from the heart. This organ is not of significance in biological terms, being "the seat of intellective and moral discrimination" (Hare, 1999, p. 28). Heart-based justice disappears in a vengeance-filled, heart-less juridical process which instead inspires fear and trembling.

Under the guise of objectivity and elimination of human bias or error, today's justice administration relies on a different kind of 'scale': the mighty sword makes right through predictive policing methods and algorithms trademarked by private companies as trade secrets; judges, towering God-like, infallible, over the proceedings, rely on 'objectivity,' unconcerned about the effects of their judgment upon the human being. Judges are not in relation with those strangers who plea for mercy. The ruse of objectivity is easily uncovered as human bias is written into the code (McQuade, 2019). Experiments also show that judges' decisions vary dramatically before and after food breaks, again, ruining the notion of objective standards applied (Danzinger, Levay, & Avnaim-Pesso, 2011).

For over 200 years, prison reformers have known that imprisonment does not make people better but instead engenders physical and mental health differences in and beyond the prison walls. Its illogic is quite *logical* within settler colonial, capitalist societies; as it seems to be quite capable of rounding up the usual suspects.[4] Of course, the Quakers who brought us the modern prison system had a noble idea: instead of maiming errant commoners and decapitating those who defy the king, they suggested to erect a dungeon, imitating the ways of the monks and nuns. Except that it was clear that the confinement wasn't quite voluntary, as one could not leave one's cell at will. After 'doing time,' the errant would return to society fully rehabilitated and penitent of their sins and offenses. Quaker idealism rested on the promising hypothesis that offensive behavior can be cured through an elaborate 'time-out' system for young adults. So far, so good, in theory. Where things turn sour is when in reality, the same 'errant' folks return again and again to the prison fortress, in part, because they were now branded as a criminal class and, not surprisingly, banded together and perfected their skills as "illegitimate capitalists" (in George Jackson's analysis).

In the abolitionist novel *Les Miserables*, Hugo's hero steals a piece of bread and gets a 20-year condemnation to the gallows (a step down from prisons?), only to go for the priest's chandelier, once released. It soon became abundantly clear to Quakers and all those tinkering with criminal justice modernization that fixed the abstract, nonviolent sanction of 'doing time' in a prison cell that their little experiment was doomed from the start. At this point, fraudulent 'science' commenced at grand scale. Prison reformers suggested to politicians that bigger and better prisons had to be built to deal with the plague of recidivism and to house really wicked people. This is a dis-ease model, housing those who have to be quarantined and mentally fixed (supposedly), but it certainly didn't amount to a public health model. Few know that Tocqueville's analysis of American democracy began as a study of its emerging prison system. The French visitors Tocqueville and Beaumont were rather critical of this American experiment, but nevertheless, the US prison system experienced worldwide rapid adoption (Benson, 2017). By contrast, a relational model would look at different parameters, as outlined in later chapters below. It would not be guided by fear and vengeance.

When I visited Mali to study why this country *underutilized* imprisonment, I was told by every learned official, from the gendarmerie, judges to the minister of justice, that the prison system is a colonial invention. Samba Sangaré, a former political prisoner who was one of very few who survived torture and imprisonment in the feared Taodénit prison camp, shared with me the following:

> To the best of my knowledge, Africa did not initially know the system of prisons. We had forms of sanctions in the social schemes which were different from imprisonment. We learned imprisonment with the colonial system. The name of prison itself has been africanized from a word which was originally French, the "cachot" which is called "kaso" in African language. Africans did not know what it was initially and since they did not speak French they called it "kaso." It did not exist traditionally. It is a new tradition that colonization introduced.
>
> (Interview with Samba Sangaré, August 12, 2002, Lafiabougou, Bamako; field notes on file with author)

Colonial prisons emerged with the French occupation force. And the coastal states experienced a transformation of slave castles into prison fortresses. My African interlocutors understood the ideology of the colonial carceral. They knew exactly that the system is about power, coercion, brings social death, and is inimical to (ludic) Ubuntu justice practices. As outlined in this chapter's epitaph, even the mural outside the wall of Bamako prison for men, erected by the French colonial regime, has an abolitionist message: "humans do not deserve punishment in form of imprisonment." Yet, in 2017, Bamako's Central Prison houses 1,200 men, when the capacity is set at 400, which amounts to torture and unsafe living conditions, according to Amnesty International (L'Indicateur du Renouveau, 2017).

I argue that a defense of carceral ethics is bound up in a deadly agonistic game, creating permanent insecurities and premature death. Fear, shaming, and stigmatization, compounded by being released into society with the lifelong Cain's scar of 'felon.' It creates mental illness and social death. It is an illogical game bound up in the paradoxical quagmire. On the one hand, one is told to behave responsibly, which presupposes a degree of freedom of choice, and on the other hand, the controlling climate engenders infantilizing behavior, where the subject under scrutiny learns to abdicate all forms of socialization. One needs to ask a captor to open the door at night for the privilege of relieving oneself if one does not have a toilet next to one's bed. There are only losers in this agonistic game of vengeance: guards' families are at higher risk of having intimate partner violence; after all, guards are also locked up all day (Rodriguez & Clark, 2022). It is time to heed the adage: 'Nobody grows up dreaming of being a zookeeper for humans.'

American Indians find themselves always already guilty, a condition of being born Indian, and Leonard Peltier motivates them to "be proud of that guilt" and to understand that they are "guilty only of being innocent": their guilt makes them holy (Peltier, 2000, p. 16). Equally, the grim legacy of "imputing crime to color," in the words of Frederick Douglass (cf. Davis, 2003), continues to hold sway in the settler colonial mindset of power and control, which denies the dignitarian demand that Black Lives Matter.

It is the rare human whose heart does not turn to stone but comes out of prison whole. To repeat, social scientists have ignored that prison itself causes PTSD with the exception of studies that reviewed long-term confinement (Cohen & Taylor, 1973). Those who emerge unscathed from the prison, or at least are presumed to be, as in the case of iconized prisoners, Nelson Mandela, tend to have endured the harsh conditions as a political prisoner (not as a stigmatized social prisoner). Fatima Meer (2001) talks explicitly about her privilege as a political prisoner during the apartheid regime. Political prisoners know that they have outside support, which motivates them to fight on. Winnie Madikizela-Mandela's long lonely stint in a filthy cell was vividly portrayed in a Hollywood film (Roodt, 2011). It captures the process of dehumanization, a near-broken spirit of a prisoner who is confronted with new sets of ghastly interrogations after a prolonged period of being refused even the basic access to maintain sanitary conditions. Yet, she is depicted as being utterly defiant, not allowing the torturers to break her.

Solitary and death row create a special kind of hell because they assure a kind of social death that is difficult to endure even for the most well-adjusted meditating person. We have known this ever since the establishment of a solitary prison, Eastern Penitentiary in Philadelphia, Pennsylvania. The 'separate system' did not produce penitent souls, instead it led to their madness. It was the Auburn system (also dubbed 'silent system') which won the day for emulating the factory work, since prisoners were working (silently) in a big hall. It was less expensive than the Pennsylvania prison experiment. But since prison officials did not learn from critics and reformers, they retorted to the separate system in its new version: The solitary prison, 'the super max,' now is reserved for 'the worst of the worst' prisoners, also labeled as 'mad' or 'bad' (Rhodes, 2004). However, that label is ever so elastic to include those who complain about prison conditions and organize. What is uncontroversial is that this carceral setting seems to be the worst of the worst forms of confining people alive—the spectacle of a living tomb. There is complete erasure of human contact, except through violent cell extraction and shackling for "recess" time in another cage, akin to a dog's pen. And what is least known is that there's a gradation of hell in the supermax prison such as Southport prison, New York. The A-block allows for privileges such as books and papers and D-block prisoners try to 'earn' their way to that level. The low-level D-block contains many mentally ill prisoners, who are labeled "screamers" by other prisoners and who are sometimes selected for special sadistic treatment. According to these guards, prisons are established for further punishment within impenetrable walls. The Angola 3 prisoners spent between 30 and 40 years in the box for the political offense of joining the Black Panther Party—and being accused of killing a white guard. Angola Penitentiary, built on the grounds of a former plantation, is a prison in Louisiana where time has stood still. White male armed overseers parade on horses over Black men who toil on the vast farm grounds as if slavery had never been abolished. It was not, as the 13th Amendment of the US Constitution reinscribes penal democracy (James, 2005).

Who are among the 'worst of the worst' besides political prisoners who organize peaceful hunger strikes or people with neurological differences, whose conditions worsen dangerously in such confinement? Solitary confinement is a preferred mode of repression for the following: a US Black prisoner who complaints that he is treated like a slave; a white woman who refuses to wear a bra; or a white prisoner who founded a National Association for the Advancement of Colored People (NAACP) chapter—for having an extra tiny piece of butter in his cell. There is always an empty solitary cell waiting to be filled by uppity prisoners, in both women's and men's prisons; more often than not, such cages are reserved for jailhouse lawyers (Abu-Jamal, 2010). Jeanette Tossounian is defiant about the threat of segregation for refusing to wear a bra:

> I don't own my own breasts. I am not in control of my own body. I have no rights concerning my body. Not only does my body have to be confined to a cell, my body parts must also be confined. Now I'm truly going to go nuts.
>
> (2016, p. 24)

A noted national writer, Jon Marc Taylor, was sent to solitary and never emerged from it. Lois Ahrens writes in her appeal for support:

> I am a friend of Jon Marc Taylor, PhD, who did path-breaking work on restoring Pell Grants. Very tragically, Jon had a severe stroke on Feb. 23, 2014 while in solitary on trumped up charges that he had contraband in his cell. As it turned out the "contraband" was butter that belonged to his cellie. He initially got some rehabilitation but not nearly what he could

> have received if he was not in prison. He can no longer write and has difficulty framing his thoughts.
>
> (Real Cost of Prisons Project, November 24, 2015)

He later died of 'natural causes.' Due to vigorous activism by people impacted by solitary, New York finally abolished the worst excesses of solitary and adopted a standard in accordance with UN guidelines. It means that William Blake, in the tomb for over three decades, is now 'released' to the general population of the prison (Casella & Ridgeway, 2013). Yet, even during the time of a pandemic, calls for compassionate release for elderly people and those who are sick with Covid do not get heeded. In fact, a nationwide survey of US prison data 2021 shows that releases went down. Many prisoners have been on 'medical' lockdown for long two years with disastrous consequences, including dying from Covid in their cells, with no medical attention provided. Commenting on such medical brutality and neglect, Leonard Peltier writes:

> In and out of lockdown last year at least meant a shower every third day, a meal beyond a sandwich wet with a little peanut butter. [...] But now with COVID for an excuse, nothing. No phone, no window, no fresh air—no humans to gather—no loved one's voice. No relief. Left alone and without attention is like a torture chamber for the sick and old.
>
> (Quandt & Altshule, 2022)

The stench of excrements is ever present, and another brilliant writer, C.F. Villa, writes vividly about the guards' "leathery faces" stinking of feces (p. 38).

Villa also describes the slow decay of the body, losing nails, teeth, and seeing helplessly that their children attacked at school—living the stigmatized life on the 'outside.' The full list of grievances is worth citing:

> Indignity. That choking filament that can cut air down to quarters and turn eyes purple, puffy, and watery. Drown skin and soul in chemical agents, outrage, some post-traumatic flashing. Manic guards off their meds. That last good photograph stamped with a boot. Classification hearings postponed for potlucks. The daughter whose eyes fill when you ask innocently, who are you? Sons who are bullied and black-eyed at school because nobody, especially sons of law enforcement, likes the son of a felon. Summers that last for three weeks, winters for ten months. And somewhere in the middle you're caught praying for global warming. Sunburn blisters from two minute's warmth. Optical nerves damaged from light. Wrists that snap wringing clothes. Tendons that tear when reaching for a towel. Knees that don't have a leg to stand on. Teeth caught in toothbrushes. Toenails that fall off into socks—rattle like loaded dice. Ankles that buckle jogging in place.
>
> (Villa, 2016, pp. 38–9)

For women the threat and reality of rape is ever present. Judith Vasquez (2016) writes that after years of sexual assault by male guards, she got pregnant and was forced to abort alone in her cell. Prior to that sexual torture, she endured solitude in complete silence, confined to a jail cell for three years, eliciting comments from guards that men break much faster than she (ever) did. Years later, during the Covid pandemic, she is again in lockdown and finds that the old demons are just as vivid and even more so that she finds herself crying for days (Vasquez, 2021).

Solitary confinement has always been the preferred method to subdue and control political prisoners. Lehlohonolo Moagi, a former member of the Azanian People's Organization, notes that Robben Island was transformed into *the* university of resistance upon the arrival of the Black Consciousness comrades in the 1970s. Outwitting the oppressor, Moagi, who was interned in Pretoria Prison, recalls:

> I remember being brutally interrogated and subsequently being charged with sabotage, abduction and attempted murder. All of these charges then carried a minimum sentence of 5-10 years on Robben Island even death penalty. I got away with 5 years conviction later suspended to three years.
>
> Robben Island has produced graduates-the university of hard knocks. [...] I also had a good read of the Bible as it was the only book we were allowed to read—the nexus of blind faith. I had these young naive racist wardens who were told I was a terrorist. So I would engage them into private talk to bounce and test how tight the security net was around me. At times depending on my moods, I would be confrontational and cause some irritation to disrupt them from focusing on me. I would shake those prison bars so so much, make so much noise that they would get mad at me, and get me out into the courtyard ... hahaha—sunshine, blue skies, fresh air. At times it's a period I look back with fond and not sad memories.
>
> (Email communication with author, November 5, 2002)

What Moagi deems "the nexus of blind faith" becomes a tool of resistance for another prisoner of conscience. In settler colonial countries, the Bible has often been allowed as the only book fit for solitary confinement, because it would create docile bodies, according to the jailers. Koigi wa Wamwere refused reading the Bible for a year but then he 'gave in' and found plenty of passages written for political prisoners like himself. Yet, he also realized later that when he cited those passages to his wife, to disguise his political disagreements with the Moi government, those letters never reached her. Laconically, he notes "The Bible had been added to the prison's list of subversive literature" (2002, p. 271).

Of course, skeptics may note that short of radical abolition, some people are better off in some humane versions of prisons such as Norway.[5] In 2018, a 100-million-pound prison was opened in Denmark, touted as looking more like a college campus than a prison (for men). Yet, it is still bleak, adorned with high gray, concrete walls lacking tree planting and no gardening prospects. Even those humane prisons have recidivism rates, which means they fail to deliver ('rehabilitating' the convict). The point is if the Quaker's game of incarceration for the betterment of the species would have worked, nobody would ever re-offend. The lack of human contact and touch, the lack of free sexual expression, and human creativity all create conditions of disorder, destabilization, and mental illness; in other words, stigmatization writ large: one is simply worth *less*. In the memorable words of Oscar Wilde's whose own life was drastically shortened by his prison stint in Reading's Gaol in England:

> For they starve the little frightened child
> Till it weeps both night and day:
> And they scourge the weak, and flog the fool,
> And gibe the old and gray,
> And some grow mad, and all grow bad,
> And none a word may say.
>
> (Wilde, 1896)

As he notes in this long prison poem, imprisonment contributes to spirit murder and dehumanization of all, especially the vulnerable ones, the young, the sick, and the aged. It is very difficult to maintain a modicum of dignity in any form of imprisonment. To me, Wilde's poem, which was a *cause célèbre* for prison reform at the turn of the 20th century in England, powerfully describes the traumatizing conditions of jail or prison. All total institutions bear responsibility for the proliferation of a specific disease: post-carceral traumatic stress disorder. Abolitionists must consider what is owed to survivors and their families (Coyle & Young, 2022). New York State is offering preferential licenses of cannabis dispensaries to those who had been convicted of cannabis possession; it is a *symbolic* step in the right direction, as it is only impacting a few of the tens of thousands of families impacted by the war on drugs.

Are Gender-Responsive Prisons the Answer?

There is one prison that I have visited that exudes a spirit of compassion: Bollé prison for women in Bamako, Mali. The walls of the building are of similar height of any private home's compound. Inside the prison, chicken run around, women tend to a garden, and young children are imprisoned with their mothers. Nobody wears a uniform—neither prisoners nor guards. A prison psychologist treats women who have committed infanticide. I learned that teenagers who leave the rural area and work as domestic laborers in rich Malian homes find themselves at risk of being raped by the patron or his son. The warden, an abolitionist, tells me that the men are never incarcerated, and because abortion services are illegal, the young women take extreme measures and kill their newborn to be spared the shame of mothering out of wedlock. I spoke with a woman in a workshop area who told me with bright eyes that the next day was her release day. Nobody wants to dwell in a golden prison. Freedom of mobility is a prized good for all humans, and these justice-involved women gain skills that they can use on the market, because they will have to support themselves.

The pressing question then is if prisons must be made more comfortable to address therapeutic and educational needs. Most prisoners are mothers, and the vast majority of all prisoners have a mental health difference *before* entering prison. In my town, a new jail was planned, and legislators and the sheriff alike wanted to design it in such a way to give 'free' people the chance to get their drug treatment plan 'in-house.' Such 'progressive punishment' favors a carceral solution to all social problems (cf. Schept, 2015). Would pregnant persons be better off being housed in a total institution? Hardly, and it shows that the patriarchal punishment system has no regard for the runaway effects of incarceration on a fetus. Why have mental health and drug treatment facilities in the 'free world,' when all kinds of people can get such services within a jail? It is important to ask court-involved people themselves regarding gender-responsive and 'progressive' solutions, especially those who are queer, trans people of color:

> This interaction between racism and trans-phobia is the basis for an anti-racist, gender-queer, anti-prison agenda promoted by black transgender and gender non-conforming activists. In contrast to calls to develop a 'normative transgender prison order,' or trans-sensitive prisons, the [activists] point to the systemic nature of gender violence as part of the structures of imprisonment and reject the possibility of gender liberation under conditions of captivity. In so doing, they seek to transform anti-prison politics by calling for the abolition of gender policing as part of a broader abolitionist agenda.
>
> (Sudbury, 2009, p. 18)

The net widening of social control and surveillance continues to vex penal abolitionists even during popular calls for defunding or even abolishing policing. Part of the problem is, as I show in the next section, the white, Euro-American paradigm governing punishment driven by attempts of rationalized vengeance.

A Note on Vengeance: Between *Noblesse Oblige* and Contempt

"So, you don't really believe in the courts," says an irritated white sheriff candidate (who later took office) to me after his debate with the other candidates. I say "well, …" thinking about what redeeming factors an ideal court might have. And he left before I could respond to such accusation. (The same candidate, who campaigned about the need for education and awareness, was not ready for a short dialogue on such a serious matter. Of course, he was provoked by my quick retort on not calling the police for (domestic) intervention, even when I was a victim of crime. He probably never heard such a thing in his life, having served as chief of police of a village that is over 95% white.)

My reasoned response to him now would demonstrate the following two contradictory conditions haunting the criminal legal system: (1) immunity from prosecution and (2) contemptuous, zealous prosecution, following settler colonial law. Put together, it creates a schizophrenic criminal justice ideology, which, on the one hand, thrives on an unstated implicit social connections model that presents 'abolitionist' verdicts to those who exemplify the art of networking or currying sympathy. On the other hand, it doles out harsh justice to those who are treated contemptuously before even entering court in shackles and orange jumpsuits. In New York State alone, on any given day, 75% of 25,000 prisoners are lingering in jail because of their inability to post bail, according to the *Justice Leadership USA* organization and their decarceration campaign *Free New York*, 2017. By 2020, over half of the remand prisoners were released in my town's jail due to bail reform. Yet, the threat of reinstating bail for nonviolent felonies and misdemeanors remains high, as the bail bond lobby in collusion with sheriffs, prosecutors, and police unions demands business as usual: bail-in those who do not have the capital.

It is important that certain interest groups marked by prestige, power, social connections, capital, and whiteness already enjoy freedom from threats of imprisonment. 'Abolitionism' confers quasi-religious absolution or sovereign immunity. (1) A protection racket is enjoyed by those who commit harm under the color of law: state actors within the punishment system, defense, and intelligence apparati; actors within environmental agencies, as well as the security/exchange commission, Bureau of Indian Affairs, politicians, and diplomats. (2) Large corporations can usually bank on the protection of their (criminal) interests protected by the settler colonial nation-state within US jurisdiction or abroad[6]. (3) In addition, transgressions by white supremacist organizations such as the Klu Klux Klan (or "alt-right") are harms perpetrated in defense of the settler state and therefore getting the dubious distinction of parastatal terrorist organizations. Two Klan members received $4,000 from a magazine when they bragged about the murder of Emmett Till in 1954 (Beauchamp, 2005). Acts of terrorism and lynching get rewarded, not with a death sentence, but with freedom, honorarium, and looting Black victims' property after pogroms (cf. Hanna-Jones, 2018). (4) The state gives great deference to the power elites with social connections and postgraduate credentials, working in respectable institutions. As police officers like to tell me (with a certain gleefulness) when we discuss police killings of civilians, that hospitals have a tremendous advantage in covering up negligence deaths and tens of thousands of patients die due to bad care or botched operations. In Germany, a nurse was found guilty of killing 85 patients in 2018 (Chappell, 2019). In the United States, during the Covid pandemic, a new term emerged: medical brutality which targets Black and

Latine patients, tracing back to a legacy of settler coloniality and slavery. (5) If they find themselves arrested, the white elites have their dream team of lawyers who can conjure up any excuse for a lighter verdict or freedom. The most dramatic example is that of the 'affluenza' defense—the white, male defendant was high on drugs and quite drunk and in a car crash killed four people (among them, a pregnant woman and a pastor). His lawyers argued successfully that because he was raised in opulence, he did not learn to take responsibility for risky behaviors. Later, he was sentenced to two years in jail, because he absconded to Mexico with his mother (Garza & Williams, 2016). White celebrities and politicians usually receive a golden parachute; upon accusations of rape or sexual assault, they check themselves into a sex addiction rehab center for a month to preempt any indictment. (6) In general, white defendants get a *carte blanche* (!) and their drug addiction is no fault of their own. It is treated as a disease, not a criminal act of personal failure. In the wake of the big pharma-induced opioid epidemic killing tens of thousands of Americans, this whitewashing of criminal addiction should fuel a popular resistance to the racist war on drugs. It is quite typical for actors of massive corporate racketeering that their affairs are a matter of tort law and not crimes against society. Witness the Sackler family, responsible for the opioid crises, and their legal team gets to have a say in the terms of the settlement payouts in class action suits. It remains to be seen if there will be a criminal prosecution (Hoffman, 2022). Over 20 years ago, Marc Mauer of the Sentencing Report (2000) estimated that whites get probation 80% of the time, while Black defendants get jail time 80% of the time for similar offenses. With Michael J. Coyle, we must ask the pertinent question: "what kind of people are selected for jail?" (2013, p. 18). The Sentencing Project provides the answer about the presence of a 'lawful' double standard:

> In a new report to the United Nations on racial disparities, we explain how the United States essentially operates two distinct criminal justice systems: one for wealthy people and another for poor people and people of color. By creating and perpetuating policies that allow racial disparities to exist in its criminal justice system, the United States is in violation of the International Covenant on Civil and Political Rights to ensure that all residents—regardless of race—are treated equally under the law.
>
> (2018)

(7) Acts of violence by leftist groups are zealously prosecuted and investigated, while state policy has not been particularly interested in investigating right-wing conspiracies and acts of terrorist violence, even though the Federal Bureau of Investigation (FBI)'s own data show that the impact of right-wing terrorism has proliferated since the Obama administration (O'Harrow, Ba Tran, & Hawkins, 2021). German socialist Otto Kirchheimer already knew in 1929 that

> the right-wing enemy of the state will be regarded by the legal justice system as a decent person, because he is not an enemy of the bourgeois order; he's only an enemy of the current form of bourgeois order, namely of parliamentary democracy.
>
> (1929/2017, p. 187)

Even where right-wing terror quite blatantly manifests itself, it does not necessarily prompt police conduct establish "law and order," including failing to arrest rioters who clearly attacked unarmed protesters. Prosecutions as the Charlottesville incident makes quite apparent: According to eyewitness reports, the riot police averted their eyes, when protesters sought their protection from Neo-Nazi brutality. Incredibly, several protesters of color received assault charges, even one who was battered by several Nazis while lying on the ground. Neo-Nazi men only faced prosecution when activists tracked down their identities, basically doing police work. One notorious predicate offender was sentenced to 360 days in prison, some 120 days suspended, for attacking the writer, Kendra Bills, a white woman activist (Bills, 2017).

The bifurcated approach to justice means 'just-us' for those whose moral flaws are minimized, even in the case of murder and a draconian wrath reserved for those who live beyond the (colonial) pale.

Colonial Justice Administration

We now arrive at two senses of justice administration. The first one defines violent administrative law (Spade, 2015) executed by violence workers who are judges, presiding in criminal court which has a "jurispathic" function (Cover, 1983–1984), generally applied to those who are victimized or terrorized by the racial contract. Groups who continue to be targeted are those whose suffering was part and parcel of the violent founding of the United States: people of African descent and Indigenous sovereign nations. The second road taken is that of legal practices among elites who recognize each other as equals: Justice is administered to friends of the court as a pathway to repair and enhanced reputation, rather than a pathway to despair and endless shame or, worse, demise. Both paths are scripted by Hobbes as the sovereign power governing by colonial might and by benign institutions. The way the police force is employed is indicative of the separate treatment of populations. One set is treated to law enforcement, the raw power of police criminalizing distant others (among whom they tend not to live), living beyond the pale. (2) The other set is treated to policing, officers who behave like social workers, de-escalating conflict and looking for lost adorable white children (in my case, as a three-year-old child). In the first case, I will describe this as Hobbes' colonial law enforcement; in the second case, I will draw on Kant's abstract-rights-bearing law, which supposedly preserves dignity and respect of persons. I will say more about Hobbes' ideology in Chapter 3.

Haunting Kant or an Ubuntu Way to Think about Dignity

> *A specter is haunting modernity—the specter of colonialism.*
>
> (Viviane Saleh-Hanna, 2015)

I am not interested in elaborating on the inner architecture of justice conceived by Immanuel Kant, considered an important figure of the European Enlightenment era. Rather, I like to focus on the elisions, who is not considered a proper subject for the cosmopolitan project and world peace. We cannot use a magic wand and wish away Kant's anthropological lectures (over 40 years of armchair pontifications), as Emmanuel Chukwudi Eze (2001) points out. Following Nikita Dhawan's (2014) analysis, I also hold that there is no epistemic turn that would make Kant's project more redeemable. There is an epistemological indulgence in the monological subject of history, victorious, white, male, possibly Prussian, the apex of the great chain of being.

I hold that Kant's social ontology gives justification to modern Western jurisprudence with its racist, colonizing, sexist gaze on othering humans in the courtroom. The law is executed in partiality, fixing epistemic supremacy on those proper subjects which deserve respect and therefore an empathic gaze. One can easily put oneself in their shoes and follow the maxim of reciprocity. Universalizing such maxim is not permitted, because the colonized, non-victorious, hence non-rational subjects of history have not proven themselves of such worthiness. Adorno's verdict about the categorical imperative leading us to the gates of Auschwitz needs its colonial correlative. The categorical imperative serves as basis for theorizing perpetual immaturity of people of African lineage; American Indians enduring the racist adage of noble savages also lack the rational, Christian, civilized ethos essential for Kant's white supremacist, patriarchal version of the cosmopolitan project. I am not convinced that Kantian ethics resembles the dignitarian ethic of Ubuntu.

Any critique of the philosophical foundation of retributive justice will have to engage with Kant. For Kant's deontological ethics which prize "duty," not "utility," has been used in dignity discussions of Ubuntu ethics (Cornell, 2014; Metz, 2022). Kant's champions propose to engage in a fruitful encounter of Western and southern perspectives on ethics and, to a lesser extent, on criminal justice. I wish to probe that uncontroversial suggestion by asking ourselves to "haunt" Kantian ethics and ideas about judgment. Why focus on a critique of Kantian ethics? He wrote at a time that the first modern prison cells were opened, and within a generation, they also introduced a women's wing, with the first women being free African Americans (in the 1830s). During the debates on chattel slavery, Kant opined that Black men *deserve* harsh, corporal punishment for insolence, to teach them a lesson. For him, Black lives did not matter, and the categorical imperative does not apply to them as a people or 'race' (Hund, 2011).

It is well known that Adolf Eichmann mistakenly invoked Kant's categorical imperative. Defending his participation in the extermination project of the Nazi final solution, Eichmann noted that Hitler ordered him to carry out the genocide against Europeans and Russians. Of course, Kant insists on the principle of autonomy, reciprocity, and universality in the categorical imperative and contrasts this maxim with the hypothetical imperative which suggests that another authority than one's moral self and goodwill is used for ethical decisions. So, it is nonsensical to will a people's genocide, as it would fail on account of reciprocity and universalization. He would have to wish to be killed, too, and the Israeli High Court ordered exactly that—Eichmann's execution.

From an Ubuntu perspective, there is something deeply bewildering about a maxim that is based on an egocentric moral grounding or *monological* reasoning. In order to engage in a universalizing mind game that is putatively based on a goodwill, many assumptions play a role. (1) For instance, parents are good-willingly abusing their children, because it will make them better equipped to face a (racist) hostile world when they grow up (a defense of paddling in schools in 19 states of the United States). Apparently, being hit helps the child mature, according to faulty reasoning. But it has a brutalization effect, and hundreds of studies on child corporal punishment all come to the same conclusion: it is harmful or even devastating to the psyche of the child, and the last effect is that such violence continues into the next generation uninterrupted. Those who have been hit as children will as adults also have a propensity to hit their children. (2) In a racist nonideal world, goodwill seems to be lost on those with diminished rational capacity and aesthetics such as African human beings. While slavery is loathsome, discrimination against African peoples is part of the Kantian Enlightenment project; Black lives do not enjoy the same moral or legal standing as whites or even other people of color, as his essay ("Of the Different Races of Humans"), which served to establish 'scientific racism,' makes clear:

> Against empiristic objections (such as those by Buffon that "nature knows neither classes nor species" or by Blumenbach that the division of humanity into races draws "very arbitrary boundaries"), Kant points out that ›race‹ does not occur as a "word" in the "description of nature" or as a "thing" in "nature" but that it is "well founded" in "reason" as a "concept." […] Even though he uses the term »prejudice« in the context of his discussion of races and warns not to "carry" one's own "ideas into the observation," his reflections are influenced by just that.
>
> (Hund, 2011, p. 79)

In the essay "Observations on the Feeling of the Beautiful and Sublime," Kant (2019) revels in white supremacy and misogynist feelings while pontificating on the graces of the white male species—himself. This is a sinister "anthropological" essay, which reveals much about his true sensibilities about ethics and punishment. It serves as a perverse advice column directed toward the reader, a white male colonizer, encouraging him to whip his indolent Black colonized subject. And given this cruel sentiment, it is perhaps clearer now how to inscribe the meaning of Black Feminist Hauntology (Saleh-Hanna, 2015) into Kant's invocation: Retributive justice defenders employ the exacting categorical imperative such that the last murderer (and last human) residing on an island, maybe in the South Sea, will have to be killed without mercy. Robinson can rid himself of an aberrant Friday without guilt. And nobody will ask the haunting question of who in turn will have to whip the colonizer?

One might ask, the author penning these grotesque examples, is it the same one who penned *Toward Perpetual Peace* or a schizophrenic Other? In fact, as Nikita Dhawan (2014) shows incisively, Kant's blind spots on racism and colonialism are factually a demonstration of its opposites: a willful discrimination against peoples who are the Enlightenment's Other. Despite Sankar Muthu's (2003) postulation of a post-racial turn in Kantian's later writings, the cosmopolitan claim does not extend beyond the European settler state to welcome unconditionally Indigenous colonized peoples into the fold of peaceful nations.

> [T]he greatest strength of the Kantian categorical imperative lies in its insistence on the fundamental equality of all moral agents. However, this is accompanied by the demand that individuals prove themselves worthy of being treated as equal by fulfilling the normative understanding of morality. Otherwise they forfeit their right to be treated equally.
>
> (Dhawan, 2014, p. 45)

The Euro-American prison and torture regimes seem not to uphold the lofty ideals of just retributive principles; white cruel colonialists were not receiving similar punishment. This logic of disparate punishment regimes continues the world over.

(3) Kant proclaims there is nothing superior to a goodwill or goodwill-generating moral maxims. Goodwill prioritizes and normalizes human action between rational male agents and is disconnected from ecological or inter-being perspectives.
(4) This Kantian assumption says explicitly: 'we are *not* interconnected.' The monological (Prussian, male) subject gets to dictate what is good for all, and especially for those who are not quite humans, i.e., rational beings. And this subject as reasonable, emotionally, secular (or spiritually impoverished) white, upper-class cisman, gets to define what rational means.
(5) Goodwill is duty-bound and is disinterested in love. Kant says that "love is a pathological feeling." Caring and sharing for family members (as filial duty) is prized in an Ubuntu ethics (cf. Metz, 2007). Valuing

disinterestedness, lack of love, and empathy are values foundational for unnested care and antithetical to Indigenous virtue ethics.

(6) Kantian accountability and judgment are backward-oriented, as we can clearly see when Kant lays out justifications for punishment, putting a premium on retribution.

Of course, all conflict resolution will have to deal with past injuries; otherwise, there would be no concern about being harmed in the future. But such taking stock of the past does not stop Indigenous, holistic justice practices with being future-oriented asking the following: how do we (not I) establish harmony for the greater good? How do the future generations interrelate as friends, partners, neighbors?

(7) One does have to wonder about this tension in Kantian ethics: Goodwill meets vengeful 'justice': even the last murderer will have to be killed because the empty formalism of a universalizing maxim dictates it. Such strange abstraction from human suffering and ending harm concerns is anathema to restorative and transformative justice. Goodwill is completely hollowed out of content. There is nothing good about this will.

(8) An ethic of compassion for kin and distant strangers is not monological and solipsistic. It is a nonideal theory by attending to the messiness of lives where feelings get hurt, and nobody occupies the reasonable 'man' perspective.

(9) Thus, a ludic Ubuntu perspective speaks back to Kant and the deontological tradition. Playfulness also matters. A ludic Ubuntu ethics is necessarily a dignitarian ethics as will be addressed in Chapter 5. Caring for one's kin, nested-care values, and prizing peace over conflict count as a life-affirming practice.

As Emmanuel Chukwudi Eze has argued, rehabilitating Kant's cosmopolitanism as antiracist is problematic. "In both the precritical and critical works, blacks are never thought of as capable of moral, intellectual, or aesthetic experience 'beyond the trifling'" (Eze, 2001, p. 81). While Kant condemns English cruelty toward colonized peoples, Eze notes "[w]hat he accused the English of doing to others *in practice*, Kant inflicts upon nonwhite peoples *in theory*" (p. 80; emphasis Eze's). Kant never publicly disavows his outright racist beliefs. Dhawan (2014) also notes that at best we see a "turn" from crass racism toward a more sophisticated racism with his critique of imperial occupation of foreign lands. Kant never wavers in his support of race as a biological category (p. 50). Hund's (2011) research strongly suggests that not only does Kant give a philosophical nod to scientific racism, he also uses his antisemitic, antiziganist, and orientalist stereotypes to map out a sinister eugenicist project. Presaging social Darwinism, Kant predicts that whites are the only ones that are meant to survive globally (Hund, 2011, p. 91). For these reasons, I find it necessary to differentiate an Ubuntu ethics from Kantian ethics; the latter fits well with carceral logic of retribution and white supremacist concerns of who is destined for incarceration and social death.

Abolition Now (for Some)

Two claims drive my argument that abolitionism already benefits the powerful and vengeance, by contrast, is exacted at the powerless.

1 *The court's ideology affirms the socially connected and powerful.* It does not matter, particularly, if this class appears as victim or as defendant. Defendant Dominique Strauss-Kahn (DSK) was able to marshal unlimited investigative resources to go after his Guinea-born accuser who dared to press charges against him for brutal sexual assault while on duty in his $3,000/night suite. In the end, the prosecutor for one of the largest criminal courts in the United States had to drop the case. The accuser (i.e., the hotel worker) was found out to have lied about her immigration status. DSK is free to roam the streets (and hotels) of Paris, while the shamed victim was accused of working as a sex worker. Cyrus Vance, Manhattan's powerful district attorney, was no match for DSK's dream legal team. Making commercial bail was no issue for the accused, and during the trial proceedings, he was allowed to reside in a golden cage in upper Manhattan—not in Rikers Island, one of the largest penal colonies in the world (Eligon, 2011). Enter the #metoo movement, which began with media expose of a serial sexual predator, Hollywood mogul Harvey Weinstein. Dozens of women dared to come forward, including those who had signed consent agreements in exchange for some monetary compensation. Where an offender is caught, the companies resort to a "well, no crime was really committed," the infamous nondisclosure agreements (NDAs): "As the cases of Harvey Weinstein, Bill O'Reilly and others show, the use of NDAs threatens workplace safety and morale, by giving repeat offenders impunity to victimize others" (Estreicher, 2017).Those who are socially connected also have capital to insulate themselves with fierce lawyers. It was clear to the US most powerful prosecutor, Cy Vance, that he could not get a guilty verdict. Many police indictments do not even go beyond grand jury stage, because these laypersons simply cannot find fault with an officer of the law who is videotaped killing an innocent Black human being.

In so many cases, we see that justice is not blind nor objective. Implicit bias is so pervasive that there is indeed contemplation about carrying predictive policing with their risk logarithms into the judicial chambers. Why not replace human judges with humanoids? Cyborgic beings might engage in exacting sanctions, and all of the sudden, jails and prisons would be filled with people from all sectors of society, not only with those who are socially disconnected and, in fact, disposable people. This is unlikely, again, because it is humans who write programs ignorant about their unconscious implicit bias. Judges may unconsciously see themselves in defendants such as the case of Brock Turner, a swimmer and student of elite Stanford University. He received a sentence of six-month jail-time because he 'is a good' person who goofed.

In drunk stupor, he raped an unconscious woman in a public space and runs away after two men intervene. (In the end, he also gets 'good time,' so effectively, he serves only three months in jail and appealed his sentence, because he did receive a lifelong sexual offender status.) Critics contrast his case with that of a Black teenager Cyntoia Brown who kills her white rapist, and it did not matter that she did sex survival work. She was tried as an adult and got a 51-year sentence for defending her life. Only after celebrities got involved and framed her as a child sex slave, she received a commutation after 16 years in prison. However, a racist system prosecuting Brown and Alisha Walker, and trans women of color confers punishment upon survivors and is not interested in innocence claims: "Cyntoia and Alisha's radical acts of self-love and preservation were criminalized by those with authority; each had the carceral weight of racism and whorephobia stacked against them" (Kaba & Schulte, 2017).

What happens to those who are not all-powerful and socially connected? In that case, a different assumption takes hold.

2 *All courts are driven by a mode of vengeance.* Of course, I am quite aware that the invention of contractarianism is meant to curtail the brute feeling of revenge that exists among humans in a fictive state of nature. Of course, feelings don't just evolve with the rule of law, but Hobbes makes a rhetorical case for their suppression. In his list of crimes and punishment, which inspired the great penal reformer Cesaire Beccaria, Hobbes favors deterrence theory, as a way to keep in check the mob who might be incited to do evil things, if justice does not come down hard at the errant subject. In no uncertain terms, Hobbes writes that punishment is "an Evill inflicted by publique Authority" on subject who has transgressed against the law, "to the end that the will of men may thereby the better be disposed to obedience" (1986, p. 353). So, it is quite clear that Hobbes imposes a penal apparatus that punishes the individual transgressor in order to deter and create conditions for a 'voluntary' submission to the sovereign. Or, if not voluntary, then obedience will be beaten into us through a myriad of sanctions or operative conditioning. This is also called schooling. Interestingly, some 19 states in the United States still perform this terrifying conditioning through corporal punishment in schools, As Jane Hall Fitz-Gibbon (2017) shows, mainline churches continue to hold up biblical justifications for punishing willful children by the paddle, and parental protest, even when a child is killed, have no legal consequences for the punishers. Where pupils were killed by the thousands, in the case of American Indian girls and boys facing the terror of the residential school system, US or Canadian school officials were never punished (Churchill, 2004; International Tribunal for the Disappeared of Canada, 2016). No transgression of the church and white settler law was apparently committed—but a great deal of extra-legal emotional and physical terrorist practices perpetrated by mainline

churches and with the blessings of the state. In March 2022, the Pope offered apologies.

In the case of using violence or resisting nonviolently state violence and all those forces who uphold white supremacy, settler nations, a logic of protection prevails. As seen in Charlottesville, Virginia, police and prosecution were completely reluctant to arrest anybody who marched as Neo-Nazi. So, a white man who pointed a gun against Black protesters was not immediately arrested and only belatedly faced charges, after a concerted media campaign. When a white man shot and killed a Black teenager for the "offense" of playing music in his car, the shooter just went home. Only when national protests were heard, the police arrested him. There is no stand-your-ground law for gunning down music lovers. But it does not matter. It is, as Paul Butler, fittingly says, the rule of the chokehold. State-sustained violence operates as outlaw when Black people are inconveniently harmed or murdered. This came forth quite blatantly when a white woman passenger nervously videotaped her police encounter, signaling to the white police officer that she was afraid of him "after all the killings." He tried to calm her down with the following remark: "But you're not black," Lieutenant Abbott replies. "Remember, we only kill black people. Yeah. We only kill black people, right?" Well, he was fired (with full pension benefits) after the media got hold of the dashcam video (Hauser & Fortin, 2017). There is a thin blue line—and it means that one does not divulge police tactics, especially those with murderous intentions, even if only meant sarcastically.

What about Alternative Courts? Gentler in Nature?

The proliferation of alternative courts to the traditional criminal court, military, immigration, and family court system, in addition to small claims courts for civil proceedings, has not really changed that general modus. Drug courts, family courts, domestic violence courts, veteran courts, or trafficking courts are supposed to do something differently from the traditional courts that focus on a top-down approach that silences the person who is on trial and gives a fake voice to the victimized person who is represented 'by the people.' Unless, of course, one is socially, politically connected and wealthy (see condition 1).

Drug treatment courts now have a proven record of being a resounding failure; at best, they show a 40% success rate. Their 'carrot-and-stick' approach and boiler-plate template creates resentful defendants who, in the words of a recovery center director, "rather take a prison term." Going through one more day of confessionals at endless meetings over a year seems like doing another jail term, on the outside, with no end in sight. Additionally, they are caught in a double bind: skip work or skip a court-mandated meeting. Of course, work means paying one's bill, and skipping the meeting entails a technical violation which leads straight to a prison bid. In fact, volunteering for drug court turns out to be a catch-22; as heightened surveillance often works to ensnare people into enlarged prison sentences, rather than shorter stints (Fluellen & Trone, 2000). Trafficking courts are meant to favor the defendant as victim, till she confesses that she is a sex worker, turning the system against her (and deportation proceedings if she has no legal papers). The kindly court is supposed to encourage the defendant to engage in meaningful licit work and provide T visas for those internationally trafficked (Nagel, 2015a).

The prevailing ideology of criminal justice is cloaked in vengeance—and in paradox. From the bully pulpit of the judge representing the mighty power of the state (the prosecution, detectives, arresting officers, parole and probation, jail captain, civil servants under the employ of the state, such as psychiatrists), the defendant is scolded for knowingly trespassing against the rule of law and worse, for not showing any remorse. A paradox arises. After all, the police/prosecutor are demanding revenge (i.e., paying one's debt to society), which clearly singles out the criminalized subject as an undesirable member of society, an outcast to be condemned to real *social death* (Price, 2015a). The court, by contrast, reminds the subject that she needs to *restore societal ties* or relationships symbolically by apologizing to the victims (if there are any), paying restitution, and, in addition, by 'doing time.' The bewildered condemned person has to sort out how to be a disposable person facing social isolation or death and how to rebirth social life at the same time. And the wrath of the judge is exacting, if he believes the 'offender' shows no sign of remorse. It is seen as a mitigating factor, if effectively employed (Maslen, 2015). A harsher sentence is usually a predictable outcome of such perceived willed defiance—in addition to implicit bias and stereotype threats based on race, color, immigration status, disability, gender identity and expression, etc.

What happens to decorative justice performance if the accused is openly defiant? Mumia Abu-Jamal worked as journalist, covering the political trials of the MOVE organization's members in Philadelphia, Pennsylvania. His own trial had all the marks of a kangaroo court, especially under the auspices of Judge Sabo, who was known in popular parlance as 'the hanging judge' in the United States. Abu-Jamal's own court-appointed lawyer, who had never defended a capital case, recalls that Sabo was completely biased toward the prosecution and would not entertain any motions of objections from the defense (Amnesty International, 2000). Sabo's judgment was finally subject to judicial review for misinstructing the jury. It is, of course, questionable, why Abu-Jamal did not deserve a new trial.

Ambiguity in Justice

Ricœur presents an interesting dilemma. He advocates an epistemic move from Kant to Hegel for accounting for contingency, namely that localized moral practices might have influence on the administration of justice. And perhaps being inspired by Hegel's master–slave dialectic, Ricœur notes that there is irreducible violence immanent to the legal apparatus. He worries about three interrelated problems in the inherent power-over dynamics on the conflictual Western paradigm. (1) While punishment may be compensation for harm done to others, it is a form of violence and expressing vengeance and blame—feelings that are supposed to be removed from the court of law (so it has the tinge of vigilante justice). (2) Justice is rational and adhering to equality for the purpose of recognition (of equal worth and dignity) of others, yet, borrowing insights from Levinas, it represents a reduction of the singularity of the other leading to exclusionary practices. (3) Administration of justice is mired in a battle over a standard bearer of ideology (rules, procedures), thus representing a power-over other ideologies, a move that is violent (cf. Dierckxsens, 2015, p. 32). So, clearly, there are enormous dilemmas at play in sorting out the merits and demerits of a justly ordered society. Power-over modality cannot be explained away.

Yet, it seems to me that Ricœur is still Kantian (and Rawlsian) enough to put forth a defense of universal rules of justice and a misplaced belief in just punishment when it occurs in the hallowed court of law. After all, justice is impersonal in its legal form. Ricœur defends justice by referring to the term "compensation" for equality in what seems to me a retributivist (Kantian) way where the judge notes the harm done to the victim (*Ibid.*, p. 36). Compensation does not have the meaning of restorative justice, and one might wonder if Ricœur would think that that term is an oxymoron. Concretely put, I must ask whether the sanction of prison time (let alone the traumatic effect of prison) is just. But prison never enters his realm of imagination. The examples presented make it seem that the parties in front of the court are actively negotiating some tort actionable issue, not criminal court proceedings where, say, the defendant is a police officer accused of killing an unarmed victim. Geoffrey Dierckxsens argues that justice aims at social peace (*Ibid.*). I take this to be another ideological defense of the Western paradigm, although the classical versions are rather less idealistic and focus mostly on deterrence and retribution (not peace). In the end, administration of justice relies on community standards, and it may privilege one group over others; yet, it is still the best thing we have in establishing peaceful coexistence, so that the state can indeed function as the "guardian of legitimate violence" (*Ibid.*, p. 38). Dierckxsens acknowledges Ricœur's deep ambivalence about justice and then moves on to defend this justice paradigm to maintain peace. Why is it that justice must be inherently about struggle, something that agrees with Hegel and Honneth, and thus opposed to love, agape, the peaceful recognition of the other (cf. p. 40)? It is because Ricœur along with other moral and political philosophers (Rawls, Hegel, Honneth) are deeply wedded to the disputational form of judicial process; settling a case always amounts to an agonistic game of winners and losers. Where Ricœur gets it right is in discussing the dynamic of ideology and utopia as a "spiral" to note an incomplete project in search of nonviolent justice practices (p. 44). But it is left up to minoritized groups to rewrite their own (utopian) histories and produce counter-commons. In the end, Ricœur holds on to a formal, objective, universal justice apparatus as a guarantor of peace (p. 45). My discussions of troubling Western justice in this chapter have given us another perspective. The rule of law is deeply interwoven with a powerful ideology that guarantees securitization to those who are well connected to the white capitalist elites and defended by Mandarin intellectuals in academe. Such ideological justice claims hold up no guarantees for peace for those who "have nothing to lose but their chains."

Negative Ubuntu and Colonial Justice as Witchcraft

Ubuntu in the negative topples the meaning of valued, peaceful intersubjectivity, of mutual recognition of humanity, and of being in relationship, being one. This sacred, social connectivity principle reverts to negative Ubuntu in the Western court of justice, especially when the adjudication involves disempowered, poor, and people of color. A primordial relationship is experienced by the fetus whose fate is varied: facing death through miscarriage or abortion or facing uncertain life through the birthing trauma; a trauma precisely, because it condemns the newborn to certain separation from the life-giving connector of the umbilical cord. But it does not amount to natal alienation per se, as the newborn remembers the sounds and even language she was exposed to in utero, and she knows to crawl to the life-giving mother's breasts for immediate nursing. If a baby is taken away from an imprisoned mother at birth, the trauma is immediate as the baby's need for attachment and nested care is severed (Bowlby, 1988; Narvaez, 2021). Lost is the trust, the bond created through nine months of gestation, and unfamiliar, frightening voices and languages, as well as strange tastes (of food, drink, and other substances) replace the familiar, and the baby may react by crying, developing colic or other dis-eases. Spiritually speaking, being-in relationship means that one is relating to something prior. In terms of Ubuntu philosophy, it also means that I am always already relating to the ancestors and ultimately to the divine spark that gives life to the universe and all within it. The ancestors may be in a supportive relationship with oneself or in a disempowering one, depending on my own thoughts and moral actions. Negative Ubuntu comes into play when colonized people are being cut off from the familiar traditions and not able to interpret the messages of the ancestors, who stand in for those who come before us and are not-yet born. Demonic forces unleash their invisible power and seek revenge on the living. In his book on South African witchcraft, Adam Ashforth (2005) notes practices that display Ubuntu in the negative. It literally kills. He defines negative Ubuntu as the practical reason of community disharmony:

> To the adage "A person is a person through other people," the negative corollary of Ubuntu adds: "because they can destroy you." That is, a person can survive only to the extent that others in the community choose

> not to destroy him or her. How they might do so is less important than the fact that they can. And when they do, whether by physical or by occult violence, the demand for justice inevitably arises.
>
> (Ashcroft, 2005, p. 86)

Ashforth laments that social scientists have no good analysis on dealing with hatred and jealousy, the drivers of witchcraft. Of course, since Freud, psychologists have looked at the devastating effects of negative emotions such as hate. "But very few have examined the broader social effects of these emotions other than as motives causing individuals to act in antisocial ways" (*Ibid.*). Scheler (2010) stands out in providing clues about *ressentiment*, which will be discussed in Chapter 4. Ashforth's complaint is echoed by psychiatrist Herbert Thomas (2006) whose book on shame response to rejection gives us a very good clue on how violence bubbles up in a prisoner and, importantly, how Thomas as prison psychiatrist was able to interrupt the violence, even with humor.

Ashforth presents narratives of life stories in Soweto, South Africa. People assisting others and facing jealousy and anger for helping with school fees, for some, but not all eligible family members. Ashforth, as a foreign-born white man, encountered this dilemma when he assisted one brother to pursue his studies but neglected to do that for the other one; thus, by not reaching out to the other brother, the two brothers developed intense resentment and even hatred toward each other. Furthermore, real harm occurs by not assisting all who have pressing needs and depend on those who earn an income, which is the minority (Ashforth, 2005, pp. 33–4). Cultivating kin relations is tightly circumscribed, and as adult child, one has an immediate duty to assist one's parents, and one has more obligations to assist a sibling than a cousin (*Ibid.*, pp. 32–3). Jealousy can literally kill the person who is better off and exudes pride. He tells of a successful business woman who built a new house in the suburbs, leaving Soweto. Within a year, she died. Those left behind in Soweto considered her proud, which they considered to be the key reason for her death (pp. 34–5). Participating in *stokvel*, a mutual aid credit association, is coupled with enormous risks. "People die, disappear, and renege on their obligations to *stokvels*" (p. 34). It is attractive to participate in order to plan for major expenses, and one can also deny credit to kin, which outside the *stokvel* obligations and safeguards, one would not be able to do so (p. 34).

> At a kangaroo court I witnessed in 1992, one of the community leaders wanted to beat a confession out of a thief. … The other members of the Street Committee restrained him, however, arguing that, once the suspect had been beaten, even if he confessed to the crime the beating itself would be taken by the culprit and the community as constituting 'payment in full' for the crime and thus preclude any chance of retrieving the stolen goods.
>
> (Ashcroft, 2005, p. 40)

Corporal violence by state actors is frowned upon within the Western criminal justice framework, unless of course it concerns the death penalty, carried out without 'cruel and unusual' sentiments, or unless it is carried out by zealous teachers and principals, paddling willful pupils (Hall Fitz-Gibbon, 2017). However, police officers' coerced confessions is so normalized that their illicit conduct is portrayed on US TV shows without any moral outrage nor a hint of criminal repercussions. Yet, when a community group in Johannesburg meets and a minority view favors a public beating, the white male Western anthropologist depicts such a group as 'kangaroo court,' replicating racial stereotyping of an apartheid past.[7] Under the auspices of the United Democratic Front (UDF) in the 1980s and 1990s, in townships, Kgotla courts meted out justice against collaborators of the apartheid state, enforce consumer boycotts, and control social crimes such as theft, rape, and gangsterism. The white settler state labeled these courts "kangaroo courts," as they defied (from below) both traditional and colonial practices. What the deliberations show in this instance is that the majority is much more interested in restitution (tort) rather than in futile imprisonment or revenge. The majoritarian view also echoes Beccaria's worry about the proportionality of punishment, i.e., that a beating would render any restorative efforts as unfair, since it would be considered an additional punitive measure. Of course, evidence of other street committees' deliberations shows that sometimes the majoritarian viewpoint is also that of the most powerful actor(s), and justice as vengeance may be the result. As I have shown, in that way, popular courts are not immune from the political power play creeping into (Western) judicial proceedings. A case in point of such power play was South African President Jacob Zuma's trial for rape of a family acquaintance, and these high-profile proceedings and his subsequent acquittal in the Western court were critiqued by feminist activist Mmatshilo Motsei in her telling book title *The Kanga and the Kangaroo Court* (2007). Her book brought much sorrow to her and her family, as she was shunned for her analysis. Yet, prior to the book's release, she had won international awards for her innovative anti-violence projects. A high price to pay for speaking truth to power.

Drawing on Viviane Saleh-Hanna's Black feminist hauntology (2015), I would add that the effects of negative Ubuntu local practices are magnified in a neoliberal, neocolonial nation-state, South Africa. Saleh-Hanna argues that the violence of the settler state continues to haunt the present: through shapeshifting the judges of slave codes of yesterday become the benign enforcers of anti-Black racist sentencing practices of today, slave patrols turn into public and private police officers and security personnel, the latter being a major employment source in South African cities.

Furthermore, a note on the use of the term "witchcraft" is in order. It is clearly a Western imposition on African social realities and should therefore be treated with much suspicion. Ashforth is quite oblivious to this objection. Does it smack of anti-African sentiments when anthropologists glibly name practices involving invisible forces witchcraft, which in other geographic locations have been labeled shamanic practices?

Turning the table, I suggest in mockery that the Western court is a practice of witchcraft. *The Witches' Hammer*, a prosecutorial guidebook written by German zealous monks (Kramer & Sprenger, 2016) providing the necessary cover (and legitimation) that lead to the medieval and early modern witch craze in Europe, shows in detail the prosecutorial force that has been perfected by modern-day policing. Without a lawyer or community advocate present, it is very easy for a suspect to confess to deeds that she clearly did not commit. Today's *Witches' Hammer* may look more benign in the form of a clandestine script written by prosecutors for others on how to eliminate Black jurors from the eligible pool during *voire dire.* But when life sentences or, worse, capital sentences are meted out by a white jury, it seems to me that the torturous process shows up in another ugly mask.

The Onto-criminological Status of Persons and Non-persons: Masks of Personhood

James Madison overtly pondered about the peculiar status of enslaved humans; are they actually persons or things (chattel); well, he decided they are a mixture of both.

So, this is how a peculiar institution became enmeshed in the juridical theater. As a chattel, they could not be charged in a court of law; as a 'person,' she could be charged, and even found guilty of violations she committed also as an object. She could even be punished to a workhouse (say, in Charleston, SC), walking the infamous treadmill for hours, when torture at the privatized site (the mine, the factory, the plantation) was not considered punishment enough.

Indigenous peoples were told that there are treaties that the colonizing power would abide by; hundreds of treatises later, none of them upheld in North America. Perhaps because they did not achieve 'personhood'? The 2006 UN Declaration on the Rights of Indigenous Peoples upholds that they have a right to their own juridical systems (cf. Art. 34). The Canadian government gave them the 'gift' of sentencing circles—with the proviso that not all cases could be administered by the native community and an unreasonable sentence would be appealed. Indigenous peoples much prefer the term 'healing or peacemaking circles' to the settler colonial concept of 'sentence.' In addition, Indigenous (re)solutions generally do not support denunciation and retribution (McConnell, 2020).

Another bewitching moment of 'personhood' in Roman law inscribes negative Ubuntu into Western jurisprudence through the art of abstraction. Persona, derived from mask, shows how the court theater masquerades:

> [Roman legal persons] do not owe each other more than what is due to them legally and they do not concern themselves with each other in other respects. Ignoring these respects is compulsory so long as one abides in the element of right; a subject, were it not abstract but only concrete,

would also not be comprehensible within the codification of law. The common formula 'without regard for the person' actually means 'without regard for the human being', that is, 'only in regard to the person'. There are no duties for persons aside from those that respect others as persons; that is, no moral, political or aesthetic duties—all such obligations, in so far as human beings experience them, derive from domains on this side of the legal masking.

(Loick, 2015, p. 194)

In the Western court of 'decorative justice,' personhood belongs to the abstract-rights-bearing individual, and the term *in propria persona*, inscribes a performative act of granting the presiding judge jurisdiction. When reviewed under the guise of personhood, the Western (Roman) court is a display of toxic performativity, "pathologies of juridicism" (*Ibid.*, p. 189). The court distorts social relations by severing ties, making intersubjective ethical comportment tremendously challenging. I argue that such pathology leads to paradoxical thinking. Prison is the worst possible place to practice sociality. The world over, prisoners report the hostility when displaying kindness, and the harsh treatment they face when incarcerated for a political crime. Political prisoners' writing is replete with examples of mobilizing within prison and of experiencing repression including solitary as a direct effect of practicing solidarity. The modern prison clearly stands for the violation of experiencing Ubuntu through recognizing the other as human and through this dance of mutual recognition, recognizing oneself as human. It is short-circuited when humans are deposited in buildings far away from parents, family, friends, and community members.

Ludic Ubuntu—Agonistic Battles

Entering the tilted maze of ludic Ubuntu at this stage, one realizes being in the throes of Justitia. Justitia stands for law and order, designed for and by the elites. They have conveyed successfully that a rule of law is preferable to its Other, painted as chaotic anarchy or dystopia. Being in this maze, one is easily drawn into the lower realms, being far from imagining a world without law 'enforcement' and harmonizing dissonance, discord in ways that stabilizes community relations (Nader, 1990).[8] One is never sure when one might get killed, as one's alliances are never so stable to trust another to defend my life and livelihood. However, the regulative ideal, depicted in front of US court houses as Lady Justice blindfolded, is far from realistic, i.e., prosecuting everybody without regard of status. If that were the case, the socially connected and wealthy would also populate the jail houses in the United States or anywhere else in the world. In her article on Black Feminist Hauntology, Saleh-Hanna reminds us of the afterlives of slavery:

The criminal justice system emerged empowered to carry on the beatings that chattel slavery and jim crow violence had performed before it

> accompanied by each generation's resistance, struggles to survive. Today, the public, recorded and endorsed police murders of Black people in the United States are confronted with ghosted words, "Hands up don't shoot" and "I can't breathe," uttered from the graves, sustained by protesters shouting back White supremacy's ultimate unspeakable sentiment: "Black Lives Matter."
>
> (Saleh-Hanna, 2015, p. 25)

The dignitarian rallying cry "Black Lives Matter" in the courthouse and on the streets refracts the ghost of slavery and Jim Crow injustice in the shapeshifting presence of the slaver into the prison wardens, the slave patrol into police officers (*Ibid.,* p. 48). The ruse of impartiality falls apart as Lady Justice is artistically decapitated (through an act of nature, no less) as Figure 1.1 captures.

'Justice,' executed under Justitia's mantle of order and security, is dispassionate and deficit oriented, devouring those who are not living up to bourgeois white standards, which hides its violence in plain sight. Canada's criminal code still condones "reasonable force" exerted against willful children, a legacy of the settler colonial, Church-run residential school system (Michaelson & Durant, 2020). The legacy of chattel slavery also provides the necessary legal impetus to destroy Black families to date (Roberts, 2022). An Ubuntu worldview embedded in dialogical relationship building, life-affirming principles comes up short in a system that celebrates antagonism, necrophilia, spirit murder through separation, hierarchization including adultism, punishment, including even the death penalty. From residential 'schooling' to today's school-to-prison pipeline, it is abundantly clear who is singled out for trafficking in children and teenagers. Abolition of imprisonment is already a reality for those who are well connected. It is not a reality for those who are

Figure 1.1 Photo taken after Hurricane Niklas, at TV Station RTL2, Munich, Germany, March 2015.

treated as disposables, toxic assets, or dispossessed peoples. Black Feminist Hauntology then presents itself as an exorcism of Western witchcraft—colonial criminal injustice (cf. Agozino, 2003; Saleh-Hanna, 2015, p. 69).

Justice as Retribution

In the ludic Ubuntu tilted maze of justice, we find a penchant for retribution or justice as vengeance driven by the emotion of fear—at level 1, symbolized by the large head of the snake (see Figure 0.2, Introduction). So far, we looked at the *emotions* of rejection, disgust, and hate, underpinning the *actions* taken at the level of vengeful justice in the criminal justice system. Provocatively put, I do not differentiate between the classical philosophical theories, namely retribution and deterrence, regarding the predictable outcome of both ideal theories, because both inevitably lead to the same result: punishment is meant to avenge a crime, and in the end, it does not matter whether such theory is formulated with backward-looking (Kant) or forward-looking intention (Mill). Retributive judgment has been described as desert based because it relies on events that happened in the past; one deserves punishment for one's criminal behavior. By contrast, punishment based on deterrence takes into consideration what the future holds for the offender and others, who should be taught to refrain from a life of criminality. Oddly, enough, forward-looking or consequentialists like John Stuart Mill defend the death penalty for the offender, making a case for deterring others from engaging in a similar criminal way that would warrant such extreme penalty.

Retributive theory is often thought to be the harsher justice model, because it relates to the ancient *lex talionis*, exacting penalty of 'an eye for an eye.' However, such substitution or equivocation is more figurative than practical in capital cases. In contemporary jurisprudence, no jurist would advocate the rape of a rapist, even though it may be routinely practiced in the prison shower stalls.[9] Yet, Larry Nasser's judge was lauded for fantasizing about delivering such state-sanctioned torture; her sentence of close to 200 years was celebrated by some as "transformative justice" (Kaba, 2021, p. 58). Within the strict terms of *lex talionis*, one might even ponder about the proportional aspect of justice of capital punishment given routinely to Black men for the false accusation of rape of white women in the postbellum South, i.e., after 1865 in the United States—the white supremacist version of honor killings. In Hammurabi's time, *lex talionis* was instituted as a reform measure, because after all, *only* one eye should be taken for another eye taken in the fit of rage. But how quickly such reforms get tossed, the original meaning of the terms ignored, and harsh justice for its own sake prevails. Even though the US Supreme Court (*Coker v. Georgia*, 1977) eliminated the death penalty for certain offenses that do not lead to the death of the victim (such as rape, usually of a white woman[10]), in the aftermath of September 11, 2001, such humane safeguards were dismissed in favor of political hysteria: The PATRIOT Act, passed by Congress soon after the events that shook the nation, includes many death-qualified offenses even without causing death to humans. It expanded upon the Anti-Terrorism and Effective Death Penalty Act, 1996, which was signed into law after several terrorist bombings, curtailed Habeas Corpus rights and increased death-penalty eligible offenses. It is instructive that the 1996 law was signed in by a lawyer-turned-president (Bill Clinton). It explicitly denies the right to effective counsel to a petitioner facing the ultimate sentence: "The ineffectiveness or incompetence of counsel during Federal or State collateral post-conviction proceedings shall not be a ground for relief in a proceeding arising under section 2254."[11] Jailhouse lawyers on death row will be left to their own devices, if they won't find a law center that will work pro bono for them (cf. Abu-Jamal, 2010).

Of the harsh penal theories concocted by male philosophers in the Western tradition, I argue that retributive justice is more honest than deterrence theory. After all, something quite inhuman and callous is embedded in a forward-looking theory that may pretend that more good can come out of executing an innocent person, if it deters the mob (*hoi polloi*) from extra-judicial killings. Of course, deterrence theory is in trouble, empirically speaking, because after publicized state executions, murder rates in area counties tend to rise, according to some studies (Bowers & Pierce, 1980). In the words of a remorseful former district attorney, whose zealous lawyering condemned an innocent man, Glenn Ford, to over three decades to Louisiana's death row:

> No one should be given the ability to impose a sentence of death in any criminal proceeding. We are simply incapable of devising a system that can fairly and impartially impose a sentence of death because we are all fallible human beings.
>
> The clear reality is that the death penalty is an anathema to any society that purports to call itself civilized. It is an abomination that continues to scar the fibers of this society and it will continue to do so until this barbaric penalty is outlawed. Until then, we will live in a land that condones state assisted revenge and that is not justice in any form or fashion.
>
> I end with the hope that providence will have more mercy for me than I showed Glenn Ford. But, I am also sobered by the realization that I certainly am not deserving of it.
>
> (Stroud, 2015)

In his interview, attorney Stroud, a white male, quotes approvingly Supreme Court Justice Stevens: "from this day on, I will no longer tinker with the machinery of death." It was actually Judge Blackmun who writes this confession in his famous dissent in *Callins v. Collins* (1994). However, retired Justice Stevens does state in a review essay that he no longer believes in a just administration of the ultimate penalty because "personnel changes on the court, coupled with 'regrettable judicial activism,' had created a system of capital punishment that is shot through with racism, skewed toward conviction, infected with politics and tinged with hysteria" (Stevens, 2010). Such political hysteria has visited upon Western punishment regimes since the reign of Terror of the French Revolution which saw the invention and industrial application of the guillotine killing machine, a befitting instrument of death for the Enlightenment era, since the Age of Reason marshaled efficient and clean ways of meting out punishment against its troubled Others. It is noteworthy that the last guillotined victim was Hamida Djandoubi, a Tunesian immigrant in 1977 who had killed his former French girlfriend (Smith, 2015).

The world over, the state's terror machine selects those who seem to have marginal status within the society; terrorism charges against members of persecuted communities stick more easily than against those who legitimately belong. Smith singles out China, Indonesia, and Saudi Arabia for executing foreign nationals and the United States for its anti-Black execution practices (*Ibid.*). Dzokhar Tsarnaev, a Caucasian immigrant to the United States, becomes a "brown Muslim" and thus cast as a terrorist so that the jury find him worthy of the death penalty for the Boston Marathon bombing, while others who are white and non-Muslims, unloading bullets on over 70 people in a movie theater, will not be marked as terrorist and may receive life without parole in a prison or psychiatric prison unit. Legitimated state terror metes out justice in such racist and Islamophobic manner—the arrogant display of an empathy deficit and vengeance game. With regard to the death penalty then, "the U.S. government adheres to international norms recognized and valued principally by its declared enemies. America stands with the warlords, whose reigns depend on the regular demonstration of power over life and death" (*Ibid.*). In other words, honor culture is an American value. In its zealous adherence to capital punishment, the United States is a pariah among UN member states.

On Slow Death Row

There are, of course, stages *below* the discussed stage 1, which will not be discussed in this book, famously put as "Abandon all hope you who enter here" (Dante's *Inferno*[12]), such as other draconian versions of justice (or hell), including extra-judicial killings such as lynchings of thousands of Black men and women in the United States (cf. Equal Justice Initiative, 2017). It is worth reiterating that US criminal justice's criminal roots are based on the twin terror ideologies and practices of chattel slavery and land theft and genocide of Indigenous peoples. Only belatedly, Indigenous People's Day is starting to get a national audience, displacing the national holiday devoted to a man who still is taught in schools as a beloved explorer and discoverer while the official record is a genocidal one—killing Taino people on Hispaniola.

In addition to the Spanish and US imperial powers, the United Kingdom and Germany are facing a moral reckoning. The British set up concentration camps in their colonies, and the Germans copied such prison camps in their colonial possessions, most notably, creating death camps for Namibian peoples (the Herrero and Nama nations), who to date are taking their reparation demands to court. It should be said that the roots of contract law are mired in violent pathologies, veritable 'legal' terrorism; the display of state power and impunity may change—yesterday's reservations are today's open-air prisons or refugee camps, imprisoning some estimated 60 million displaced peoples worldwide. And the century-old and ongoing devastation of the Congo and multiple genocides began with King Leopold of Belgium and continue with today's multination raids, rampant rapes, and killings of Congolese people, in the hot pursuit of Congo's natural resources. The methods change but the ideology of 'humanitarian aid' rings hollow while thousands perish in the Sahara, Libya's dungeons, and at sea; at the same time, the military apparatus of Frontex continues to uphold the external borders of fortress Europe with a vengeance.

At level 1 of the ludic Ubuntu tilted maze, a veritable Hegelian master–slave dialectic reveals a dancing-toward-death, signifying a social death spiral.

Masking Reciprocity

Ethicists such as Kant emphasize the value of reciprocity—the need of mutual recognition to affirm the humanity of each person. Social psychologists add a theory of mind approach that holds each human is ideally capable of taking an observer's perspective. In moral decision-making, it means that we wish to follow a golden rule because we are able to put ourselves in the other person's shoes. It seems when it comes to punishment, these good principles are easily forgotten. Prisoners and returning citizens encourage anybody who wields power over others (police, prosecutors, judges, jurors, and even defense attorneys who pressure the defendant to take a plea).

What if a judge takes on the judgment that he has given others? That way he could reflect on the meaning of reciprocity and "life-trashing sentences" (Price, 2015a, p. 53)? Most will find a week of jail too much of an ordeal, let alone the life or 60-year sentences they give carelessly or vindictively to those they do not consider human. An undercover agent spending a week in jail quit his police job when he got released. He no longer had the heart of locking away substance users (Abadi, 2018). Of course, one is not always assured that reciprocal intuition will work; after all, several jailed-freedom-fighters-turned-statesmen, e.g., Fidel Castro, Kwame Nkrumah, and Jomo Kenyatta, had no qualms about treating their political opponents to stints of imprisonment (cf. Asumah, 2007). President Mandela was a notable exception to this dire trend, even treating his former jailors with mercy.

United States as Penal Capitalist Democracy

In order to ground reciprocity in political and economic terms, we have to review the many tentacles of the prison-industrial complex spiraling out of control. Joy James (2005b) describes the US system as a penal democracy. As

Michel Foucault (1975) famously notes, all schooling systems are implicated in providing systems of control, especially those that make truancy a status-crime or even those who expel unruly children from school premises. We can add to such institutional forms of social control the following: residential centers for youth or reform schools and personnel such as drug/alcohol counselors or PINS officers: these are probation officers who supervise children (persons in need of supervision, i.e., PINS). The following institutions provide the necessary ideologies to buttress the penal character of US 'democracy': law schools, preparing lawyers for prosecutorial and judicial office, military academies, police academies, academies for dictators (Western Hemisphere Institute for Security Cooperation) so that the US penal version of 'democracy' can be exported.

Children of prisoners are often targeted by the family regulation system, another arm of the policing apparatus which sets up traumatized children for the foster-to-prison pipeline. Other forgotten people impacted by the criminal system of justice administration are traumatized family members (of police officers and guards). All may rely on psychological counseling and/or legal or illicit psychopharmacology.

The list for carceral structures and policing-like functions and those who aid and abet it in the United States continues:

Social Services prosecutors and social workers, the other arm of the PIC, who play a huge role in family court proceedings.
Judges and justices (including rural officers without law degree)
Police patrol and detectives, privatized police, college/university and school police (resource officers)
Parole and probation
ATI—alternatives to incarceration (linked to probation)
FBI, ATI, DEA, NSA and other federal anti-terrorism units
DA, large number of ADA
Private bond industry
Privatized prisons and detention centers for immigrants and asylum seekers
Civil confinement structures
Half-way houses
Therapeutic communities
Walmart lock-up cells
Private university lock-up cells
Schools "time-out" [*sic*] spaces
Residential treatment centers and homes for youth
military police, tribal police
Guards, wardens
Civilians working in prisons
Public safety complex, civilians and sheriff, undersheriff, secretaries, maintenance staff

Judges' clerical staff
Justice administrators for veterans
Forensic psychologists working for the courts and prison systems
NGOs Catholic Charities, another arm of DSS
Family counseling services, deal with traumatized kids)
Probation
ATI—assessing risk factor and recommending bail and other pretrial measures
Public Defenders office
Assigned counsel and private attorneys
Private attorneys—ordering their own forensic and psychiatric services
Prison industries (clothing; hygiene; bedding; food)
Transport services (including former prisoners' buses for families—prison visits)
Health care personnel (including labs)
Pharma industry
Locked facilities in public hospitals
Forensic prison hospitals
Civil confinement prisons
Canine units (training dogs for forensic work)
Recovery services
Half-way housing
Prison architectural services and their lawyers (plus secretarial services)
Construction services
Routine maintenance: electricians, plumbing, other suppliers
Security equipment (riot gear)
IT industries (computers, surveillance cameras, security and prediction models for offending)
Scanning devices (entering jails/prisons)
Electronic chains and other IT equipments of surveillance (e-carceration)
Typewriter industry
Copy centers (all that legal stuff has to be printed)
Mail services
Food industry
Small weapons industry, including tasers
National guard (in service of prison during revolts or uprising)
Coast guard (to rescue and deport migrants at high sea)

A narrow perspective on prison costs puts annual expenditure at $85 billion. The Prison Policy Initiative (2017) has given us a more honest appraisal: the cost of the prison-industrial complex amounts to $182 billion annually. Perhaps, it is time to envision with creative artists from the Vermont-based Bread and Puppet Theater collective a decommissioning and composting industry as Figure 1.2 portrays.

Figure 1.2 Prison demolition and composting services.
Source: Printed with permission from Soffiyah Elijah.

Conclusion

Malian children know about the danger of natal alienation and social death. A judge and former head of the corrections system, Bourama Sidibé, shared with me that he used to be very tough on crime, sentencing every offender to long prison terms: "One day my son was stopped on the street and told, 'Your father is a thief! He is stealing people.'" The child was humiliated and came home crying that nobody wanted to play with him. "Then I had a change of heart and am now rethinking punishment" (interview, 2002). Reflecting on this personal experience of shaming, he also took action by attending the International Conference on Penal Abolition (ICOPA) in Toronto, 2000, to gather information from scholars and practitioners internationally on how to minimize the use of imprisonment. The focus must be on real existing alternatives to carceral realities. It is ironic that a judge shares such a confession, since Mali has one of the lowest incarceration rates in the world, far lower than Sweden or Germany.

US penal abolitionist Mariama Kaba (2021) points out that there is a pattern of street rebellion that occurs after the acquittal of police agents who kill civilians, often unarmed. Police are the visible symbol of a racist penal system which arbitrarily enforces the violence of the law. While the current social movement's focus is on prison abolition, already articulated in the Black Panther Party's platform, the invisible prison is overlooked. Chapter 2 deals with the family regulation system to bring to light a biopolitics of surveillance which eerily parallels and works in conjunction with the criminal punishment system.

Notes

1 Such sentiment is echoed in literature of imprisoned intellectuals in the United States and France. Nobody could have imagined that the prison population would explode in the way the United States, now the prison nation of the world, exemplifies.

2 ACES Too High News (n.d.) also notes that the effects of high ACE scores can be mitigated by Positive Childhood Experiences (PCEs) scores.

3 It should give us pause that *only* 42% of violent crimes were reported to the police in 2017 (Lopez, 2017). Would it be differently if we had a justice system based on restitution rather than prisons?

4 And criminal organizations may indeed collude with the police and judges to round up an innocent man to serve time. In a village (in India), running a protection racket in the service of goonda raj ("the rule of hoodlums") may look like this: an important political operator, a raj, heckled an enemy of his boss to pay full price. The man refused and got stabbed in the gut with a pair of scissors by the raj, dying of his wounds. The raj brags:

> I was clever; I gave the scissors to another man, excused myself and ran to another village. I stayed away for three or four months, and my boss's people finished this matter. I said to my boss: 'I did your work; don't send me to jail'. So *he named a different man, a poor lad with no money*. They told him they'd feed his family while he was in jail. And they did. He was in for two and a half years, and for two and a half years they fed his family. Then he got out on bail.'
>
> (Piliavsky & Sbriccoli, 2016, p. 5, emphasis mine)

5 There is even an interactive media site that asks viewers whether they know the difference between a US corporate office or a Scandinavian prison. Most US students of mine fail the test. The site features a Danish prison where a man enjoys a sauna, and it showcases the cell of Norway's most notorious prisoner Breitvick, replete with a computer. It is also noteworthy that he has lost his appeal, demanding the end of isolation from other prisoners. He received the maximum sentence (21 years, a life sentence) for his offense of killing over 70 people, motivated by his white supremacist, Nazi ideology.

6 Latin American 'banana republics' got the dubious distinction of having their democratic governments replaced by politicians, friendly to US corporate interests such as banana plantations controlled by Dole corporation and others. Among the most egregious such cases is the CIA-sponsored coup of Chile's social-democratic government under the leadership of Salvador Allende in 1973. He dared to nationalize mining and other industries that were owned by US corporations.

7 Thanks to Peter Kankonde's insights about street committees and Kgotla courts (personal communication, December 7, 2015).

8 Laura Nader notes that Indigenous bargain model is "neither disintegrated nor disorganized," and it discourages dependency on the nation-state (p. 132). Among the semi-autonomous Zapotec villagers prize the proverb: "A bad agreement is better than a good fight." The focus is on re-establishing harmony rather than winning a settlement (pp. 127–9).

9 However, creative judges become cause célèbres when they dole out unusual punishment in lieu of jail time. And they claim that it cuts recidivism to low Norwegian levels. "Why an Ohio Judge Is Using Unusual Punishments to Keep People Out of Jail" (Aris Pinedo, Jasmine Brown, Alexa Valiente, ABC news), September 1, 2015, http://news.yahoo.com/why-ohio-judge-using-unusual-punishments-keep-people-144054880--abc-news-topstories.html?soc_src=mediacontentstory&soc_trk=ma.

10

> [The U.S. state of] Georgia has employed capital punishment since colonial times, with executions recorded at least as early as 1735. Crimes punishable by capital punishment in Georgia have historically included murder, robbery, rape, horse stealing, and aiding a runaway slave.
>
> (Death Penalty Information Center, n.d., www.deathpenaltyinfo.org/georgia-1)

11 28 U.S. Code § 2254—state custody; remedies in federal courts, 2 (i), Legal Information Institute, Cornell Law School (www.law.cornell.edu/uscode/text/28/2254).

12

> Through me is the way to the city of woe.
> Through me is the way to sorrow eternal.
> Through me is the way to the lost below. Justice moved my architect supernal.
> I was constructed by divine power,
> supreme wisdom, and love primordial.
> Before me no created things were.
> Save those eternal, and eternal I abide. Abandon all hope, you who enter.
>
> (Dante Alighieri, *Inferno*, III, 1–9)

2 Policing Families

The Many-Headed Hydra of Surveillance[1]

The child froze and didn't say another word. At the entrance of the park, a police car pulled in.

Prior to seeing the car, she had talked easily to the emergency medical staff who had arrived ahead of the police. Her mother Nancy whispered to me, "Jasmine is terrified of cops." The event where this took place was an emergency-preparedness workshop organized by a social justice group for parents who had run-ins with the 'system.' It was by invitation only, because most of the parents had been 'indicated' by Child Protective Service workers, and their status as 'fallen' parents meant that they couldn't congregate with others similarly situated. A United Way staff member gave the training in the shed next to the playground, a convenient location for parents to bring their children along. However, the staff member had dialed 9-1-1 when Jasmine fell from a slide and hit her head. That call triggered a visit from both emergency medical service and city police. A trip to the hospital would have triggered another call—to the much-hated Child Protective Services (CPS), a division within the Department of Social Services (DSS), considered by economically-disadvantaged parents to be worse than the police. And then Nancy would have had to get have gotten affidavits from all of us adults (who were not 'indicated') stating that she had not pushed her child. So, in light of this hypothetical scenario, Nancy refused all services and did not give her name to the medics. A healing salve fortunately worked wonders for Jasmine who was pain-free the next day.*

Nancy knew all about the DSS. She had tried to escape their grip before. When pregnant, she had fled to another jurisdiction to give birth, but to no avail: since she used her proper name and Medicaid card, DSS was able to find and 'hotline' the mother and demand that the hospital hold the baby until a CPS worker could come and whisk the child away. Due to vigorous legal defense, she is one of the few parents who succeeded in being reunited with her children in Sunshine County. However, the trauma of separation is quite significant and was compounded for the children when they faced abuse, allegedly, in the foster home.

DOI: 10.4324/9781003055327-3

This narrative, based on a situation which I witnessed in 2014, gives a glimpse of the effects of social services' policing powers on poor families. In what follows, I offer reflections on policing of poor families by focusing on one county in the United States (which I call Sunshine County). As Chapter 1 dealt with the visible aspects of punitive 'justice,' it is now important to reveal several aspects of the shadow side of the criminal punishment system in the United States. Increasingly, critics of mass incarceration have come to appreciate and even embrace prison abolition as a goal in the distant future. Many understand that the tentacles of the criminal court reach far and wide, including the punitive institutions of probation and parole which focus on moralism and produce net widening of surveillance, replete with electronic chains, which are relics of a chattel slavery regime (Kilgore, 2022). Criminal justice research focuses almost exclusively on the role of police officers and argues that although they do not intend to, police do end up in roles and processes that often result in criminalizing certain communities. My modest proposal serves to shed light onto the invisible realm of mass criminalization of Black, Indigenous, and poor families. The family regulation system is supported by policy and law. Yet, a carceral feminist lens might argue that in its guise as a foster care institution, this branch of government has uplifted scores of families and benefited marginalized children. There are important implications for how feminist scholarship on criminal justice and policing develops in the next decade. Very little attention is still paid to the surveillance function of the Child Protective Services (CPS) and how it not only controls families but also entire communities.

I argue that the policing arm of CPS intends to keep children safe but does not review carefully the impact of their polices and processes on the families targeted. The modern nation-state invokes the right to broad policing power in order to protect individuals, groups, and property; to deter individuals and groups from committing harm; and to seek appropriate punishment for those who committed harm within the constraints of the rule of law. Police officers who do not uphold the law appropriately may be prosecuted, and even if they do not face conviction, they may lose their jobs. What kind of equivalent policing roles exists for CPS workers? Does it even make sense to compare their jobs, which deal exclusively with child welfare and protection, to police officers' duties? There is indeed at least one significant difference: the standard for suing. While one can sue officers if they do not follow the law, the caseworkers can only be sued if they failed to act in good faith—something that no one could really prove. And if it is the case that there are similarities and even overlapping responsibilities between the two agencies, how does their work affect parents' parenting strategies?

This chapter focuses primarily on the policing role of CPS within the context of US child welfare practice and family law. Drawing on Miranda Fricker's (2007) theory of epistemic injustice, I argue that the testimonies of stigmatized parents cannot be heard within social services and the legal community.

Subjected to intense behavior modification, such parents also smother their truth, even when it would it be in their best interest for accessing quality mental health services. Here Kristie Dotson's (2011) theory of oppression is relevant in order to understand such paradox. Furthermore, the child welfare system is experienced as oppressive by mothers and is practically immune to resistance. Part of the problem is that, until recently, law schools rarely offer courses in family defense[2] or child welfare (Guggenheim & Sankaran, 2015, pp. xix–xxi). Even human rights advocacy groups are almost nonexistent in the family defense context. The technical term of 'child welfare' or 'child protection' refers to a number of government actions, namely, "investigations of allegations of child abuse or neglect, the placement of children in foster care, and the termination of parental rights to make children eligible for adoption" (Guggenheim, 2005, p. 175). Guggenheim argues that there is undue attention paid to abused and murdered children, and it entails a number of policies that are intended to provide an early alert system, but state actors are overzealous in implementation by denying parents fundamental protection against an invasive state bureaucracy.

I argue that the family regulation system tends to subscribe to an elitist ideology, combined with racist and neocolonial practices of targeting the poor, families of color, and those who are socially stigmatized because of criminal records. Those parents targeted and ensnared by CPS workers often find them to be far more menacing than the repressive tactics and criminalization practices employed by police officers. The CPS' own dragnet depends on the complicity of county therapists, mental health service providers, drug counselors, and, of course, school personnel who are also mandated reporters (cf. Mack, 2021). Worst of all, parents who are 'hotlined'[3] by neighbors or family members, considered to be 'permissive reporters,'[4] will never know who targets them with a false allegation. The hotline policy was instituted in 1974 through the Child Abuse Prevention and Treatment Act (CAPTA), which, in part, accomplished an overhaul of the child welfare system. It is perhaps not too far-fetched to call these 'hotlines' our contemporary *lettres de cachet*: Some 6.3 million hotline calls were placed in 2012, and some 40% of caregivers are found to be 'indicated,' which means that child protection investigation substantiated "some credible evidence" of child neglect or abuse. Black parents are differentially impacted in terms of being hotlined more and facing child removal disproportionately (Mack, 2019, pp. 779–80; Roberts, 2022). Millions of parents join the child abuse registry (called, the register) every year, and even if they win in court, their name is often not automatically expunged from the state registers. Many indicated parents may even stay on the register for life (Redleaf, 2015, pp. 390–1). Today, the register is clearly used to stigmatize parents and prevent them from pursuing jobs where they would interact with children or teens. The original intent of the register was for epidemiological purposes and to target state funding for children deemed most at risk. It was not meant to criminalize caretakers (Redleaf, 2015, p. 393). Due to vigorous advocacy by family defenders such as Joyce McMillan, founder of Parent Legislative Action Network (PLAN), New York's registry must expunge parents' names after eight years or earlier, as a result of a family court outcome (Franklin & Werner, 2020).

Child Welfare Rights or Wrongs

A central issue relating to CPS is whether an agency's policy of child removal really is in the best interest of the child. In this section, I focus on two traumatic effects of "policing" families and children. Sunshine County has the highest child placement rate in the state since a new commissioner was hired over a decade ago.[5] Prior to the local punitive era, the Department of Social Services (DSS) used a strength-based approach, keeping families together and using the draconian measure of removal as a last resort. This was in line with the state's policy toward preventive services (Mack, 2021, p. 800). Today, DSS uses removal as 'the first resort,' where no cruelty or negligence can be established and even where less disruptive measures (such as supervision) could be employed. Retired DSS workers have reported to me that at annual parties, workers chant the slogan "They hatch them, we'll snatch them," referring to their first-resort policy of breaking up families without cause. Sunshine's CPS workers, many of whom do not have an associate's degree in social work, target poor families. As such, these case workers assume superpowers being "investigator, prosecutor, and adjudicator" when they determine the parents' compliance (Mack, 2021, p. 803). Generally speaking, Sunshine County's rates of punitive foster care is an outlier in the state, and there is no shortage of egregious, wrongful removals. A neighboring county's CPS worker gasped, after one such removal, "I think I am seeing legal kidnapping here!" A Sunshine CPS worker removed a newborn baby and allegedly told the mother, "You have been in the system as a foster child, your mother was no good, and so you will be a bad mother, too!" However, in this case, no hospital worker had reported any evidence of neglect or abuse. Thus, a preemptive strike against the right to motherhood takes its traumatic course. At that early point of separation, irreparable harm in the child's socio-psychological development had already been committed, because the baby's first two years are considered a critical period: Proponents of attachment theory note the occurrence of an *ur-trauma* of even a brief separation at birth (some five days), which effects negatively the mother–child relationship and contributes to the child's increased propensity toward aggressive behavior (Howard *et al.*, 2011).

Additional trauma occurs when a toddler or schoolchild encounters either the shackling of their parent or when they themselves are deposited in the police car and driven to complete strangers and new environments, forcing change on all levels, including changing school systems. Jasmine experienced forced removal from a home by police officers and thus developed a distrust of police in general. Her mother worries about a future time when Jasmine might have to face a 'resource officer,' in high school, patrolling the school and frisking students at will. The child's post-traumatic stress disorder (PTSD) is real. Nancy reports:

> my oldest is still concerned about it a bit—she made a comment back a few months ago of why she picked her seat in the spot it is at the table … so she can see both doors just in case they ever come back: 'I'll see 'em 'n be ready for them. Nobody will ever tear my family apart again or take me from my mom …'
>
> (Personal communication, October 16, 2016)

This behavior is akin to that of returning soldiers, or returning citizens (from prison), coping with the stress of (surviving) war or witnessing others being shanked in mess hall. As already mentioned, the trauma is often compounded when children face abuse in the foster family. In Nancy's children's case, egregious abuse allegedly occurred in the foster home. One of the daughters vows never to have a child or partner, to protect herself from having anybody close to her be exposed to violence by strangers (personal communication, October 16, 2016).

Critics of the foster care system and foster carers alike are concerned about the prevalence of psychotropic medication: the majority of foster children receive multiple drugs a day often having severe side effects (Edelman, 2015). Andrew Fitz-Gibbon and Jane Hall Fitz-Gibbon (2019) share that a child in their care was on nine medications; six of them were for daily use treating psychosis, attention-deficit hyperactivity disorder (ADHD), bipolar disorder, and acid reflux, and three drugs for allergies, nausea, and asthma (as needed). Children respond differently to the pharmacological treatment: One outright rejected them: "I don't feel like myself when I take it." Another could not cope without them (pp. 8–9). In another case in Sunshine County, a nine-year-old Black girl shared with a white teacher that she was tired of babysitting. The teacher never called the parents. Instead, she engaged CPS who came to the house with three police cars. Actually, an adult babysitter opened the door, and, still, all six children were taken to different foster homes, only to be united with their grandmother after two years. The girl has been on psychotropic drugs ever since, and on the day that the appeals court was supposed to rule whether the seven children would return to their parents, the father shot his wife and succumbed to death after months in coma from a self-inflicted wound. Since the parents had moved away that teacher initiating the call may never know that her report prompted such tragedy. In mandated reporting trainings, teachers and school social workers are primed for looking at signs of abuse and neglect in children. They are not given compassionate tools to interact with parents and caregivers *first* before initiating a call to CPS that has traumatic effects for the extended family.

State agencies openly discuss how removal causes anxiety and trauma for children of all ages; CPS workers and foster caretakers are being taught in trauma care (OCFS, 2015). What is not adequately being discussed is how to minimize CPS workers' vast discretion with removal proceedings and how to strengthen families and disrupt the foster care-to-prison pipeline. And, of course, parents are also deeply traumatized and are not given meaningful, material support to overcome the obstacles in order to reunite the family. The Family First Prevention Services Act (2018) is supposed to provide relief from punitive supervision in favor of offering services and material support to families in need. But in the end, even this reform turns out to be a net widening of control which serves to patronize, punish, and patrol Black families (Mack, 2021). Protective factors include living wage, safe housing, subsidized or free daycare, and being free from environmental pollution. Studies show that an increase in minimum wage jobs leads to less contact with the family regulation system (Mack, 2021, p. 790).

Chapter 3 addresses the imperial concept of sovereign immunity. Here, I note that sovereign immunity conceals sovereign impunity. In cases of severe child maltreatment and death, the courts hesitate imposing penalties on CPS administrators and caseworkers. In *Smathers v. Perry County Children's Services,* a caseworker knew of the child torture and could have removed her; he did not and covered up his negligence by tampering with case files *after* the girl's death. The courts preferred to look the other way and gave immunity to agents of the CPS system (Miller, 2021). Similarly, parents or kin have no right to demand government protection and redress from government negligence using 14th Amendment's Due Process Clause (cf. *Castle Rock v. Gonzales*, 2005 and *DeShaney v. Winnebago County Dept. of Social Services*, 1989). Wealth, whiteness, and heteronormative status are protective factors in minimizing state surveillance, intervention, and removal of children. As Mariam Mack notes, the state monitoring system is "unimaginable for those with racial and class privilege" (2021, p. 798).

The Meaning of Surveillance

Surveillance of poor families strikes at the heart of the unjust practice of policing. They might as well be sitting in the "digital poorhouse," having their data mined for risk assessment predictions (Eubanks, 2018). Parents whose children are in the family and child services system are rendered powerless in the choices of whom their children consort with and whom they date. Those who are educated in the law may practice low-level resistance. Such parents give their children 'the talk,' i.e., teaching them Miranda rights, when they have to interact with mandated reporters at school. Children learn to distrust adults and may have anxieties about encountering the school nurse, resource officer, or their own psychiatrist. Parents and children alike who are 'in the system' do not have right to privacy. In fact, the parents must sign release forms for a broad range of medical services (and others), and information gathered from counseling sessions may be used against them in court. In the case highlighted at the beginning of the article, Nancy had to weigh the benefits of medical intervention for Jasmine with the cost of losing the child (again) to 'the system.' Nancy is an 'indicated' parent, which means that 'some credible evidence' was found supporting the allegation of abuse or neglect. Armed with this 'indicated' report, the CPS investigators can remove a child without court order, but they then have to seek court order within 24 hours confirming it. The CPS version of the situation is almost always confirmed by the courts in Sunshine County. The 'indicated' parent also suffers other stigmatizing consequences, similar to a person who is on probation or parole. The parent must avoid other indicated parents, including dating an adult who has children removed or is a felon. This is even the case when the individual's charges are unrelated to child abuse. However, the pool of eligible adults to socialize with is sometimes limited, and the state often accuses the parent of engaging in 'inappropriate' socializing practices as the last straw to deny the return of children, even if the parent was otherwise docile, compliant, and finished successfully all boilerplate parent programming. In Sunshine County, there is such a prevalence of indicated parents that in one school, there is nobody left to participate in parent–teacher (PTA) meetings. Parental involvement in children's learning is key to children's success in staying in school and graduating with a diploma. Systematically disrupting such essential opportunities of PTA conferences prepares the child for the social services-to-prison pipeline (cf. Decker, 2015). Children who are shuttled to different foster homes or group homes tend to lack a steady adult advocate and are more likely to be caught engaging in illicit behavior or statute offenses such as truancy than children who do not face removal proceedings.

Again, it is important to point out that the policing mechanism of surveillance affects more children in poor and racialized homes than those who grow up in wealthy neighborhoods.[6] Controlled by the system means opening their "homes to family family regulation system workers wherever those workers appear, answer far-reaching inquires into their mental health, medical, sexual, and romantic histories" (Mack, 2021, p. 798). More often than not, the state's controlling gaze veers away from the original charges placed on the parent and invents new ones during the long period of continuous supervision and enforcement of parental improvement programs (Roberts, 2021).

In rare cases, parents who are part of the new 'free-range' parenting movement become policed by the family regulation system. What is novel is that a few wealthy white parents are all of a sudden charged with neglect when they fail to supervise their children who walk alone to a park. In 2015, one couple was found "responsible for unsubstantiated child neglect," a judgment that was argued to be "Orwellian" and "a legal purgatory" by their lawyer (Goldstein, 2015). It was the first case of its kind, not because it was an overreaction by CPS but because the family targeted is wealthy and highly educated. Nationwide, investigators who work for the family regulation system concentrate on poor Black neighborhoods, and studies have shown that CPS workers are more than three times as likely to report Black children's accidental injuries as suspicious than accidents involving white children (Roberts, 2002; Goldstein, 2015).

> Although Black children were only 14% of children in the United States in 2018, they made up 23% of children in foster care. More telling are recent data indicating children's chances of landing in foster care at some point while growing up. According to a 2014 study, about 15% of Native children and 11% of Black children could expect to enter foster care before their eighteenth birthday. The rate for white children, about one in twenty, was remarkably lower, reflecting America's racial hierarchy, but still incredibly high.
>
> (Roberts, 2021)

In the Tentacles of Family Court and Criminal Court

The field of family defense, which advocates for indicated parents, is considered to be in its infancy (Guggenheim & Sankaran, 2015, p. xxiii). Lawyers who file appeals on behalf of the aggrieved parents are stigmatized as "parents' advocates" or, worse, they may no longer receive assigned cases in family court. In Sunshine County, the family court judge assigns cases, not a third party; thus, there is the appearance of favoritism. Lawyers also tell me that a bigger problem is that, in general, the appellate courts grant too much deference to the rulings of family court so that the level of oversight is not the same as it is in criminal court. Furthermore, standards of evidence are more ambiguous—family court always falls back on 'credibility determinations' made by the judge.

Guggenheim and Sankaran argue that criminal prosecutions and child protection cases are treated very differently in the United States. The state does prosecute the rich and socially connected in criminal court, but it never pursues them in family court. The state only targets poor and marginalized parents for neglect and abuse of their children (2015, p. xx). Guggenheim and Sankaran's findings support the claim of penal abolitionist Hal Pepinsky (who co-created the term of criminology as peacemaking) that there is no social pressure whatsoever for prosecutors to

> lay child sexual assault charges against a well-established biological father and extraordinarily rare for child protection workers and family judges to believe children who allege they are being sexually abused by their fathers, especially by fathers who otherwise have impeccable community reputation.
>
> (Pepinsky, 2006, p. 67)

By contrast, in Sunshine County, parents who face neglect charges in family court have been thrown into jail for far less serious charges than those Pepinsky mentions. In some cases, the CPS worker reported that they suspected the parent abusing drugs, because they (a) appeared too thin or (b) had missing teeth or acne. Thus, family court may not protect a parent facing spurious allegations from incarceration and losing their child to the family policing system.

Most prison justice activists never focus on the punitive sphere of family courts, even though public defenders report having a larger case load in family court than in criminal court. Notably, of the hundreds of cases litigated every year by the public defender's office in Sunshine County, few are ever appealed, even though the judge mostly sides with the DSS lawyer and adjudicates against the errant parent. In the case of Nancy, mentioned in the beginning of this paper, a tenacious counsel assigned to the children appealed successfully and was able to reunite Nancy with Jasmine and the other children.

When criminal justice activists neglect their focus on the punitive tentacles of family court, they also ignore a gendered reality. Family law cases are bigger chunk of court proceedings and inevitably target women. DSS polices poor women through mandatory drug tests, and mothers who are on Medicaid are policed by the hospitals who report positive drug test results to DSS. Hence, poor women actually are more affected by the surveillance mechanisms of the judicial system than men. This fact is obscured because policing is usually seen in terms of police officers issuing arrests; however, in jurisdictions like Sunshine that are hostile to a poor parent's right to raise their children, policing also occurs in the following manner. A CPS worker is accompanied by police officers, who tend to terrify the children with long-lasting effects. Thus, the policing is double-pronged: the supposedly benign face of a CPS investigator who takes away children under the protective gaze of a police officer, who typically supports the CPS worker's account. And the cynical reality of such quotas means that CPS workers find parents neglectful rather than devise ways to strengthen family bonds or dismiss frivolous hotline charges altogether.

Family law remains largely unaddressed by prison critics, even though the United States is the number one jailor of the world. A majority of women in prison are mothers, and they face serious consequences in family court such as automatically losing their child to the state when they face long-term conviction. Black women were especially targeted during the war on drugs and the rate of incarceration outpaced that of white men. Worldwide, women are about 6% of prisoners. Prisoners' advocates such as the Sentencing Project, the Vera Institute, Prison Policy Initiative, and the Movement for Black Lives need to raise consciousness that many more millions of Americans are under extraordinary state supervision when family court cases placement are counted. After all, these organizations already examine the parole/probation status of American residents, which is considered an extension of prison regime. Sanctions meted out in family court also involve the curtailment of individual rights, and therefore, the abstract-rights-bearing defendant should be afforded the same protections that exist in criminal court. Along with PLAN, New York's Movement for Family Power is leading the way in raising consciousness and even calling for the abolition of the family regulation system (MFP, 2019).

The state is starting to acknowledge that "[r]emoval from the home is a difficult and traumatic experience for a child" (OCFS, 2015). Foster caregivers and DSS officials all need to be trained in safeguarding the needs of the child. However, there are no guidelines for CPS workers counseling aggrieved parents whose children are removed abruptly from their home. The best they can hope for is being forced to take anger management courses. The problem is that all these DSS mandated programs tend to focus on a deficit model of parenting. Moreover, all too often, mothers are so traumatized that they start to self-medicate with opioids. But every aspect of their behaviors is policed, so that they find themselves in criminal court with drug dealing charges. CPS workers use this as another example of their proven failure as mothers. What starts with civil proceedings in family court in pursuit of the 'best interest of the child' without criminal threat by the court often cascades into criminal court procedures which entail threats of a felony charge. Again, it appears that family law enables the policing of criminal law that leads to criminal court penalties. In such cases, a parent is stuck in two courts, family and criminal, where different defense strategies operate (deQuattro, 2015), and the parent is set up to lose custody of her children.

The family court system was originally set up to keep children away from the adversarial and difficult procedural justice of criminal court, in which family court decisions are to be made using 'the best interest of the child' standard. In reality, family law is also antagonistic. Parents' lawyers face DSS counsel who is hired to advocate for the agency. Their CPS workers, who do the initial investigation, routinely bring along police officers as additional witnesses, clearly designed as intimidation of the parent who is facing allegations. But lawyers have noted that family law simply is in the pre-*Gideon* state of legal procedure, which means that there are no fundamental protections (innocent till proven guilty, etc.) from accusations. In Sunshine County, when CPS workers show up at the door of a parent with the intent to remove a child or children, they often bring along the local police, who also enter the premises. The police officer serves two purposes for the DSS: intimidating the parent and serving as witness for the state in family court. The unfounded report does not disappear from the register. In the end, the parent is at an enormous disadvantage when two state agencies corroborate and testify against the parent. It is a case of epistemic injustice, as the parent's testimony has no worth against the privileged testimonial voices of the state enforcing an unwritten white middle-class moral codex.

Martin Guggenheim (2005) critiques forcefully such epistemic invalidation of parents and the largely invisible breakup of poor families and of families of color within the past decades. He makes a case that this policy started with the birth of the 'children's rights' movement in the 1960s and several US Supreme Court rulings that began to give preference to a "best interest for the child" ideology. Oddly enough, such 'child's rights' perspective prompted state action, state intrusion into sacrosanct parental decision-making, and the consideration of poverty as an actionable indicator of parental neglect. Only in recent years, when the state made the 'mistake' of occasionally arresting the 'wrong' kind of parents, i.e., those with social and legal connections and bourgeois community status, has there been a corrective lens to this endemic crisis faced by thousands of poor families and families of color (Goldberg, 2015; Nagel, 2016). The crisis has reached a veritable tipping point where advocates, such as law professor Guggenheim, may finally get their day in court: shining light on a system which is corrupt and bankrupt and callously undermines family values of targeted parents, i.e., their constitutionally protected right against state intrusion and the right to rear children beyond the normative purview of white upper-class values. However, the hurdles are many to undo federal policy which pours money mainly into child abuse but not into child welfare:

> The unfortunate turn federal legislation took in child protection in the early 1970s was to make it into an arm of the police with primary investigative and removal powers. A great opportunity was lost to transform child welfare into a program that served the needs of vulnerable families. From the investigative function, it was a short step to becoming a removal and prosecutorial agency. Although many in the field lament this shift and work in child welfare to provide services to bolster vulnerable families, child protection today, more than at any time in the past hundred years, stresses the virtue of breaking up families and freeing children for adoption.
>
> (Guggenheim, 2005, pp. 211–2)

Guggenheim does not exaggerate. Even though in recent years, social services policy notes that child removal is traumatizing for the child—and their policies are completely silent on parents being traumatized—many resources are spent on making foster homes safer and providing trauma care for children. However, there are no substantive, specialized support services for homeless families; parents dealing with addiction; with felony status, which makes them ineligible for work; with mental delay and mental disabilities, which has been used against parents' ability to care for their infants, etc.

The Patriarchal State Apparatus: Policing Families through the Adoption and Safe Family Act

Defenders of social services that control the family regulation system claim that state intervention is necessary to rescue kids from cruel and negligent parents. However, in 21 states, corporal punishment is still legal when carried out in schools, and parents are usually not able to challenge the paddle, Taser or chemical spray (PBS Newshour, 2016). Black children are twice as likely to face corporal punishment than white children in school (Startz, 2016). The long-term harmful effects have been well documented in several hundred studies, yet there is no relief in sight from such cruel and very common state violence (Gershoff, 2016; Hall-Fitz-Gibbon, 2017). This is due to popular support for adultism, a system of oppression that accepts that adults are entitled to break children's will, even resorting to physical and emotional abuse. A poll from 2015 shows that over 90% of parents admit to hitting their young children (Fitz-Gibbon & Hall Fitz-Gibbon, 2019, p. 3). It did not have to be this way. Child-rearing practices in Indigenous communities showcased a nested-care philosophy which was contrary to the disciplinary protocol of settler colonial Pilgrims:

> there is in all children [...] a stubbornness, and stoutness of mind arising from natural pride, which must, in the first place, be broken and beaten down; that so the foundation of their education being laid in humility and tractableness, other virtues may, in their time, be built thereon.
>
> (Zinn, 1980, p. 21)

Drawing on Roman law, which considers children as property of their parents, white children could be subjected to death if considered unruly (van Schilfgaarde & Shelton, 2021, p. 690). Indigenous nested-care pedagogy shunned violence and humiliation against children (Narvaez, 2021). Among the Iroquois, women enjoyed egalitarian status and children were raised to value bodily autonomy, dignity, and interdependence including sharing of property. The child determined when breastfeeding ended, not the mother. The child did not "submit to overbearing authority" (Zinn, 1980, p. 20). Yesterday's draconian, 'civilizing' measures are today's sign of barbarity, and its habits are difficult to break. Today, governments have to spend millions of dollars to educate adults about the dangers of corporal punishment. In the United States, this colonial practice is still legal in schools in many states and supported by a US Supreme Court decision *Ingraham v. Wright* in 1977. And private, largely religious, schools are not regulated at all (Hall Fitz-Gibbon, 2017). By contrast, most countries in the world have pledged to stop corporal punishment, and in March 2022, Wales has joined over 120 nations who have prohibited corporal punishment (End Violence against Children, 2022).

Children's advocates argue that children's 'rescue' ought to be carried out by impartial actors of the state who are trained professionals because they know what is in the best interest of the child. Placement no longer occurs in 'orphan trains,' or other ghostly institutions of the past, including the colonial practice of removing American Indian[7] children and placing them in 'boarding schools'—a euphemism for children's garrisons and places of torture. Today, CPS workers place small children into families that are immediately urged to file adoption proceedings. Sometimes, siblings are separated, even though it increases the traumatic experience of being severed from one's parent. The most egregious case of such breaking up of dozens of families involved Lakota families (*Oglala Sioux Tribe v. Van Hunnik*, 2015)—a haunting colonial reminder of the racist child-removal policies of the past century. It also echoes the violent family breakup of Black families under chattel slavery.

The federal Adoption and Safe Family Act (ASFA, 1997) brought back the ghosts of the colonial past. Politicians voted for the act because it is known that children who linger in foster care throughout their teens are at greater danger of graduating into adult prisons rather than graduating high school. So ASFA has a noteworthy child welfare goal: reduce children's time spent in foster care. However, it also limits parents' ability to achieve reunification (which must be accomplished in 15 months) and increases adoption incentives. This has especially created havoc for incarcerated parents and those on parole. Prisoners have difficulty in showing due diligence to maintain bonds with children given the resistance of CPS workers facilitating children's prison visits to remote areas. Furthermore, for returning citizens with drug felony convictions, it is very difficult to obtain public housing and a job in order to repay the state in child support debt incurred during incarceration. Given that the average parent with a felony conviction owes $20,000 in child support, a minimum wage job would not even be enough to cover expenses for the adult, let alone her child (Bernstein, 2010, pp. 154–5). In addition, ASFA did little to curb the ever-increasing number of teens who are not adoptable, including over 100,000 children who aged out of the system and became legal orphans in the last decade alone (Guggenheim, 2015, p. 18).

The passage of ASFA (in 1997) increased the policing power of CPS and judges who rubber-stamp their decisions. In 2002, over 600,000 children were placed in foster care (Guggenheim, 2005). By 2011, 'only' 400,000 kids remained as wards of the state because some states (Arizona and Indiana) abolished family court and dispersed the children to kin (but not to parents) (Children's Bureau, 2016). Foster care can also be experienced as a prison sentence, even if foster caretakers are not abusive. A new policy recommends to place children with relatives. For example, since 2016, it appears that Sunshine County has reduced its cases by relying increasingly on caretakers who are relatives of the biological parents. The law allows DSS to place children with relatives and then those relatives can petition (and get) full custody from parents, thus relieving the DSS of the legal obligation of trying to reunite the children with parents.

In addition to the United States having the unfortunate status as the world's largest jailor, it also holds the record in foster placement the world over, but this fact is rarely mentioned in prison statistics. But the children who are currently in foster care, as well as those who have been adopted, need to show up in statistics that showcase the massive 'legal' transfer of children from parents to others. Such excessive transfer would be labeled child trafficking if it were not done by the power of the paternalist state (Nagel, 2016). Furthermore, the biological parents caught up in such punitive state intervention also need to be counted as lifelong probationers—who, along with their children (and grandparents), are subjected to intergenerational stigmatization.

Family court proceedings have inflicted much damage since 1997. In the beginning, the main critiques of 1997 ASFA Act came from prisoners' rights organizations, fighting on behalf of incarcerated parents, who have tried to stay in touch with their children beyond the 15-month limit allotted to 'overcome the obstacles' so that they could stay bona fide parents. Often, prison sentences are much longer; therefore, they automatically forfeit their parental status. In Sunshine County, no significant effort is made to bus children to their incarcerated parents, even though it may be the express wish of both parties. Sadly, such resistance to visitation requests by both children and parents is not out of the ordinary, as it would require the cooperation of child welfare agencies and the corrections department (Woolman, 2015, p. 52). The family court judge is in a position to ensure that those two entities collaborate, but this does not happen in many cases.

A child's loss of her parent to the carceral regime is tremendously traumatic to the child and affects some 2.7 million children annually (Bernstein, 2005). Compounding this trauma is foster care placement, and children of incarcerated parents are four times more likely to be in contact with CPS than those who do not have parents in prison (Woolman, 2015, p. 51). The risk factor of spending life behind bars is already increased for children of prisoners, and even more so if those children cycle into the foster care system. The foster care-to-prison pipeline becomes almost inevitable. It is no coincidence that the United States "leads the industrialized world in the rate at which we lock up our young," and it is often "for nonviolent offenses such as truancy, low-level property offenses, and technical probation violations" (Bernstein, 2014, p. 223). My first encounter with a CPS worker of Sunshine County provided a first glimpse at these intersecting controlling systems. A white caseworker wagged her finger wildly at a young Black teenager, threatening him with violent words: "you will amount to nothing and go to prison when you grow up." She placed him in foster care in a remote rural area, and an adult Black male mentor was not allowed to interact with the teen. The young man 'graduated' to the adult jail a few years later and did not finish high school. By contrast, the system works for those who are socially connected to the powerful: a few years after the young man was sent into 'exile' (i.e., placed with a rural white family, and he was the only Black child in the elementary school), the CPS worker's husband was caught with marijuana, yet the district attorney's office did not prosecute; no charge of child endangerment was brought up against the couple who have children, and she also retained her job with the agency.

Childcare in the Crossfire of Cultural Clashes

As it stands now, child welfare is practiced inconsistently and targets children of poor and minority families. Poor children have a much more extensive experience with the policing apparatus of DSS, probation, parole, and schools than their wealthier counterparts. According to my own observations and review of court documents and CPS workers' reports of supervised visitations between indicated parents and their children, it is apparent that the DSS favors a white middle-class cultural perspective on what constitutes 'appropriate' parenting skills. A young woman reports that she was carted off to 40 different alienating institutional settings and only wished that she could have been placed with her grandmother instead, and for a fraction of the foster care and youth prisons expenditures, her mother's addiction could have been treated (Bernstein, 2005, p. 177). Do we really need to throw away the 'usual suspects,' the poor and socially disconnected? As Smith Ledesma (2015) argues, the ideological driver of punitive child removal constitutes the systemic destruction of the Black family. Black children are disproportionately represented in the foster care industry and are also the children who are least likely to find an adoptive home. Natal alienation, the systematic breakup of Black families, was a pernicious feature of US slavery that continues to haunt the American republic which is indeed exceptional in policing its residents to a much greater extent than other countries. "[T]he intersection of tougher sentencing and child welfare laws has set in motion 'the greatest separation of families since slavery'" (McCray, cited in Bernstein, 2010, p. 156).

So, is the solution to pour more money into foster arrangements with strangers, or is there a better way? What kinds of governmental reforms are necessary to ensure that poor children are not the collateral damage of a broken family law system? Norway has been a leader in restorative justice practices. Its government has taken advice from its premier criminologist Nils Christie. In "Conflict as Property," Christie (1977) argues boldly that solving conflict belongs to community members, and he opposes rigorously reliance on professionals and bureaucrats in dealing with offenses. While he had in mind the criminal justice system, one can easily translate his concern into the realm of family law. Incidentally, Norway has made international headlines in recent years for targeting immigrant families, whose values seem to be out of step with Norwegian secular humanism. A Romanian couple lost their five children to the state for using corporal punishment and being too doctrinaire about Christian teachings (Whewell, 2016). In this case, the immigrant family was criminalized because of their cultural values. So, again, those who are socially disconnected may find themselves policed more harshly.

In the same way that poor people make up the vast majority of prisoners around the world, the benign police apparatus of CPS workers targets poor and socially displaced parents who apparently do not *deserve* to keep their children from state intervention because of 'inappropriate' cultural values (such as corporal punishment). For example, Norway could take a strength-based approach in assisting immigrant families who do not know or understand the Nordic countries' cultural norms that proscribe all acts of corporal punishment. CPS workers could become cultural translators and educators instead of using their policing power to stigmatize immigrant parents. Furthermore, to build trust with newcomers, it would be effective to have a mentoring system in place, employing older immigrants to facilitate cultural and political integration. Such a mentoring system could make use of parent advocates, who have been successfully reunited with their children. Peer-mentoring is already in place in other domains, e.g., recovery programs.

Not surprisingly, the US court's cultural values reflect those of the dominant culture. It has been labeled as a *staircase culture* of middle-class whites versus the *roller coaster culture* of those who are othered by the system for the crime of holding 'inappropriate' family values. Members of the staircase culture believe in the ameliorating force of the American Dream and the optimistic belief in upward mobility whereas those who subscribe to the roller coaster culture believe that outside forces control things and life is a constant up-and-down struggle (Rosga, 1999). This is especially true for children who have been severely impacted by years of separation from parents and the effects of institutionalization moving from foster care to group homes to detention centers, as this young prisoner decries:

> *You don't know what it feels like to come up in the world with parents that can't stay out of jail.*
> *You don't know what it's like to have your sisters and brothers took from you and placed in a group home.*
> *You don't know what it's like to have no family to be by your side when you need them in a time of hurt.*
> *You don't know what it's like to be me and never will, so I'll tell you ...*
> *It feels like a forever going rollercoaster ride through fire and water that ends when you fall.*
>
> (cited in Bernstein, 2005, pp. 147–8; her italics)

The child laments the loss of parental and sibling ties and ultimately faces the profound trauma of being 'all alone in the world.'

The problem is that without additional training or reflection on whether standards of appropriate parenting skills are rooted in biased cultural norms, CPS investigators may never understand what the young foster child's life on the roller coaster is like. In Sunshine County, CPS reports are replete with reprimands of the following kind: the mother makes insufficient eye contact with her children during a supervised visit or does not hug the child. Her parenting skills are considered 'inappropriate' or outright dangerous: take the case of a mother being cited for bringing chicken nuggets to a supervised lunch visit. Family court judges rarely wonder why 'appropriateness' is used as a standard when the law specifies 'neglect' or 'imminent danger' as grounds for removal of a child. It seems to be the case that the judges have also bought into the DSS' 'staircase' ideology. CPS reports specify more or less the following recommendation using a cookie-cutter patriarchal approach: a mother submits to dozens of programs that focus on anger management or nutrition classes. Often, even mothers who are lauded for their cooking skills are still required to take nutrition classes, because there is no individualized tailored approach to family reunification. However, such a system fosters dependency, as the mother has to go through a dozen different programs a week, which means typically that she loses her minimum-wage job. Wages also are garnished to pay for foster care, even when she has permanently lost her right to her child. A better solution seems to be cultural competence training for DSS and similar agencies such as Probation and Parole. AnnJanette Rosga describes an innovative multicultural awareness session with police recruits who get to reflect on their own unconscious biases when they interact with those marked with outsider status (1999, p. 164). Exposing workers to anti-bias training may lead to developing strength-based programming instead of breaking up a family. But DSS is guided by a paradoxical stance of providing social service assistance and being an enforcer of 'suitable homes' and 'appropriate' child-rearing techniques, and cultural competence trainings will not eradicate such split allegiance.

Finally, poor families are policed heavily through the state which uses surveillance methods of mothers on government assistance. The biopolitics of the paternal state are at work here: due to the government-issued health insurance card, a woman can easily be 'hotlined' if she escapes to another state in order to give birth. Such resistance is obviously futile, because the computer system of the hospital alerts DSS of the fugitive of justice. And promptly, a call for the return of the newborn is placed to the hospital. In Georgia, where foster placement is a matter of last resort, the state is working with an innovative approach: stakeholder group work. All parties to the system were invited to rewrite the Juvenile Code completely, and parents' attorneys were at the table as well (Moore, 2015, p. 419). New York City has also used a new, strength-based approach to help families overcome the obstacles and reunite, thanks to the advocacy of the Center for Family Representation. Since 2014, teams of CPS workers, parent advocates, and lawyers work together with the explicit goal to prevent foster placement (Moore, 2015, p. 425). Equally, The Bronx Defenders have social workers and lawyers for families and provide support. Thanks to such persistent efforts thousands of Black families have been able to fight state charges (in family court) successfully, which meant that much fewer Black children faced the trauma of removal (Mack, 2021). Different jurisdictions across the country face different outcomes; simply put, it is the marked difference between those living on the roller coaster and those who walk with ease on stairs. Such epistemic injustice is difficult to overcome, but the self-organizing of parents, peer mentors, and parents' advocates is beginning to occur at a small-scale level and may bring about incremental change.

But is such advocacy sufficient to reform the system? Similar to a growing movement that demands prison abolition, activists with the Movement for Family Power are arguing that true change only can be envisioned outside the system of family regulation. Even a law journal of Columbia University, featuring Dorothy Roberts' keynote in a special issue, has come out in favor of abolishing the child welfare system (Galván, 2021). As long as the state plays a role in training 'mandated reporters' supervising poor, Black, Latine, and Indigenous communities, its agents will not relinquish control over what they consider 'proper' family values. Most likely, they will continue to object to nested care such as co-sleeping with infants and remove the children from suffering from 'abuse.' Twenty years after publishing her groundbreaking book *Shattered Bonds* (2002), Roberts has now come out as an abolitionist. She no longer believes that the system is able to reform and reinvent itself to serve and protect Black families and communities (2021). As Laura Briggs (2021) argues, much can be learned from native nations' abolitionist activism against cultural genocide. Family regulation ideology is put on notice for interfering with Indigenous cultures when it propounds 'humane' carceral logic: The settler colonial state will argue that removal is for the best interest of the Indian child and place them with distant white strangers. Native activist lawyers and members of tribal councils disagreed critiquing the imperial state logic for denigrating kin relationships and culture. "When state officials criticized the absence of indoor plumbing, overcrowding, and poor housing as child neglect, Native activists argued that state social workers were trying to make life on the reservation itself a crime" (p. 628). Challenging the system meant not succumbing to a politics of respectability. After decades of native activism, Congress passed the Indian Child Welfare Act in 1978, which grants sovereignty/jurisdiction to Indian tribal courts. Demanding freedom from white social workers' intrusion on sovereign lands and Indian homes helped to reduce the epidemic of child removal which included some one fourth to one third of Indian children (*Ibid.*, p. 628).

Indigenous communities are setting up peace circles to respond to families in crisis. Theirs is a nested-care approach which focuses on needs of children, not rights. In fact, the abstract-rights-bearing individualist ideology based on Roman law is foreign to Indigenous worldviews in North America and beyond.

> Much like a child welfare system rooted in an individual-centric, property-based framework, specialists had emphasized the perspective of the individual while failing to account for the influence of the community. Like an old-growth forest, Indigenous families are not isolated trees. They are part of a vast, ancient, and intricate society that is connected, communicative, and interdependent. These connections should be leveraged.
>
> (van Schilfgaarde & Shelton, 2021, p. 702)

A circle process does not adhere to an adversarial or deficit-based logic of social work. It does not involve outsiders as experts in law but draws on community stakeholders and extended family members to problem solve and build consensus, thus assuring that the outcome is beneficial for all involved. Peace circles are models for non-Indian people as well and have already found adherents in a court in Michigan where, as a result, fewer children are removed from their homes (*Ibid.*, pp. 705–6).

Conclusion: The Way Forward

Family law was set up to keep family matters out of criminal court. In this chapter, I have highlighted practices and policies in one county to show that such good intentions have not served children well. State agencies, including social services, acknowledge that it is traumatic for any child to be removed from home. Feminist philosophers who wish to engage with this hidden care industry must ask who gets to decide and on what grounds a child may be forcibly removed from their home. Simply put, one must question the entire family court apparatus with its attendant policing apparatus such as CPS, lawyers for the DSS, semi-privatized psychological services who do evaluations solely in favor of CPS, and other services that claim to work for the 'best interest of the child.' In the end, one thing is clear: the industries associated with the family regulation system are thriving at the expense of the child and the parents.

The federal ASFA (1997) has exacerbated the state's intrusion into families instead of solving the crisis of thousands of children failing to get adoptive homes. Rather than reducing time spent in foster care, children spend exactly the same time: 33 months. In 1997, there were about 6,000 legal orphans; a mere seven years later, there were 129,000 legal orphans (Bernstein, 2010, pp. 156–7). In Sunshine County, there are entire streets where each house has parents who are indicated. It is disturbing to overhear young children taunting each other with: "I will hotline your parents!" The experience of CPS workers and police visiting a home on their block at least once a week is so normalized, that the children build this new policing reality into their (agonistic) games. Additionally, family advocates must be vigilant in anticipating the biopolitical effects of new technologies. Child development advocates note the large word gap between poor and rich children by 18 months (Aggarval, 2016), and studies are now in place to monitor 'at-risk' children with word pedometers (Neergard, 2017). It is not too far-fetched to assume that Sunshine Country might use these monitors on 'high-risk' children and cite the persistence of word gap as an indication of child neglect. Elsewhere, predictive policing of families has already been utilized to increase surveillance and break up poor families and targets Black families for 'neglect' investigations. Its defenders say that the algorithm is just one of many tools, and social workers can always override it (Ho & Burke, 2022).

The Lakota class action lawsuit challenging the breakup of families shows two major issues: (1) it is important to continuously litigate so that state jurisdiction does not trump that of a sovereign nation; (2) legislative victories at the federal level do not mean that they are *de facto* enforced, safeguarding the rights of Indian families. Too many Indigenous children are still removed from their homes considered 'inappropriate' or 'unsuitable.' The adversarial logic of CPS is what should be considered 'inappropriate' and out of step with traditional Indigenous approaches to family wellness and nested care.

Iris M. Young's essay "House and Home" (1997) gives us an inkling of what it means to fall victim to 'inappropriate' child-rearing in a New Jersey suburb in the 1960s. Her white mother lost custody for several years of Young and her sister for reasons similar to those that Sunshine County uses to indicate parents. A few empty bottles of alcohol on the floor were enough evidence to substantiate claims of child neglect. In Young's case, once they reunited, the mother moved with her daughters to New York City. Martin Guggenheim suggests that if child welfare were treated holistically as a

> public health or shared social problem, rather than an issue focused solely on child abuse, we could develop policies that address directly and proactively those conditions that adversely affect the health and welfare of poor children in the United States.
>
> (2005, p. 211)

The 'child-advocacy-focused' state—under the guise of *parens patriae*, the power of the state to intervene in the affairs of families—sounds good in theory, but in practice, it means that the state investigates, almost exclusively, families that are not socially connected to powerful stakeholders in their communities. Women who call police to protect them from physical violence are at risk of child removal because the state assuming the role of patriarch argues that such mothers are inept to protect their children from witnessing violence in the home.

Dorothy Roberts (2002) notes that it costs 11 times more to remove a child to foster care than to overcome obstacles and to strengthen family bonds. She notes that 95% of children in foster care in Chicago are Black. The state's attack of the Black family has historical roots in the Middle Passage and chattel slavery. It should shock the conscience that more than half of Black children will be subjected to state investigation during their childhood (Roberts, 2021, p. 460). If we were to see a transformation in welfare politics, we need to invest in non-punitive practices such as community-based advocacy for families and a public health approach to child welfare. Taking inspiration from an Indigenous model of peace circles, such approach would center healing conflicts within families, intergenerational trauma, and eschew humiliation practices of any kind.

The point of view presented here may not be popular with those who are engaged in the noble pursuit of rescuing children from corporal punishment and other serious cases of abuse. The National No Hit Zone Committee (2022) has become a leading child advocate in the abolition of corporal punishment and developed a toolkit for various child-centered organizations. Its philosophy fits within a restorative justice reform movement which still draws on the policing power of the state (CPS, school police officers) in order to assure a zero tolerance for emotional and physical abuse in child advocacy centers, schools, hospitals, etc.

Anecdotal evidence from Sunshine County suggests that arbitrary and capricious removal practices are far more prevalent than justifiable removal of young children. So, I agree with Stephanie Smith Ledesma (2015) who argues that

> until children are protected from the 'master narrative' of child welfare that plays out in hundreds of courtrooms across this nation on a daily basis through the inconsistent application of 'reasonable efforts,' our children stand desperately in need of protection from the very child protective service agencies that are charged with protecting them.

The lives of millions of children are at stake, and racialized and poor families' lives matter. Parents and children deserve more than the relentless *policing* gaze of social workers whose rescue mission seems benign but does not fool any of the targeted recipients who get sucked into the invisible dragnet of total social control with no escape hatch in sight. Dorothy Roberts (2018) warns of the runaway effects of policing reforms that emerged from calls to defund the police. If police are replaced with social workers who perform 'wellness checks' on families, it would inevitably ensnare such families in systems of control, supervision, and punitive measures.

> As with prison abolition, the aim is not to reform the child protection system; the aim is to replace it with a society that attends to children's welfare in a radically different way. With a common vision for meeting human needs and ensuring safety, we can build a world where caging people and tearing families apart are unimaginable.
>
> (Roberts, 2018)

Such vision of ludic Ubuntu transformative justice which takes note of Indigenous nested care is further explored in Chapter 5. Chapter 3 sheds a critical light on sovereign immunity and outlaw settler colonial legacies.

Notes

* All names and places have been anonymized to protect the families and advocates. The cases I discuss here include those in which mother-respondents have reported directly to me or those in which I have been involved as a witness.

1 This chapter draws upon a published article: "Policing Families: The Many-Headed Hydra of Surveillance." *APA Newsletter for Feminism and Philosophy*, 17(2), 2018, pp. 2–11. (https://cdn.ymaws.com/www.apaonline.org/resource/collection/D03EBDAB-82D7-4B28-B897-C050FDC1ACB4/FeminismV17n2.pdf).

2 Family defense refers to "working on behalf of adults threatened by state intervention with the temporary and permanent loss of the custody and rights to their children" (Guggenheim & Sankaran, 2015, p. xix).

3 Hotlining refers to the practice of placing an anonymous call to Child Protective Services to report child endangerment, which may trigger investigation (Redleaf, 2015, p. 390).
4 Permissive reporters are those who encouraged to report any suspicion of child abuse (Redleaf, 2015, p. 392).
5 While Sunshine County's placement rates are disproportionately higher than other counties in the state, the rate of removal of children has dramatically increased across the United States since 1997.
6 One Texas courtroom even permitted the criminal defense counsel use of "affluenza syndrome" for his wealthy client Ethan Couch who killed several persons while driving under the influence of several drugs in 2013. The judge agreed and sentenced him to probation and drug rehabilitation (Chicago Defender, 2013).
7 I use "American Indian," not "Native American," to make the following point: "Native American" became the official term adopted by the Clinton administration, an ethnic group designation that is not a self-chosen term by many Indian people and one that deliberately denies sovereignty.

3 The Context of Insurrectionist Justice

Resisting the Looting of Black Bodies[1]

At this stage, we enter the realm of righteous anger of the dispossessed who confront state violence. In this deadly dance for recognition, those who control the master narrative need to ascertain how the deployment of legalized bondage is the most effective. In a white supremacist polity such as the United States, those who are beneficiaries of the racial contract learn to naturalize 'rights' and even call them 'inalienable.' They accuse the racialized insurrectionists as wallowing in a distant past, instead of picking themselves up by their bootstraps. By contrast, marooned freedom fighters living beyond the pale have a Janus face—they know the past is not dead. It is not even past. They know of the afterlives of slavery and continue to speak and enact truth to power. They may inspire symbolic or material uprisings, and they have a second sight that the arc of the universe does indeed bend toward justice.

The year 1619 is an important year, as it marks the arrival of 20 African women and men in the North American territory, now known as the United States. I argue that it marks the beginning of an outlaw nation. Chased, chained, traded, and forced into a death march in Angola, these African human beings were then kidnapped from the Portuguese slavers' ship only to end up on the shores of the British colony against their will. The pirates traded in the Africans in exchange for food, marking the violent advent of chattel slavery. Over the next 400 years, slave codes, black codes, convict lease, and Jim Crow, and other targeted disenfranchisement policies, laws, and statutes, have been carefully designed to accomplish two goals: (1) to protect the white polity in the United States from a population that has been systematically denied rights and benefits that white citizens enjoy (and demand) from their state institutions; and (2) to shield the white polity from accountability for the individual and social harms white people through the political-legal process caused to these populations. In this chapter, I critique the state's legal reasoning as fundamentally Hobbesian and Manichean. This means that the state defends sovereign immunity reserved for white property owners and, in turn, practices legal subjugation of racialized subjects, especially those of African descent. Ultimately, such ideology critique is meant to showcase that an investment in legal protection for subjugated people is futile; specifically, the concept of an abstract-rights-bearing individual is a ruse, and the

DOI: 10.4324/9781003055327-4

belief of the race-neutral rule of law has been used to buttress white supremacist practices. Yet, people of African descent have always resisted subjugation and servitude, and here, I turn to the ideal and practice of insurrectionist justice (Harris, 2002; McBride, 2020) and contrast it with carceral feminism (Bernstein, 2010; 2012).

My analysis acknowledges the insights of scholars who have critiqued the settler colonial criminalizing system that has targeted Indigenous peoples the world over. Viviane Saleh-Hanna (2017) characterizes the system as racist, imperialist, and (hetero)patriarchal. I turn to historiographies of the United States which give us histories "from below" (e.g., Zinn, 1980; Davis, 1983; Takaki, 1994; Miller, 1995; Mogul *et al.*, 2011; Dunbar-Ortiz, 2014; Sinha, 2016; Thuma, 2019). Building on their critiques, I want to draw the line between the law which circumscribes the procedural system for those deemed citizens (white, colonial, straight cis men) and what I label as an outlaw criminal legal system reserved for subjects residing beyond the pale: subjugated, racialized as Other, disposable, Indigenous peoples, in other words, those who live beyond the protection of the law. According to English law, an outlaw is someone who willfully does not submit to the rule of law, someone who engages in acts of treason and sedition (Bellamy, 1973).

Importantly, I argue that it is the state itself that is devoted to strategic lawlessness, designating certain groups to live "beyond the pale" (Nagel, 2014). Such status is reserved for those who do not benefit from the state's protection, in other words, living 'inside the pale.' They are rendered disposable, caught up in the vagaries of capitalist exploitation, racism, colonialism, and empire-building. Thus, the project of outlaw nation-building is defined as a set of contradictory practices which are designed to ensnare a racialized and impoverished Other. The outlaw nation-state decrees by law that the caste of disposable people be thrown into a permanent status of insecurity and vulnerability, condemning them to a life beyond the pale, unworthy of protection or rights-bearing privileges. The outlaw state is not bound by universal principles of morality. Insurrectionist ethicists charge that it is a moral duty to support resistance to the state's outlawry through uprisings and escapes, pointing to the legacy of abolitionist struggles against chattel slavery (Harris, 2002, p. 192).

In the final analysis, we are dealing with a paradox: a law that is committed to supporting lawlessness. This is the definitive characteristic of the *outlaw nation-state*: the use of statutory law, legal precedent, and discretionary legal procedures that keep people of African descent "in their proper place"—their right to life is strictly determined by those who formulate contract theory and decide who is worthy of receiving contracts. Black people are not even permitted second-class citizenship; they are the denizens of a republic that continues to wage war on Black lives and livelihood. Their chattel slave and subject status continues through the invisible and invincible dragnet of surveillance, occupation, and submission to the white supremacist, capitalist police state of the colonizer. My social justice abolitionist reasoning draws on the brilliant insights of those who have been subject to the 'laws' of a captive nation, hunted down by the state and its charges. From David Walker to Ida B. Wells-Barnett, Assata Shakur, and Angela Y Davis, marooned intellectuals serve as way-showers for insurrectionist justice and abolition democracy. As organic intellectuals, they resist by putting their bodies on the line and protest the state's looting of the Black body and property. Black Lives Matter movements notwithstanding, as Trevor Noah points out, Black bodies are looted daily (Moran, 2020). Such persistent necrophilic transgression goes unnoticed, because it is white America's entitlement since 1619. *White Lives Matter Most—and Other "Little" White Lies* (Meyer, 2018).

Outlaw Origins of Nation-Building

In 1845, Stand Watie, a member of the Cherokee nation, describes poignantly that the white man's conquest is imperial and genocidal.

> If there was a crime ... it was more your crime than ours. ... You abolished our government, annihilated our laws, suppressed our authorities, took away our lands, turned us out of our houses, denied us the rights of men, made us outcasts and outlaws in our own land, plunging us at the same time into an abyss of moral degradation which was hurling our people to swift destruction.
>
> (Stand Watie, cited in Miller, 1995, p. 344)

Stand Watie's analysis points out the legal contortionism inherent in the imperial project: The colonial settlers (a polite descriptor for English invaders committed to outlawry) are the real outlaws, deny the harm of their behaviors, and place their behaviors within the law while victimizing and harming the colonized whom the settlers deem the 'outlaws.' Genocidal practices are part and parcel of the nation-building project.

Progressive historians note that the US republic is founded upon genocide (of Indigenous peoples[2]) and slavery (of African peoples). What is forgotten in this sober account is that both peoples faced both evils. It is forgotten that Indigenous human beings were not only enslaved on their own territory on both coasts, but they were transported to the Caribbean islands by the slavers. It is also forgotten that peoples of Africa not only lost their lives in the Maafa (i.e., the transatlantic holocaust) but that the conditions of enslavement meet criteria of the United Nations (UN) genocide convention. Mainstream historians defend the Enlightenment ideals of liberty and equality as overriding progressive principles of the US republic's social contract. Some try to complicate it somewhat, as told by Matthew Desmond in the celebrated (and controversial) "1619 Project" of the *New York Times*:

> What made the cotton economy boom in the United States, [...], was our nation's unflinching willingness to use violence on nonwhite people and

> to exert its will on seemingly endless supplies of land and labor. Given the choice between modernity and barbarism, prosperity and poverty, lawfulness and cruelty, democracy and totalitarianism, America chose all of the above.
>
> (Desmond, 2019)

I argue that the founders of the US republic chose *lawlessness* for their new outlaw national project. It is a well-disguised endeavor. The criminal logic of enslaving human beings and their descendants in perpetuity was based on the enduring ideological claim that the plantation served as a civilizing mission for human beings of African descent. To be effective and quell unrest outlaw economic policies were buttressed by a theological promise: through pious submission, enslaved humans would earn salvation.

However, there were protest voices 'from below.' As early as 1635, a leader of the Patuxent Nation wrote a pointed letter to settler colonial occupiers protesting their imposition of English law on all Indians accused of taking the lives of English persons. He argued that "since that you are here strangers, and come into our Countrey, you should rather conform yourselves to the Customes of our Countrey, [than] impose yours upon us" (unnamed Patuxent leader, cited in Miller, 1995, p. 121). A certain Captain John Odber had been killed in retaliation for his murder of a Wiccomiss woman. Indian people knew very well that a white captain would never face any colonial court of law for crimes committed against them. Two scenarios showcase the impossibility of imposing Indigenous legal standards. (1) If a member of an Indian nation retaliated, the English simply proclaimed total warfare on the nation, killing most and enslaving all survivors. (2) If Indian people did not resist colonial transgressions and violence, the English declared that they were savages who did not have a system of punishments. In the case of Odber, what started as an interpersonal conflict and personal harm ended up in harming the entire community: By 1669, the extermination of the Wiccomiss was assured. They were "hunted down in swamps and mires and sold as slaves in Barbados. Jubilantly, the English report their total annihilation" on the shores of the territory, now known as Maryland (Miller, 1995, p. 120).

Sovereign immunity—*The king can do no wrong*. Such is the elegant outlaw language of English common law; its logic is extended to settler colonial commoners who not only trespass on 'foreign' soil but also commit genocidal crimes against 'foreign' peoples, dubbed 'natives.' Colonial 'law' was ever so exacting even when a trifle offense occurred such as theft of a single silver cup in 1585. Such 'property crime' leads to the torching of an entire Indian village, and the villagers had to seek refuge with neighboring peoples (Zinn, 1980, p. 12). Indian generosity toward starving strangers was taken for granted by the English. The invaders' own grand theft, clear-cutting, and massive dispossession could literally not be seen as major transgression (and barbarism). Here, it is helpful to study Hobbes' *Leviathan.* It seems to serve as a blueprint for settler colonial outlawry. Sovereign power is granted by (a) "natural force" (i.e., by waging wars against hostile peoples) or (b) a social contract, where men qua subjects submit voluntarily to the sovereign. Governing by force describes a "commonwealth by *acquisition,*" whereas peaceful consent is called a "commonwealth by *institution*" (Hobbes, 1986, p. 228, emphasis in original). Hobbes gives us a hypothetical case:

> [I]nto what place soever a man shall come, if he do anything contrary to that law, it is a crime. If a man come from the *Indies* hither, and perswade men here to receive a new Religion, or teach them anything that tendeth to disobedience of the Laws of this Country, though he be never so well perswaded of the truth of what he teacheth, he commits a Crime, and may be justly punished for the same, [...] because he does that which he would not approve in another [...].
>
> (Ibid., p. 338)

Hobbes seems to make a moral case for respecting sovereign customs while using the principle of reciprocity. Applied to the case of the Patuxent leader's petition, the English colonials should have submitted to the Wiccomiss' sovereign legal system. For failing to do so, it is the English who exemplify outlaw behavior. However, Hobbes does not really think of Indigenous peoples as sovereign nations. Legitimating a commonwealth by acquisition means that the Wiccomiss are not legally entitled to the land and must submit to English common law.

Long before social contract theory found its way into the Declaration of Independence, outlaw ideology was firmly rooted in Hobbes' ideas of commonwealth and dominion. *The Leviathan* serves as a blueprint and stern warning: those who are endowed with inalienable rights such as legal and civic personhood may give their consent to be governed and included into the (white) brotherhood. In its US contract version, it brings civilizing measures such as the rule of law, free and equal treatment under the law, habeas corpus, and the right to a trial of a jury of one's peers. These are to be 'controls' on the sovereign's power, but they are used to solidify power over those controlled in the mythology of law. In other words, a commonwealth that keeps all in awe, by balancing rights and security. However, there are indeed those who Hobbes believes are not endowed with such precious inalienable rights. What shall be done to them? In no uncertain terms, he decrees that they simply be conquered—their lives can even be sacrificed to preserve law and order for those who are rightful participants in the social contract. This is how Manichean outlaw ideology creeps into a text defending a social/civic contract. Why is such conquest legitimate? Hobbes justifies it because these "savages" do not consent to the social contract. Later, contractarian philosophers have more subtle ways of expressing their racism and imperialism, but the point is made. As Charles Mills (1997) argues, the social contract is a racial contract, and philosopher John Locke provided the necessary legitimation: Indians had merely a natural right, but not a "civil right" to the land. Thus, Governor Winthrop was able to expropriate Indian nations living in the Massachusetts Bay Colony. I argue that Winthrop used outlaw logic to declare their land a legal vacuum. With a stroke of genius, they were landless, because natural rights do not have legal standing (Zinn, 1980, p. 13). The social contract was also used to legitimize a plutocracy—personal wealth dictates that laws are only legitimate when they serve and protect the interest of the white male elites, and the legal punitive, i.e., criminalizing law binds the 'unruly' masses by force. (The elites, by contrast, enjoy sovereign immunity in the event they do harm to others, not socially connected to them.)

Much has been made of the Doctrine of Discovery and the fiction of *terra nullius*—the idea that colonialization is justifiable when land does not belong to anyone. Of course, the Americas were already occupied by peoples having diverse justice systems. I suggest an additional focus on the claim of sovereign immunity is needed to legitimate the nullification of Indigenous legal practices. Outlaw colonials with blessings of their religious leaders impose colonial law on subjects who do not consent (especially Indigenous and Black subjects). Witness the kingdom of Hawai'i which lost its sovereign status when the queen was overthrown and jailed by US military forces in the 19th century. Apologies were made under the Clinton administration, but no mention of reparations accompanied that symbolic gesture. (And Puerto Rico and other islands are still considered 'dominions,' or captive nations, of US empire.) Today, sovereign immunity is legally invoked in order to deny claims by torture victims of CIA agents, military, and private mercenaries, who operate in (secret) prisons the world over (e.g., Abu Ghraib prison in Iraq).

To summarize, the US republic is founded on multiple layers of outlaw violence—the embodiment of a well-disguised 'legal' hegemonic apparatus.

1 Freed from the empire in the east (England), it pursued its own empire building in the West (Zinn, 1980, p. 85). Territorial expansion meant elimination of peoples by any means necessary, including systematic genocide such as the Cherokee Nation's death march, known as Trail of Tears, and brutal containment into "reservations." Furthermore, genocidal practices included forced "assimilation" of Indian children into a "boarding school" system that led to thousands of children's premature death and intergenerational trauma. The outlaw state has violated and continues to dismiss Indigenous nations' self-determination and right to peaceful coexistence. Treaties were supposed to preserve such mutually agreed principles. Every single treaty between the government and Indian nations was systematically broken through various devious practices by one side—the agents representing the settler colonial nation-state (Miller, 1995).

2 The US government built on the British colonial legal instruments justifying and expanding enslavement of human beings. The US government stands alone in the world defending chattel slavery for adjudication purposes.

3 The US government maintains an obstinate belief in the "possessive investment in whiteness" (Lipsitz, 2006), which means that whites and their families benefit in cumulative ways while Black people are systematically disadvantaged, oppressed, and punished.[3] Marc Mauer (2000) of the Sentencing Project estimates that during the height of the war on drugs 80% of adolescent whites received probation while 80% of young Black people were sentenced to prison terms. The benefits of whiteness carry structural, enduring life-affirming advantages. Anti-Black racism, by contrast, leads to "premature death" (Gilmore, 2007).

Applying the logic of sovereign immunity to the white imaginary gives us a special insight into the performativity of lawlessness. When whites turn their hatred toward the racialized Other, they enjoy immunity from prosecution for instigating race riots, coordinating lynching, and violently boycotting desegregation. While others have analyzed the violence of the law, I focus on the violence of lawlessness—the systematic lack of federal, state, local enforcement of constitutional law, statutes, and ordinances. Sovereign immunity is, of course, hegemonic ideology, giving such outlaws the irresistible pleasure of never having to say "sorry." For the (white) hegemonic, Manichean nation-building logic to succeed, it needs diversionary fear-mongering strategies by inventing black criminality, black-on-black crime, and black superpredators. Imprisonment then becomes the right and proper tool of white supremacist carceral logic and law (enforcement) inflicted on those who will never become white (enough).

I turn to specific examples to resisting state-sanctioned violence: the law's support for chattel slavery and its legacy, the criminal legal system since 1865, the date of the supposed abolition of slavery.

Enslavement Codes and the Battle Cry for Dignity

Numerous appellate courts in slave states had to deal with the following paradox: Judges ruled that enslaved humans were considered personal (movable) property and incapable of making rational decisions. Enslavers offered them the choice of staying enslaved or moving to another state to be freed. A Virginia decision, *Bailey v. Poindexter* (1858), opposed such offer because the enslaved "have no civil or social rights." Furthermore, giving enslaved persons a choice was "an effort to accomplish a legal impossibility" (Kennington, 2019, p. 234). Alabama judges considered enslaved persons as humans endowed with intelligence and could therefore be found "capable of committing crimes." But they are "in respect of all civil rights and relations, not persons, but things" and could not possibly make choices regarding their civil status, i.e., choosing freedom (*Ibid.*, p. 235). Enforcement of slave codes meant that rebellious people who committed crimes of insurrection, large and small offenses, on the plantation, faced the full weight of the law. Yet, slavers who punished excessively never faced legal consequences. Over six decades, some 800 people filed freedom suits across Southern states. Fairly uniformly, antebellum judges considered them chattel, not humans or the courts prized upholding the rule of (slave) law higher than moral values (*Ibid.*, passim). Kelly Kennington's analysis also shows that judges supported slavery, even when the slavers' will granted manumission and material inheritance. In that case, the law was ignored due to judges' fears of a free Black populace (pp. 233–4).

The formal strategy of appealing to the courts for freedom was one avenue that was usually unsuccessful. From a maroon's perspective, the struggle for liberation by other means was more practical, if not, more dangerous. In his autobiography, Frederick Douglass (1855) shares what precipitated his decision to run away. He describes one epic fight with a notorious enslaver Edward Covey, "as though we stood as equals before the law. The very color of the man was forgotten" (Douglass, 1855). Covey never punished him again and did not report Douglass to 'authorities.' Douglass (1855) speculates that Covey was too ashamed to admit to other whites that a 16-year-old teenager fought back—and 'won.'

Radical abolitionist David Walker, a businessman from Boston, fought in another way with his incendiary manifesto for all Black people. His *Appeal to the Colored Citizens of the World* (1830) was deemed so dangerous that anybody caught with the tract would be severely punished; for Black people—swift execution. Walker's manifesto rallies Black people to commit a concerted insurrection against the institution of slavery (David Walker Memorial Project, n.d.). It represents a first-rate indictment of the 'Christian' nation-state's outlaw ideology. Walker addresses fellow brothers as citizens, even though the nation-state has only treated him and others as subjects. He died under suspicious circumstances. Georgia's governor had promised a reward of $10,000 for his capture. Walker, born free, was not entitled to free speech (guaranteed by the First Amendment), and his manifesto was considered seditious, dangerous literature: "The crackdown against the *Appeal* was swift and harsh. Authorities also passed new and stricter laws against anti-slavery material and against slave education" (David Walker Memorial Project, n.d.). Black abolitionist groups took on the US republic's promises of liberty, representation, and free speech to demand liberation from all shackles. This is best exemplified in Frederick Douglass' speech: "What to the Slave is the fourth of July?" Its ideology critique of the fugitive slave law serves as an expression of exquisite moral outrage, indebted to David Walker's *Appeal.*

> What, to the American slave, is your 4th of July? I answer: a day that reveals to him, more than all other days in the year, the gross injustice and cruelty to which he is the constant victim. To him, your celebration is a sham; your boasted liberty, an unholy license; your national greatness, swelling vanity; your sounds of rejoicing are empty and heartless; your denunciations of tyrants, brass fronted impudence; your shouts of liberty an equality, hollow mockery; your prayers and hymns, your sermons and

> thanksgivings, with all your religious parade, and solemnity, are, to him, mere bombast, fraud, deception, impiety, and hypocrisy—a thin veil to cover up crimes which would disgrace a nation of savages. There is not a nation on the earth guilty of practices, more shocking and bloody, than are the people of these United States, at this very hour.
>
> (Douglass, 1852/1999)

Douglass also looked at the Haitian Revolution with great admiration and conceded that the liberated Haitians paid dearly for taking to heart *liberté, fraternité, egalité*, overthrowing the French colonial and slave system all at once. As a result of such victorious insurrectionist revolution, the global imperial regimes conspired to penalize the Black republic economically from which Haiti has not recovered till today (Alexander, 2022).

In the United States, the outlaw behavior of the slavers' empire starts in 1619 before the legal codification of enslaving Africans and their descendants. The arrival of Africans in Virginia was an event unlike the transports of indentured servants from Ireland and England (cf. Zinn, 1980, pp. 23–5). These 20 African women and men were exchanged by hungry pirates for food stuffs. The colonial masters did not take the pirates into custody charging them for trafficking in human beings and returning the Africans to their ancestral lands. However, mainstream historians take a narrow view arguing that these trafficked Africans were not reduced to property and were therefore not slaves (for life) (Takaki, 2008, p. 52). But contracts and punishment regimes showcase one (*de facto*) reality for Africans and a different one for servants (whites). Where they mingle, cohabitate, and run off to maroon communities, racist laws proscribe such fraternization beginning in the 1660s (Zinn, 1980, p. 31). The defeat of the multiracial Bacon's rebellion, which had targeted both friendly Pamunkey Indians and austere English aristocrats in 1676, meant that differential punishment and incentives had to be instituted for Black enslaved persons and white servants to avoid such dangerous liaison in perpetuity. In the Carolinas, outlaw statutes prohibited Black persons' travel to Indian land—a policy to "create aversion" rather than fraternization and revolt against whites (*Ibid.*, p. 54). Virginia instituted a systematic outlaw framework that proscribed interracial marriage and slave codes specified that children born to an enslaved woman would follow her 'condition.' A century later, the US federal government followed suit by giving maximum protection to slavers to thwart off slave insurrections (*Ibid.*, pp. 89–90).

A case could be made that there existed protections for the subjugated and racialized Other. The transatlantic slave trade (Maafa) was abolished within a decade of the Declaration of Independence. Slavers could not torture, rape, or kill enslaved persons, including children. However, as most texts laconically state—such fancy legal protections were never enforced. Such *de facto* disregard for the law is never described as outlaw. There is one notable exception. When the fugitive slave law was passed, one insurrectionist rebel, J.W. Loguen, declares in 1850 that "it outlaws me, and I outlaw it!" (*Ibid.*, p. 177).

He provided for some 1,500 people safe housing in Syracuse, New York, *en route* to Canada. Loguen taunted his former slaver Sarah Logue, who wanted him to return or pay her $1,000 in compensation: "Have you got to learn that human rights are mutual and reciprocal, and if you take my liberty and life, you forfeit your own liberty and life?" (*Ibid.*). In fact, enslavers received ample compensation, especially during times of crisis, while freed people's legal petitions for reparations did not materialize (Hunter, 2019).

Possessive Investment in Whiteness—Black Lives Matter?

From 1619 to 1669 to the 3/5th compromise, to US Supreme Court decisions *Dred Scott*, *Plessy*, and *McCleskey*—the outlaw nation continues to disguise its exceptionalism. "The history of the United States has been a history of successive and cumulative racial projects" benefiting whites in every aspect of their lives and setting prohibitions regarding interracial fraternization or marriages (Lipsitz, 2011, p. 41). Specifically, Lipsitz faults the US Constitution for setting up "an elaborate federal system designed to protect the power of slaveholders" and for restricting rights of free Black people (*Ibid.*). In fact, as freedom and whiteness are coterminous, so are bondage and criminality inscribed on the Black body (Muhammad, 2010). Slavery and indentured servitude remain codified in the amendment that was supposed to set enslaved people free. Many critics of the "abolition" [*sic*] amendment (i.e., 13th Amendment to the constitution, 1865) have noted that slavery merely morphed from private to state-sponsored legal codification. However, the state has always been involved in the "peculiar institution," since slave codes and the US constitution granted slavers policing power over their human chattel (Walters, 2013).[4] The Amendment along with the other two Reconstruction era amendments (14th and 15th) signified a bit of victors' justice, a hard-won demand by freed men who fought in the Union army to outlaw slavery and bondage. In 1864, Senator Charles Sumner of Massachusetts proposed this abolitionist language: "All persons are equal before the law, so that no person can hold another as a slave" (Walters, 2013, p. 309). In the end, the compromise abolitionist language imitates other emancipation laws such as Vermont's 1777 Constitution, which includes this exception: "bound by law, for the payment of debts, damages, fines, costs, or the like" (Walters, p. 309). The Amendment's first section declares slavery and indentured servitude abolished, except "where duly convicted of a crime." Thus, the federal government preserves bondage under due process. Thus, the constitutional amendment magnifies the paradox of the outlaw state, which is the guarantor of the rule of law. The Reconstruction Amendments could rein in white supremacy, especially since they are the only amendments that each conclude with this imposition: "Congress shall have the power to enforce this article by appropriate legislation." However, Congress never made use of its power of enforcement mechanism—again, the hallmark of the outlaw state, which enforces laws only when it conveniently serves as severe punishment of the already dispossessed and soon-to-be disembodied. No Southern government was ever punished by Congress for systematically violating the Reconstruction Amendments. However, it has also been a convenient myth to suggest that Northern states were free from race prejudice in antebellum decades. Legal disenfranchisement and extra-legal pogroms took place while the abolition movement took off as elite whites incited the rabble that whiteness signals freedom, and African-descending people are undeserving (Clark-Pujara & Cox, 2020).

How is it possible to enslave human beings at the same time to promise freedom from bondage? As Senator Sumner demanded, abolition of slavery must be categorical and absolute, binding. The United States is exceptional in this regard since the 1920s—when the League of Nations abolished slavery. The slave patrols and jails, the plantation, the slave codes all morph into police patrols who enforced the black codes and the convict-lease system, considered as "worse than slavery" (Oshinsky, 1996). Texas finally abolished the murderous convict-lease system in 1912, when its prisoner mortality rate got too high—3,500 prisoners died within a 40-year span. A mass grave of 95 prisoners was recently discovered (Groetzinger, 2019). Neoslavery through debt peonage and convict-leasing continued into the 1970s. By the 1980s, rural African Americans in Georgia still received a peculiar 'choice.' Sheriffs offered the following punishment to parolees or probationers: work on a farm or in logging or go to jail. White farmers also paid bonds and fees, and if the workers slipped, coming late to work, they were sent back to jail. Often, Black women and men worked for an indefinite period, since they somehow could never pay back the debt (Thompson & Copeland, 1987).

Federal complicity with the Jim Crow system was made explicit with the US Supreme Court decision *Plessy v. Ferguson* (1896). Journalist anti-lynching crusader, Ida B. Wells-Barnett (1892, 1895), also legally challenged the racist transportation system—unsuccessfully. In three books and pamphlets, spanning decades, she issues her damning judgment about the savage reality of white supremacist terror in the streets and the courts. White men hiding in Ku Klux Klan (KKK) uniform justified torture and murder to control Black people's desire for uprisings, control their desire in political participation and economic uplift, and, most provocatively, proscribe consensual interracial relationships.

> Negroes were whipped, scourged, exiled, shot and hung whenever and wherever it pleased the white man so to treat them, and as the civilized world with increasing persistency held the white people of the South to account for its outlawry, the murderers invented a third excuse—that Negroes had to be killed to avenge their assaults upon women.
>
> (Wells-Barnett, 1895/2005)

Especially, the last charge, the invention of the myth of the rapist, triggered a concerted response by the white elites. For daring to speak truth, Southerners put a bounty on her head. Undeterred, Wells-Barnett practiced strategic insurrectionist justice demands by proposing a consumer boycott of white business. In the footsteps of another great female abolitionist, Harriet Tubman, Wells-Barnett was successful in encouraging a great migration of Black people, who left Jim Crow Memphis for Kansas and Oklahoma. She carried her anti-lynching message to London, following the intercontinental path much traveled by abolitionists decades earlier (Greaves, 1989). Brilliantly, Wells-Barnett was able to invert the charge of criminality, foisting it directly on white supremacists, in a way that centuries earlier, Stand Watie charged the colonial system with committing outlawry. She understood that "one tool of white supremacy is its inversion of predation: the victim is costumed as criminal, the criminal as victim" (Murakawa, 2021, p. 218).

The Jim Crow outlaw decision, *Plessy v. Ferguson* (1896), made it clear that whites found it intolerable to share *public* spaces with Black free citizens. Equally important is the *de facto* proscription of sharing *intimate* spaces. Until 2000, interracial dating was prohibited in the state of Alabama—41% of voters fought to keep it that way—even though this law had already been overturned by the US Supreme Court in *Loving v. Virginia* (1967). Categorically and defiantly, the state law warned: "The legislature shall never pass any law to authorize or legalize any marriage between any white person and a Negro or descendant of a Negro" (cited in Stevenson, 2019, p. 29). Bryan Stevenson's courageous Equal Justice Initiative unearthed hundreds of lynching victims in the *Lynching in America* report (2017), and his organization initiated a first national memorial, the Museum for Peace and Justice, which opened in 2018. It memorializes victims of white supremacist terrorism. Lynch terror signaled to Black citizens that they would never receive the protection of the white supremacist legal system.

By suggesting that white women freely consorted with Black men, Wells-Barnett had to escape the South. To this day, the myth of the Black rapist has endured (Davis, 1983) and morphed into its own species: the trope of the "criminalblackman" (Russell-Brown, 2008). A powerful example of this moral panic is the recent attempt of eroding bail reform in New York state. A month before its enactment in 2020, police union and prosecutors warned about the premature release of violent people (without bail). In reality, bail serves to contain the poor, especially Black and Latine people, presumed guilty *before* the court and plea system fix their sentence. New York's penal abolitionist groups continue to protest legislative proposals that seek to introduce a prediction of dangerousness as a new condition of confinement, which would inevitably lead to higher incarceration rates of Black men.

Insurrectionist Justice Meets Carceral Feminism[5]

Those advocating a pragmatist ethics of insurrection hold that there is no progress without struggle, following Douglass, Walker, and philosopher Leonard

Harris. On the other hand, there were civic-minded abolitionists who follow the polite discourse of respectability politics, using petitions, dialogue, and voting (Harris, 2002, p. 206). Yet, civil discourse did not overthrow the outlaw system of chattel slavery. What are some lessons for today? The carceral system is exactly working as it is designed, namely, steeped in outlawry and disorder. This is a common rallying cry of prison and policing critics, although some suggest that the erosion of the Bill of Rights protections only occurred within the last decades which brought on mass incarceration (Alexander, 2010; Karakatsanis, 2019, p. 37). As I have argued, the criminalizing system is steeped in apartheid reality; one system for whites: lawlessness, disguised as police discretion; another operating system for policing Black bodies that is disguised in the fictitious euphemism of "law and order." Outlawry and disorder are more honest terms, and this describes quite perfectly the century-old complaints of terrorized Black communities: every "riot" [*sic*] commission issued the same recommendations from the "Red Summer" racist pogroms of 1919–1965 and beyond. Stop police brutality, demilitarize the police, and invest in fair, safe, affordable housing, jobs, community health centers, and quality education. What is novel today is a nationwide demand to "defund the police" which comes from the streets, not expert commissions. What has also become painfully clear is that all Black bodies are under attack. George Floyd's lynching, witnessed and filmed by a courageous 17-year-old Black woman, Darnella Frazier, highlights the system's casual extinction of Black lives. In the case of Michael Brown, a white police officer persuaded a grand jury simply by professing that the Black male body looked threatening, painted as a 'monster.' Such jury tends to be unwilling to pronounce indictments of those acting under the color of law. The indictment and successful prosecution leading to long sentences, as in the case of Derek Chauvin in 2021, is truly exceptional. Three decades earlier, the Orange County jury could not see an act of attempted murder viewing filmed evidence that Rodney King was lying on the ground, facing batons and kicks to his head. For some, Chauvin's conviction on state and federal charges shows that the system works, but penal abolitionists know that the criminal legal system is not designed to secure accountability or justice. It is not a coincidence, that those who birthed the hashtag #Black Lives Matter after the acquittal of a neighborhood vigilante are Black women. In the tradition of Wells-Barnett, Patrisse Cullors, Alicia Garza, and Opal Tometi called for active resistance after Trayvon Martin's mother received no justice from the courts. This call was finally heeded in national mass protest after another young Black man was shot in the streets of Ferguson, Missouri. The state responded by painting movement activists as terrorist, choosing to focus on "looting" and "vandalism" (German, 2020). But with Trevor Noah we must ask, who is looting whom? Insurrectionist ethics defended on pragmatist grounds holds that urban uprisings, "organized and spontaneous, are important and influential features helping to create social change" (Harris, 2002, p. 200).

Sovereign immunity meets US Supreme Court's 'qualified immunity': a member of the policing brotherhood is declared immune to conviction unless there is an identical case where an officer has been found guilty. This legal reasoning should be studied as a case of epistemological smothering and circular logic, because no two police brutality cases are identical to each other. George Floyd had to die by the choke hold—Paul Butler's term for the systematic brutalization of Black men's bodies by police—in order for US Congress to contemplate two laws: abolish choke hold torture and abolish qualified immunity within a month of his murder. Butler (2018) is pessimistic that the abolition of the choke hold could usher in lasting change to a corrupt system which started with the slavers patrols in the 17th century. After all, the US Supreme Court has been very firmly ensconced on the side of police, sometimes even with unanimity. The nine judges literally see nothing wrong with officers' overreach who, after all, make deadly decisions "within a split second." Morally speaking, they might also be incapable of seeing themselves on the receiving end of a police officer's pepper spray, baton, and bullets. (Here it is noteworthy that Paul Butler changed his mindset, quitting the district attorney's office after he found himself arrested over a parking spot that he had paid for.) The judges do not consult international policing standards which would alert them that the US police force kills citizens at a vastly higher rate than other countries. The reporting of 'justified' killings by uniformed police is optional. Remarkably, there is no rubric for 'unjustified' homicide. And the underreporting does not address the collusion with local coroners, who often certify that the 'suspect' died of natural causes: police is responsible for some 30,800 deaths between 1980 and 2018, of which about 17,100 were not reported (GBD, 2021). Coroners hold elected positions, and rarely, they are trained physicians. Attributing a death to a colleague in the police force apparently can be a political decision, as was made apparent in the certification of George Floyd's death. According to the medical examiner, he died due to drug use and underlying health conditions. Movement activists and scholars alike (such as the Global Burden of Disease (GBD) group) call attention to officers of the state being outlaws with badges. Sovereign immunity shows up in many faces of the carceral state.

Fugitive knowledge draws from an acute sense of urgency, as the 'outlaw' speaks back to the power structure from an informed lived existence in the margins and the spaces of invisibility from the surveillance apparatus. In fact, maroon activists are keenly aware of how surveillance creates normalized conditioning—docile bodies who do not question the system. On the one hand, US Communist Party member, Angela Y. Davis, could theorize abstractly about Marxism and liberation, but it was another to learn from fellow prisoners how to practice resistance within the carceral. The Movement for Black Lives envisions a transformation of the legal system from the bottom-up. Marooned in Cuba, Black Panther freedom fighter Assata Shakur still inspires young revolutionaries who organically created a pledge to radical transformation and liberation in the streets from her autobiography's call for action:

> It is our duty to fight for our freedom.
> It is our duty to win.
> We must love each other and support each other.
> We have nothing to lose but our chains.
> (Shakur, 1987, p. 52)

And then, tellingly, Assata calls out the revolutionary ancestors (#say their names), who were killed in captivity by the outlaw state such as imprisoned intellectual George Jackson and those who were murdered while sleeping such as the charismatic Panther leader Fred Hampton. In the same book, she shares "Affirmation," a poem that anchors her biography in life and loving:

> I have been locked by the lawless.
> Handcuffed by the haters.
> gagged by the greedy,
> and, if I know any thing at all,
> it's that *a wall is just a wall*
> *and nothing more at all.*
> *It can be broken down.*
>
> I believe in living
> I believe in birth.
> I believe in the sweat of love
> and in the fire of truth.
> (p. 2, emphasis mine)

Maroon fighters believe fiercely in revolutionary love. Transformative justice community-based groups internalize the duty to love one another by developing safety networks beyond the surveillance apparati of the state. They do so out of necessity: when the state intervenes in conflict situations in a home or public space, they often escalate the violence and traumatize all involved. The call for defunding the police is not an empty slogan, as Black cis gender and trans folks only know too well. Broken-down walls must not be reassembled into even shinier palaces of securitization.

Putting the legacy of Assata Shakur into context of Michael Brown's legal lynching, Davis alerts us to the state's language of violence, labeling a revolutionary thinker a 'terrorist':

> Four decades after the original campaign against her, the FBI decided to demonise her once more. Last year, on the 40th anniversary of the New Jersey turnpike shoot-out during which state trooper Werner Foerster was killed, Assata was ceremoniously added to the FBO's Ten Most

> Wanted Terrorist list. To many, this move by the FBI was bizarre and incomprehensible, leading to the obvious question: what interest would the FBI have in designating a 66-year-old black woman, who has lived quietly in Cuba for the last three and a half decades, as one of the most dangerous terrorists in the world—sharing space on the list with individuals whose alleged actions have provoked military assaults on Iraq, Afghanistan and Syria?
>
> (Davis, 2014)

Davis answers the question why Shakur's struggle is important to us today:

> The global response to the police killing of a black teenager in a small midwestern town suggests a growing consciousness regarding the persistence of US racism at a time when it is supposed to be on the decline. Assata's legacy represents a mandate to broaden and deepen anti-racist struggles. In her autobiography [...], evoking the black radical tradition of struggle, she asks us to "Carry it on. / Pass it down to the children. /Pass it down. Carry it on ... / To Freedom!"
>
> (Ibid.)

A Chicago-based group, Hands off Assata! Campaign, raises awareness about the danger Shakur faces being sought by the US government with a "blood bounty" of two million dollars—as a fugitive slave and newly labeled "terrorist." However, Angela Y. Davis and Assata Olugbala Shakur, both appearing on the Federal Bureau of Investigation (FBI)'s Most Wanted List, are still committed to anti-capitalism and consistently speak out about the dangers of criminal 'justice' reforms. Thus, these women will continue to have outlaw status while speaking truth to power. Davis could not conceive of what countless other Black revolutionaries have done—leaving the country while she was underground—after the shoot-out in the Marin County courthouse:

> But each time I considered going abroad, the thought of being indefinitely exiled in some other country was even more horrible than the idea of being locked up in jail. *At least in jail I would be closer to my people, closer to the movement.*
>
> (1988, p. 12, emphasis added)

Shakur was broken out of prison successfully because her supporters believed that she would be killed. This is what happened to another revolutionary, George Jackson, whose murder prompted the Attica Rebellion of 1971.

Righteous anger may also be channeled into call for national reckoning or popular tribunals. In the tradition of Walker and Wells-Barnett's pamphlets, the document "We charge genocide!" is a modern-day wake-up call to the genocidal system that ignores its own crimes while criminalizing racialized other, one of the many effects of the afterlives of slavery. This petition was presented by Paul Robeson to the UN in New York City and by William L. Paterson to the UN in Paris in 1951, yet, it found no acknowledgment or hearing, as the US government strongly opposed its originator—Civil Rights Congress, a "communist"-leaning organization. The McCarthy era effectively muzzled all critique of state violence, but the manifesto has had its cyclical reappearance at the end of the 1970s and again during the renewed anti-police brutality era since 2014. Importantly, in 1996, the National Black United Front petitioned the UN, among other charges, for the over-criminalization of Black and Latino youth, and they foresaw the vast expansion of the prison-industrial complex (Kennedy, 2019). In a chapter, "A People's History of Prisons in the United States," Mariame Kaba defines herself as an abolitionist in a holistic way:

> Abolition for me is a long-term project and a practice around creating the conditions that would allow for the dismantling of prisons, policing, and surveillance and the creation of new institutions that actually work to keep us safe and are not fundamentally oppressive. What you need to make those conditions happen, you have to be for addressing environmental issues, you have to be for making sure people have a living wage economically. I know for me it's important to be anticapitalist.
>
> (Kaba, 2021, p. 72)

Founder of the grassroots organization Survived and Punished, Kaba, is an organic intellectual, organizing in Chicago, the hometown of Ida Wells-Barnett and Fred Hampton. She points out the roots of urban uprisings leading straight to incidences of police brutality: "It's the clearest way that almost every Black person can see that they are second class. In other things it's diffused" (*Ibid.*, p. 75). Kaba has repeatedly mentioned that she works only with survivors of violence. At the same time, as abolitionist, she puts no faith in the criminal legal system and makes it clear that convictions of police officers are no panacea. Oppressive policing "rooted in anti-Blackness, social control, and containment" does not vanish with a few guilty verdicts, but a starting point for her is never to call the police (pp. 55–6, 64–5). However, demanding reparations is consistent with transformative justice tenets (repair, restoration, acknowledgment, cessation, and nonrepetition); it was successfully achieved in the case of over 100 torture survivors at the hands of now-convicted Chicago police commander Jon Burge (p. 66). The Movement for Black Lives advocates for reparations for families impacted by police violence and the drug war (p. 67). Black feminist organizers such as Kaba and Loretta Ross are able to mobilize rage into productive outrage against the system. As a member of the National Black United Front, Ross organized a "People's Grand Jury Hearing" in Washington, DC, in 1981, which "indicted" for genocide city council members and the mayor, Marion Barry, as well as key figures of the criminal legal system.

Activists investigated the targeted killing of a charismatic young leader Yulanda Ward and put the murder into context of the FBI's continued COINTELPRO's murder of Black organizers and leaders (Thuma, 2019, pp. 152–4). Street trials or tribunals uplift local activism against state violence and show that it is the state that is involved in outlawry. Calling the police to investigate street violence or intimate partner harm is not an option for insurrectionist struggle. However, protecting oneself against racist policing and profiling is common sense for African-descending men. Black boys are given 'the talk' by their loving parents, so that they internalize or, at least, perform according to the expectations of the white supremacist politics of respectability. Paul Butler outlines 'the talk' for adult men in how to avoid police surveillance, how to make oneself invisible:

> Three or more black men in a car at any time
> Black man in a new or late-model car
> Black man in a black SUV
> Black man in a car with tinted windows
> Black man with a white woman
> Black men in a group laughing too loudly
> Black men play-fighting or joking around physically
> Black men raising their voices
> Black men in any sort of disagreement or argument
> Black men running fast
> Black men in a hoodie
> Black men with low pants
> Black men with a T-shirt that says "Black Lives Matter"
> "Racial incongruity"—a legal term meaning being in a place where members of your race usually are not
>
> (Butler, 2017, pp. 202–3)

Marooned freedom fighter Assata Shakur blamed herself for using the New Jersey turnpike, when she faced her final confrontation with police before her imprisonment. It was well known that Black motorists, including women, were under intense surveillance (Shakur, 1987). Activists labeled this profiling routine practice as 'Driving while Black' and the federal government critiqued the state police for racist surveillance decades later (OJP, 1999).

Then, there are other voices who call themselves feminists, who work very closely with state institutions. Enter carceral feminism. This designation created by Elizabeth Bernstein (2010) characterizes those who advocate for women's rights by supporting harsh punitive laws and cooperation with the criminal legal system. Additionally, feminist campaigns support involvement of border patrol and supranational criminalizing agencies and a greater role of the UN and International Labor Organization to prohibit sex work, which becomes redefined as traffic in women (Bernstein, 2010; 2012; Nagel, 2015). It could have been otherwise. Emily Thuma's feminist genealogy showcases examples of political campaigns that are explicitly abolitionist, without a middle-class moralizing ideology. In Boston, the Prostitutes Union of Massachusetts and the Combahee River Collective were part of a broad-based Take Back the Night (TBTN) coalition that organized around women's safety and to free Willy Sanders of rape charges, which was part of an explicit anti-rape, Black feminist campaign. He was freed after an 18-month protracted struggle. This TBTN coalition also demanded reallocation of funds from a prison for "violent" women toward shelters for women in crisis (Thuma, 2019, pp. 137–8). Decades later, a shift toward 'feminist' support of carceral solutions occurred which coincided with an increasing punitive turn, culminating in the omnibus crime bill during the Clinton administration in 1994. A feminist demand of violence prevention became attached to crime control, and Hillary Clinton used her platform to shore up moral panic against superpredators, rehashing racist stereotypes of Black masculinity. Professionalizing services, tying funding formulas for women's shelters to carceral budgets undermined options for community mutual aid strategies favored by women of color involved in the anti-violence movement. The call for "law and order" was meted out with mandatory arrests in intimate partner violence situations (Kim, 2018). This also meant an even greater surveillance of intimate spaces in the Black community, including of children's welfare, as I discuss in Chapter 2.

Liberal feminists also called for hate law legislation which was supposed to benefit members of the LGBTQ community. However, such carceral feminist efforts make false promises as they individualize acts of violence and intensify policing instead of problematizing systemic homophobia, transphobia, and its dynamics with respect the political climate that prepares fertile ground for such harm. LGBT people who turn to the police for help may find themselves assaulted, violated, and criminalized by such officers of the homophobic, transphobic state (Mogul *et al.*, 2011, pp. 126–9). Anti-lynching law passed in South Carolina in 1951 is race-neutral, and today, it is Black youth who is disproportionately targeted, "even in cases less serious or comparable to those involving whites" (*Ibid.*, pp. 127–8). Clearly, 'protective' legislation may backfire as it is not designed to historicize power relations; instead, it is the usual narrative that protects those who already reap all the benefits as abstract-rights-bearing individuals in a heteronormative, capitalist settler-colonial nation-state.

A kinder, gentler touch to policing in the times of #Black Lives Matter is also part and parcel of the carceral feminist agenda. Naomi Murakawa critiques the police's new caring ethos as "weaponized empathy" which functions to "dull resistance to the routine racial terror of policing—racialized suspicion and the processing of mass citations and arrests" (2017, p. 108). Even though it is the case that some police brutality cases receive media attention, the quotidian enforcement of the violence of the law ensnares over 11 million people annually, including a disproportionate number of Black and Latine residents (pp. 103–5). Thus, "the sincerity of police empathy is irrelevant to the violence of policing" (p. 103). Furthermore, every police department, including state police, masks its quota policy of tickets and arrests in "department averages," tying promotion to zealous enforcement data. Every three seconds an arrest of a human being is made in the United States, and the drug war continues unabated (Neusteter & O'Toole, 2019).

A Call for Abolition Democracy

We need to write histories of the state's own outlaw behavior, exposing their legal reasoning in ideological terms. Their lawyers and judges use any rationale to "divide and conquer," make laws upon the subjugated Other, and they pass over in silence when it comes to their own terrorist behavior. Jailhouse lawyers know this only too well, as Mumia Abu-Jamal breaks it down to another prisoner: "the System just make and break laws as it see fit!" (2009, p. 28). The elites' acts of transgression and acts committed by the imperial state are simply rendered invisible with impunity.

When penal abolitionists parse through the annals of history written from the perspective of the elites, they must note the Manichean logic which dictates that there are laws for 'decent' people who write and execute the laws, as much as they remain above the law. These laws are foisted upon 'indecent' people: the rabble, the racialized, and the stateless denizens of the world. The club of the law comes down hard on the downtrodden, who are banished into carceral fortresses, warehoused in psychiatric hospitals, reform schools, boot camps, and other total institutions. The law is cavalier toward those who commit atrocities but exist within the pale—safeguarded by capital and social connections to those who write or administer the law.

I choose the Japanese knotweed plant as a metaphor for concerted struggle and resistance at this insurrectionist stage. No matter how much the state seeks to punish politicized lawbreakers and insurgent armies, they will regroup and reconnect and fight back. Violent struggle in modern times is romanticized (or vilified, depending on who's side one is) when it is David versus Goliath: Fidel Castro's revolutionary war; the Haitian liberation wars leading to the defeat of colonialism *and* slavery—a first in human history; the Vietcong's humiliating defeat of the empire's army. The knotweed's rhizomatic root structure and resilience even in the face of fire and herbicides is unparalleled in this relentless fight to life, breaking concrete, asphalt structures. Interestingly, the British government fines or imprisons gardeners who plant knotweed: housing structures become unstable thanks to its amazing power to undermine foundations.

A commitment to abolition democracy (Davis, 2005) entails a recognition and critique of the outlaw nature of a juridical state that *says* it enforces the rule of law and exacts punishment fairly but *acts* otherwise. The critical voices of Stand Watie, David Walker, and Ida B. Wells-Barnett still ring true today since the criminalizing system still has no ethical foundation in a rule of law that applies to all equally. Justice as fairness cannot be realized as long as the imperial, racist, and heteropatriarchal system continues to serve as bedrock for the outlaw nation-state's *raison-d'être.*

What is to be done? I join the choir of abolitionist voices who resist state and corporate violence; who use maroon strategies, unplugging and opting out of the surveillance machine; who establish sovereign and autonomous spaces and cooperatives and community structures with the call for dignity and abolitionist care practices (Kaba, 2017). Exploring visions for liberation, Julia Oparah (Sudbury, 2009) foregrounds the work of 'maroon abolitionists,' trans and gender-nonconforming activists of color, who contest the penal system (and gender-responsive prisons) and take their inspiration from the ancestors. Specifically, I support a call for *radical* maroonage, since, historically, some (treaty) maroon communities collaborated with the hegemonic colonial state (cf. Lebrón Ortiz, 2020). These treaty maroon towns had to chase freedom-seeking Black folks into the arms of the slavers (Saul, 2018). Radical maroonage is necessarily abolitionist because it rejects the Hobbesian, colonial legal ideology that criminalizes Indigenous and Black existence. Today, the Movement for Black Lives challenges us to work for transformative (social) justice:

> This agenda continues the legacy of our ancestors who pushed for reparations, Black self-determination and community control; and also propels new iterations of movements such as efforts for reproductive justice, holistic healing and reconciliation, and ending violence against Black cis, queer, and trans people.
>
> (Platform, n.d.)

Abolition democracy means nothing less than tearing down the entire criminalizing system and investing in healing praxis. The next chapters will showcase such commitment and explore the differences between restorative and transformative justice perspectives.

Notes

1 This chapter draws in part on a published chapter: "The Lawlessness of Law: Outlaw Nation, Settler Colonialism, and a Possessive Investment in Whiteness." *Contesting Carceral Logic* (M.C. Coyle & M. Nagel, eds.), Routledge, 2022, pp. 36–49.

2 I use Indian peoples or American Indian peoples to refer to *self-naming* nomenclature. "Native American" was popularized during the Clinton administration in the 1990s. Note, for example, self-naming practices regarding American Indian Movement (AIM) and the National Museum of the American Indian.

3 Lipsitz (2011) expands on the racial logic in the following way:

> Largely because of racialized space, whiteness in this society is not so much a color as a condition. It is a structured advantage that channels unfair gains and unjust enrichments to whites while imposing unearned and unjust obstacles in the way of Blacks. Of course, not all whites benefit equally

from the possessive investment in whiteness, but even the poorest of the poor among whites do not face the degree of concentration in impoverished neighborhoods and schools or the levels of exposure to environmental hazards that routinely confront middle-income Blacks.

(p. 3)

4

The institution of slavery was created by positive law and could not exist without it. Slavery required that the general tort and criminal laws against kidnapping, false imprisonment, assault, and battery be exempted from applying to actions of the master toward the slave. The master-slave relationship was not necessarily about exploiting the labor of another; it was about the positive legal grant of the power, from the state to the master, to physically control and coerce the slave.

(Walters, 2013, pp. 302–3)

5 This section draws from my previously published article: "Angela Y Davis and Assata Shakur as Women Outlaws: Resisting U.S. State Violence," *Wagadu*, 13, Summer 2015, pp. 43–78.

4 Between *Ressentiment* and Forgiveness

Transitional Justice in Rwanda and South Africa

In Chapter 3, the rule of law, sacrosanct in Western capitalist democracies, is turned on its head. The question then is whether Indigenous restorative justice processes offer a way out of the impasse of 'outlaw' legal frameworks indebted to the Roman tradition. To that end, I will offer a case study of the New Rwanda's Gacaca model and compare it with the New South Africa's 'tribunal,' set up to investigate state and political violence committed during the apartheid era.

Specifically, this chapter analyzes ideological claims made regarding South Africa's Truth and Reconciliation Commission (TRC) and Rwanda's National Unity and Reconciliation Commission (NURC). Both transitional justice practices have been praised as restorative or even therapeutic. The TRC popularized the ethics of Ubuntu engendering feelings of forgiveness in victims of apartheid injustice. Similarly, the NURC's Gacaca informal justice proceedings have been considered by restorative justice advocates as a paradigm case of overcoming ethnic hatred. I will argue that the TRC may have fallen short of such lofty goal of forgiveness, but in the end, it did not succumb to a logic of revenge. By contrast, the Gacaca courts, set up by a Tutsi-dominated government with approval of the world (legal) community, unraveled a retributive victors' justice while eliding true restorative justice. However, Rwanda's authoritarian government presented quite successfully Gacaca as a restorative justice model. The comparative analysis will show that the Rwandan experience of tarrying with transitional justice could be characterized as *negative Ubuntu* or victor's justice ideology, while the South African experience can be portrayed as Ubuntu in the positive, championing *authentic Ubuntu ethics*, which avoids an Othering process that often leads to further violence between aggrieved parties. In principle, it could have been possible to conceive of a precolonial conflict resolution in abolitionist terms, as it has been done elsewhere on the African continent. But penal abolitionists should avoid romanticizing the past and carefully review how 'customary' practices are deployed and whether they serve opportunistic purposes. Rather than being restorative, Gacaca has 'outlaw' character, which propagated violence at the same time as it was supposed to investigate violence.

DOI: 10.4324/9781003055327-5

In the early 2000s, human rights experts were cautiously optimistic when the Rwandan government decided to set up community courts, called Gacaca, to address serious overcrowding in its prisons. Hundreds of thousands of Hutu were accused of being *genocidaires*, committing killings and rape against Tutsi and moderate Hutu during 100 days in 1994 while the United Nations (UN) watched and did nothing to stop the genocide in Rwanda and Burundi. The Tutsi-led rebel army, Revolutionary Patriotic Front, under the leadership of Paul Kagame takes credit for liberating the country, thus stopping the genocide. In subsequent years, thousands of remand prisoners perished while awaiting trial because of overcrowding. So, urgent legal measures had to be taken to alleviate the prison and humanitarian crisis, while the country's legal infrastructure was in ruins. Tutsi lawyers and judges also were among the genocide victims, so the remaining judges were unable to adjudicate the enormous case load. The International Criminal Court of Rwanda was set up in Tanzania to try the architects of genocide and eventually found some 60 people guilty, all of them Hutu (BBC, 2014). To the chagrin of Hutu survivors and critical human rights observers, neither Kagame nor any of his generals were put on trial for atrocities committed against the civilian Hutu population.

Rwanda abolished the death penalty in 2007 after the Gacaca courts were in full swing. The results were impressive: a commutation of capital cases to life imprisonment for over 1,300 Rwandans who were convicted for genocide (Horovitz, 2016). Furthermore, the Gacaca courts conducted proceedings for two types of offenses associated with the 1994 atrocities: (1) having committed some acts of violence or aided and abetted others who murdered and (2) having stolen goods from genocide victims' homesteads (Burnet, 2009).

There are parallels with the way the New South Africa attempted to engineer peace and reconciliation, but it went down a dramatically different path. President Nelson Mandela set up a TRC and appointed Archbishop Desmond Tutu as its chair along with other commissioners who listened to thousands of testimonials. Famously, Tutu invoked Ubuntu ethics during the process. It suggests that I am only human because you recognize me as such (Tutu, 1999). It is a dignitarian appeal to shared humanity and interdependence of all relations. Tutu vigorously encouraged participants (victims' families and petitioners, i.e., the offending party) to recognize each other's humanity and commit to forgiveness, not retributive justice. The commission recommended amnesty to many who committed atrocities, including murder during the apartheid period. These publicized proceedings also mesmerized the global human rights community because it was seen as an effective transitional justice tool to shine a light on state violence and prevent retributive extralegal violence against state actors. For victims' families in both countries, it was important to hear the truth, specifically what happened to the bodies of their loved ones and in the South African case if proper burial arrangements could be made (even decades later).[1] In fact, very soon, the TRC was renamed by its critics as 'Truth Commission' because they could not see how it could possibly address reconciliation. For penal abolitionists and restorative justice advocates, it is important to see whether therapeutic justice through reconciliatory measures could be achieved through these transitional justice institutions.

The Case of Rwanda—Negative Ubuntu Ideology

History of ethnic strife in Rwanda (and neighboring Burundi) is not new. European colonizers exploited simmering tensions with the colonial divide-and-rule principle. For over two generations, the minority group, the Tutsi, got to control the majority, the Hutu, as well as the Twas. The 1959 Hutu revolution drove out the Tutsi king and elites, including the current president's family. The 1994 genocide and the other violent events preceding the genocide have to be analyzed from that historical vantage points of victors and victimized populations (Geraghty, 2016; 2020). After Paul Kagame's military forces established control over all institutions in the country, it did not take them long to hunt down Hutu who fled to neighboring Congo. It is an open secret that Tutsi soldiers killed those Hutu *genocidaires* and their families, even attacking UN-organized refugee camps in the Congo. Victors' justice was quite genocidal itself because hundreds of thousands of people were extra-judicially executed (BBC, 2014). It goes beyond the scope of this chapter to provide a more detailed overview of the complex historical and postcolonial context for Rwanda and the Central Africa region.

When the Gacaca court system was set up, over 100,000 Hutu suspected of genocide were imprisoned in dangerously overcrowded prisons. Therefore, restorative justice advocates enthusiastically supported an alternative dispute resolution system that would expedite hearings and decarceration. Gacaca means 'short grass' in Kinyarwanda, and prior to European colonization, only nonviolent, minor conflicts were discussed and resolved in open grassy areas (Geraghty, 2020).

> [T]he hearings were traditionally held outside in empty markets, school yards, and other public places within each community. In an ideal hearing, defendants would confess their crimes, express remorse, ask for forgiveness, provide restitution, and then offer food and drink to all parties as a symbol of reconciliation.
>
> (Nyseth Brehm, 2014, p. 336)

Serious (violent) crimes were adjudicated by the (Tutsi) king. Gacaca hearings have not been practiced in a century beginning with the introduction of the colonial legal system. While the Gacaca legal process began as early as 2001, the government also abandoned the death penalty, in 2007. By the time the Gacaca trials ended in 2012, thousands of lay judges had tried almost two million cases and the prison population plummeted, representing a resounding success for a country's attempt to deal with a murderous recent past.

The aims of Gacaca were to:

1. uncover the truth of what happened during the genocide;
2. address a culture of impunity by prosecuting the genocide's perpetrators;
3. reconcile Rwandans and support their unity; and
4. prove that Rwandans had the capacity to settle their own problems through a system of justice based on Rwandan custom.

(Rwanda Preamble to the Organic Law No. 40/2000 of 26/01/2001)

The installation of thousands of these popular courts that involved the entire adult population in the countryside and the cities brought about swift justice, which, in the Western court system, would have taken hundreds of years. The Rwandan government was praised for abolishing the death penalty and setting up the Gacaca process across the country. They were lauded for instituting swift justice, emptying the jails of remand prisoners. At least in the beginning of the proceedings, lenient sentences were given to Hutu. It seemed quite the miracle that former foes could now live peaceably next to each other. Indeed, the prisons were emptied out and deadly overcrowding was halted, but today, Rwanda's imprisonment rate is still more than twice as high as the next contender, South Africa. Rwanda imprisons more people (76,000) than Nigeria (70,700), Africa's most populous country (ICPR, 2020). I argue that, for many reasons, the Gacaca courts were quite retributive; it was not uncommon for convicted Hutu to receive life sentences (up to 30 years). This would not have been possible under the traditional way that Gacaca was used to settle nonviolent disputes. In addition, observers noted that coercion and intimidation was used against witnesses including revenge killings (Le Mon, 2007; Human Rights Watch, 2011). Le Mon speculates that given the government's repression of critique of the Gacaca system, the putative goal for both justice and reconciliation may yield neither one (Le Mon, 2007, p. 5).

Emil Towner (2013, p. 292) traces four common characteristics of a successful apology in Rwandan culture:

- a detailed narrative of the crime or offense
- a statement of sorrow combined with a request for forgiveness
- the demonstration of sincerity and heartfelt remorse
- symbolic or real reparations

These seem to be fairly typical traits of restorative justice practices elsewhere, especially when they are performed in a voluntary manner (Murithi, 2006). In the Gacaca context, the emphasis is on reintegrative shaming (cf. Braithwaite, 1989). In the judicial "Record of Confession, Guilty Plea, Repentance and Apology" at the conclusion of the trial, the guilty plea must include a formulaic request for "forgiveness to God, to the Government of Rwanda and to all Rwandese particularly the victims." What does that look like in practice? The classes of victims and perpetrators are predetermined. Every Tutsi is a victim, and every Hutu is a perpetrator. Even the government's own phrase "genocide against Tutsi and moderate Hutu" was rewritten by the time the Gacaca trials commenced: any references to moderate Hutu and prosecution of war crimes (i.e., crimes committed by Tutsi soldiers) were eliminated (Waldorf, 2009). Passive bystanders become criminalized as the following testimony of a Hutu prisoner indicates:

> One day I decided to tell them that I realized that I took part in what happened. They asked me "do you admit your crimes?" and I said "yes." They said "OK, tell us more." I told them that I did not help them and "you were brothers and I did not sensitize Hutus not to kill you." So their hearts were relieved. And then, when we walked out, some thanked me for doing that, and they said they wished I would have done that before. They said "*we knew you didn't eat our cows or destroy our houses or kill any of our family members, but you were watching when it happened and you knew about the plans and this is what we were looking for.*"
>
> (Horovitz, 2016, p. 542, emphasis added)

If Gacaca tribunals were truly restorative, why is an innocent prisoner confessing to crimes of genocide while also protesting the terms of his punishment, his incarceration, to the Western interviewer, a lawyer intent on asking leading questions about 'reconciliation'? It shows that the categories for criminalization to warrant an indictment (and punishment) were broad enough to include a large population of adults (older than 14 years of age) who were punished for practicing negative Ubuntu, i.e., of being passive bystanders and thus apparently closing ranks as Hutu. (In this case, the Ubuntu principle of shared humanity is only extended to ethnic kin, not to others, even if those are Tutsi who intermarried with Hutu.) Bystanders are faulted for not recognizing the humanity of Tutsi exposed to the ravages of genocide. In turn, ironically, the proceedings show that the state's zealous assignation of collective guilt (of Hutu) showcases that the shared humanity does not extend to 'moderate' Hutu, after all. Hutu 'boundary crossers' were also killed or tortured for refusing to wield machetes on strangers, neighbors, or family members. Poor Hutu could not desist from killing Tutsi because the poor did not have means to buy themselves out of this ghastly work expected of them by Hutu authorities (Luft, 2015).

Doughty (2015) notes that Gacaca indeed was used to settle scores and redistribution of wealth, often with theft charges being more contentious than murder charges (p. 425). Gacaca was used to debate 'genocide citizenship' with respect to the categories of who is a genocide victim and who is a genocide perpetrator. Once these lines were drawn, it set the parameter who has access to resources and opportunities in the new Rwanda and who does not (p. 113). It demonstrates to the world that reconciliation should not be romanticized but that violence and divisiveness are part and parcel of the steps involved negotiating sociality (p. 432).

What of 'genocide citizenship' afforded to survivors of sexual assault and mutilation? Chitra Nagarajan (2012) reports that some women do not even use the term 'survivor' because daily living conditions are intolerable. In addition to dealing with abject poverty, and abortion being illegal, it is shameful rearing unwanted children ('children of bad memories' or 'little interahamwe') who resemble neighbors who in turn carry on with their life with impunity. The government has refused to recognize rape by soldiers as a war crime and thus denied such rape survivors' compensation. Furthermore, when victims protested and spoke up, the regime is faulted for exposing the women to further shame, retraumatization or loss of life through Gacaca: "82% of survivors say they feel threatened during the process with insecurity voiced particularly by female survivors .... Indeed there have been reports of survivors threatened and murdered" (Nagarajan, 2012, p. 117). The government's concerted effort to silence sexual assault survivors is demonstrated in its preference of providing relief for genocide widows instead. Those who are in an interethnic family constellation have little hope for redress or compensation. Sepharime, a Hutu who hid her severely tortured Tutsi husband from the killers in 1994, was forced to "entertain" a Hutu commander during that time. In the New Rwanda, as a Hutu, she was not only stigmatized as a loose woman but she and her ethnically mixed family had no entitlement to reparations (Burnet, 2009, pp. 90–1).

Mark Geraghty's (2016) extensive research on Gacaca courts documents a case of egregious miscarriage of justice, where the defendant Gahutu received a merciful sentence of five years of manual labor (a sign of restorative justice, if he were actually guilty of the charges). However, the vindictive judge decided to void the sentence and retry him for the apparent offense that he and his son celebrated his light sentence and thus angered the community of (Tutsi) survivors. Without presenting evidence of wrongdoing that would satisfy any of the three categories of genocide participation, the first sentence was altered, and the farmer was condemned to a 15-year prison term, akin to a death sentence given the terrible prison conditions. During the first trial, he comported himself in a way suggesting humility and respect for the Tutsi survivors, hardly speaking on his behalf. By contrast, Gahutu's wife gave bold witness testimony during the first trial, which earned her the wrath of the judges: soldiers removed her from the court, and she spent six months in detention for the crime of defending her husband's innocence. Gahutu gave in, asked for a pardon for the offense of speaking ill about the Rwandan Patriotic Front (RPF) as liberation force to a neighbor. To secure the farmer's second conviction (of 15 years), Geraghty (2020) argues that it sufficed to appeal to the defendant's putative support of 'genocide ideology,' thus turning these proceedings into a witch-hunting theater. After all, the guilt was already presumed from the onset and any protestations of innocence, as Gahutu's wife continued to do, even after her imprisonment, only showcased their guilt and being a danger to the community. Even Tutsi survivors speaking on behalf of Gahutu were sternly silenced by the president of the court (Geraghty, 2020). The key contradiction of the 'traditional' court is thus: "in the guise of 'allowing the ordinary people to speak,' it came to operate as a strategy of silencing" (Geraghty, 2020, p. 608). Whoever is found guilty of supporting the events of 1994 or denies that a genocide against Tutsi occurred is zealously criminalized in the aftermath of a basic law about genocide ideology propagation in 2008, which was passed during the height of Gacaca proceedings. Hutu survivors, who protested their exclusion from annual commemorations or their guilt, do not understand that the New Rwanda excises their ontological status and rights as citizens. They have lost the war of liberation and must pay tribute in perpetuity, as Mitterand's case clearly shows. Gacaca served as an instrument of repression and victor's justice.

Waldorf (2009, p. 289) adds a realistic and critical assessment of the purpose and achievements of Gacaca. He acknowledges Rwanda's president Kagame's mystification of *Gacaca* as "restorative justice." I argue that its purpose was to make the practice palatable to those who advocate President Mandela's pursuit of African harmony (Ubuntu) through South Africans' process of reckoning with the violent past. After all, Gacaca was a precolonial institution to solve (minor) conflicts among neighbors and families, often by resorting to restitution. Waldorf claims that "modern Gacaca bears no resemblance to pre-colonial dispute resolution—other than the name" (*Ibid.*). It is codified law, not customary practice; serious crimes are adjudicated, not low-level ones; imprisonment takes the place of restitution while the former system focused on repair and harmony (*Ibid.*). Waldorf indicts the current regime as perpetrating one-sided victor's justice with no prospect of amnesty (unlike the TRC) and avoiding any truth-telling regarding war crimes committed by the Tutsi army (RPF) that liberated the country from Hutu *génocidaires*; unlike at the TRC hearings, attendance at Gacaca trials was mandatory and refusal resulted in fines or imprisonment (p. 289).

Thousands of Gacaca courts were launched after 2005 and continued into 2012. Over one million persons were tried in upper-level Gacaca courts (violent offenses), and over half of the cases dealt with property offenses adjudicated by lay judges in the lower-level Gacaca courts. To be eligible for a judge, one had to be a person of integrity (Organic Law, 2004). But in reality, it was more likely that they had to have membership in the ruling party, which suggests that rather than being of the people, they were representatives of the state (Geraghty, 2020). Critics note that in the beginning, there was a bit of enthusiasm to attend the trials, and perpetrators were eager to confess in exchange for release from prisons or lighter prison sentences, including reeducation and work camps. However, as more and more cases were tried, the enthusiasm waned and a culture of fear propagated the forces of negative Ubuntu: mass denunciations quickly replaced (incentivized) confessions (cf. Ingelaere & Verpoorten, 2016). The dragnet drew from many indictable Hutu, including returning Hutu, who had left the country before the genocide, and produced almost two million cases, with the vast majority focusing on property offenses, in the Gacaca courts. 'Genocide' accusation became a tool for redistribution of scarce resources, and the Hutu neighbors' economic well-being drew wrath and jealousy. With a new law proscribing 'genocide ideology,' it was easy enough to accuse a Hutu adult of committing a grave offense to be adjudicated by his peers of Tutsi neighbors. It all came to a crisis point by 2007, as a Gacaca judge, who wished to live up to the moral principle of integrity, confided:

> What I wanted to say is this, there are people who are afraid of Gacaca justice. These trials cause fear because those who are in a financially strong position will be accused and brought before the Gacaca Court, even if they have never done anything. All you need to do is just check: those against whom charges were brought after August, were never accused during the preliminary investigatory stage. It is obvious that the very purpose of the Gacaca has been misappropriated. Today, over 80% of the people here are afraid. Anyone who has the means tries to get away.
>
> (PRI interview with an *Inyangamugayo* ["person of integrity"; a judge], September 9, 2007; cited in *The Rwandan Lawyer*, 2021)

Mark Geraghty also mentions the egregious case of François Mbarute "Mitterand" (which at the defendant's own request is his real name) who saved almost 100 Tutsi from certain death and still was retried six times till a Gacaca judge produced a guilty verdict: condemned to life imprisonment in solitary confinement (the clear marking of a political prisoner). Geraghty (2016, p. 491) provocatively argues that the Gacaca process was a state-engineered witch persecution, not so much for the crimes of 1994 but for the 1959 Hutu revolution that drove elite Tutsi such as Kagame's family into exile. It is quite obvious not only that Gacaca then ensnared over one million Rwandan people as defendants, but it ended up being seen as benefiting a Tutsi elite that now controls all aspects of government (Kuradusenge, 2016). It provided a useful ruse but, in reality, it did not benefit the survivors of genocide, nor did it contribute to truth-telling and reconciliation. On the contrary, Gacaca proceedings sowed suspicion and distrust among current neighbors and within families, so that appeals to positive Ubuntu and restorative justice are completely far-fetched.

Yet, this mystification of Gacaca as an African restorative justice model continues unabated. Desmond Tutu extols the restorative power of Gacaca community courts, even after the end of these trials:

> The justice they sought was often restorative rather than punitive. Those who had planned and incited the genocide were punished, but those who

> were swept up in the internecine conflict were given lower sentences, especially if the perpetrators were repentant and sought reconciliation with the community. The goal was to rebuild the communities and the country, to heal and prevent further revenge and violence.
>
> (Tutu, 2016)

Tutu was not alone in describing Gacaca as a model supremely suited for forgiveness and peace-building. US penal abolitionists also laud Gacaca as a positive Ubuntu model for restorative justice practices. It is easy to be deceived, perhaps due to confirmation bias. That means, abolitionists generally favor restorative justice processes which are organic, using popular (and traditional) conflict resolution rather than the state's regulatory system. So, in that sense, Gacaca trumps South Africa's TRC. But a jail cell was never far away from the grassy or gravel yards (Geraghty, 2020). Very few were acquitted of all charges, which explains, in part, that Rwanda is the only African country that deserves the label prison nation. Some jurists tend to be more skeptical about the benefits but appreciate its potential for reconciliation (Bilchitz, Metz, & Oyowe, 2017, p. 245). They are silent on the element of coercion, but they emphasize the salutary effect of giving a community ownership of the process of conflict resolution. Elsewhere, Thaddeus Metz's (2019) support for therapeutic justice mirrors the Gacaca formula of demanding of the convicted to show genuine remorse and to do significant burdensome work benefiting the victim and/or the community. In Chapter 5, I will explore a critique of accountability that is the basis for these 'thera-punitive' demands.

Restorative justice in the ideal always is voluntary for all participants, which was not the case in Rwanda. Neither was the goal of autonomous community justice attained. In fact, the Gacaca courts had greater affinity with public show trials with docile defendants admitting to guilt than with Indigenous precolonial dispute resolution. The RPF openly admitted to their allegiance to Maoist ideology, which would also explain the installation of "re-education" camps targeting not only party members but the entire non-elite population (Geraghty, 2020).

Cui bono? In the end, the controlling frame of the Gacaca narrative and the selective archival preservation of trial proceedings benefited the returning elite Tutsi, not those who survived the genocide. International scholars or journalists who dared to critique Gacaca as fostering revenge, corruption, and impunity among zealous judges faced the serious charge of promoting genocide ideology. They not only faced expulsion from the country but even reeducation in prison-like camps. Dissidents who reframed the 1994 genocide as a fratricide have also been convicted to life sentences. The invention of a tradition that seeks to disguise victor's justice is deeply problematic. However, is restorative justice ever a possibility in the postcolony?

Amnesty and Forgiveness: The Case of South Africa's TRC

It is understandable that Western legal experts and others marvel at the possibilities of Gacaca. While legal standards of the West may be resistant to change, African jurisprudence "resonates with a global explosion in the resort to tort law to settle scores that elude conventional political and legal mechanisms" (Comaroff & Comaroff, 2004, p. 199). Therefore, it should be appealing to abolitionist activists and scholars. In 1994, South Africa inaugurated its new democratically elected government, and many members of formerly banned organizations assumed the responsibility of governance. While the transition to a rule of law was marred with some level of political violence, it was not accompanied by an outright civil war, thanks to the charismatic leadership of former prisoner, peacebuilder, and Nobel laureate, Nelson Mandela. The TRC, chaired by Desmond Tutu, was one of the negotiated outcomes of bridging the gap between starkly different ideological demands for justice, on the one hand, and blanket amnesty, on the other hand. TRC member Piet Meiring (1999) highlights the promises of healing and focuses on the testimonies of heroic forgiveness by many mothers. Fellow commission member Pumla Gobodo-Madikizela (2003) also notes that some victim families were willing to be reconciled with amnesty seekers who showed genuine signs of remorse.

Many veterans of the liberation struggle eschewed the negotiated peace process and remained skeptical about the use of the TRC as therapeutic tool (cf. A. Allan & M. Allan, 2000). Many Black South Africans critiqued the process, as they saw it catering to the needs of the applicants for amnesty and ignoring the demands for justice and meaningful reparation by the victims and survivors of apartheid (Lyons, 1997; Wilson, 2000). The commission was criticized for prematurely promoting reconciliation by making encouraging gestures toward victims' families who forgave the agents of apartheid (Hamber & Wilson, 2002). Consider this example of Charity Kondile, whose son was tortured and killed by an agent of apartheid: Dirk Coetzee asked Kondile for forgiveness. Kondile's lawyer responds to his request:

> You said that you would like to meet Mrs. Kondile and look her in the eye. She asked me to tell you that she feels it is an honour [...] you do not deserve. If you are really sorry, you would stand trial for the deeds you did.

To which Mrs. Kondile adds: "It is easy for [Nelson] Mandela and [Desmond] Tutu to forgive [...] they live vindicated lives. In my life nothing, not a single thing has changed since my son was burnt by barbarians ... nothing. Therefore I cannot forgive" (cited in Moellendorf, 1997, p. 286). In this case, a mother's mourning over the untimely death of her son leads to an expression of rage toward the perpetrator rather than the conciliatory sentiment of forgiveness. Mandela and Tutu's call for forgiveness, embedded in the call to embrace Ubuntu—"the essence of being human" (Tutu, 1999)—is consistent with the clarion call of the African National Congress' freedom charter: "that South Africa belongs to all who live in it, black and white, and that no government can justly claim authority unless it is based on the will of the people" (cited in Lyons, 1997). White perpetrators of injustice were not going to be asked to leave the country but, if found guilty of political, rather than personal, violence, they would be able to receive amnesty for their crimes and be welcomed back to build a new nation. The new South Africa, according to Mandela and Tutu, would be a 'rainbow nation' and acts of remorse, forgiveness, and reconciliation were key to transcending a violent, century-old path. Survivors, such as the Khulumani Support Group (2005), agree with these political goals, but they tend to disagree with the range and timing of reparations; thus, the therapeutic aspect of the TRC is contested.

The creators of the TRC felt that they combined Western and African approaches to justice, where the goal of justice is seen as restorative rather than as retributivist. Both victims (survivors) and perpetrators (amnesty-seekers) shared their stories with the TRC seeking either justice/reparation or amnesty. Nonetheless, fewer than 10% of victims were chosen for public testimony (A. Allan & M. Allan, 2000), and the TRC initially made no provisions for the mental health needs of those who testified and were overwhelmed by recurring trauma. The emphasis on investigation of crimes gave the TRC "a truth-finding, rather than a conciliatory, role" (A. Allan & M. Allan, 2000, p. 470). Its makeup was seen by many as partial to one political side (as Inkatha members tended to stay away from the process). Because of these and other shortcomings, the TRC did not contribute to healing individuals or the nation (Allan, 2000). Survivors tend to believe that the goals for the TRC should encompass all of the following: telling one's story, finding the truth, restitution or reparation, and justice—not amnesty. Some also had strong feelings about just deserts, harboring revenge (Hamber & Wilson, 2002). Survivors felt that the perpetrators gained immensely throughout the process by being granted amnesty if their crime was of a political nature, whereas reparations for the victims fell short of expectations (Hamber, 2000; Allan & Allan, 2000).

While reconciliation is a challenging goal for many survivors, a few have actually had a meaningful encounter with perpetrators' families, such as Johan and Ann-Marie Smit who reconciled with the parents of the person who took the life of their son Cornio (mentioned in the TRC Final Report and quoted in Hamber, 2000). Might reparation be a more attainable goal? The key issue, as Hamber notes, is that survivors do not want to accept monetary compensation for past crimes if it is used to buy their silence in the absence of truth-finding.

> Reparations and truth recovery must be linked, because without this link any form of reparations runs the danger of being seen by the survivors as

> a governmental strategy to close the chapter on the past prematurely and leave the secrets of the past hidden.
>
> (Hamber, 2000, p. 220)

Another reason for refusing payments may lie in the symptom of the survivor's guilt, who feels that she is betraying the memory of the dead by accepting monetary 'repair' for the irreparable (Hamber, 2000). This sentiment of expressing revenge as a way of respecting the dead may have been present in the families who, along with the Azanian People's Organization (AZAPO), challenged the sweeping amnesty proclamations of the TRC but ended up losing this battle in the constitutional court. Yet, Hamber claims that AZAPO's action did shift the ideological focus of the TRC from reparation as a symbolic gesture to reparation as a monetary and symbolic gesture. The TRC originally did not intend to make payments to individuals and families who lost loved ones, a stance that changed in the aftermath of the AZAPO and Biko family lawsuit (Hamber, 2000). Some survivors may have experienced the TRC hearings as a space where remorse by the amnesty-seekers brought about feelings of forgiveness and healing in the survivors (cf. Gobodo-Madikizela, 2003). This suggests that in some cases, the TRC fostered therapeutic justice where expressions of remorse were of voluntary nature.

Of note is the case of Amy Biehl's parents reconciling with young South African men who apologized for the killing of their daughter and received amnesty through the TRC hearings. This case gives hope to intercontinental (United States and South Africa) transformative justice practices at a micro level. Most astounding perhaps is the goodwill gesture and internalization of positive Ubuntu by all parties to commemorate Amy's violent death. The Biehls, US white citizens, provided significant material support for those who took their daughter's life to assist them in becoming role models for others (cf. Davis, 2003; Nagel, 2013). It is telling that the Biehls' gesture of positive Ubuntu occurred within the framework of the TRC. I argue that whenever such practices of forgiveness occurred in Rwanda, it was despite the practice of Gacaca, not because of it.

Between Resentment and *Ressentiment*

If we had to characterize the transitional justice models into two major affects, I argue that resentment was a prevailing sentiment during the Truth commission in South Africa, whereas *ressentiment* was predominant in Gacaca's community courts in Rwanda, with very different results: Ubuntu in the positive (South Africa) and decidedly negative Ubuntu, magnified as negative ethnicity, in the case of Rwanda. In the following, highlighting the differences between the two affects might be useful in clarifying the transitional justice models in their geopolitical and historical importance. Just as moral shaming has seen a comeback in moral and affect studies, I argue that we have seen a similar trend with a defense of resentment or even *ressentiment*. It coincides with a renewed (and important) interest in Holocaust survivor Jean Améry's (1986) defense of *ressentiment* in response to a very specific historical context: the 1960s optimism of West Germans and their indifference toward past atrocities.

How to make sense of resentment and *ressentiment*? They are an oppositional couple perhaps similar to the emotions of guilt and shame. The former couple denotes victims' feelings about injustice and being wronged and being expressed in feeling of outrage (resentment), not in seething rage and repressed vengefulness consuming the self (*ressentiment*). Similarly, victimizers may feel guilty about the act of harming someone; but in a sense, it is act-focused and thus externalized. Feeling shame, by contrast, expresses as sharp pain of internalized humiliation. Resentment relates to an averting type of energy (avoiding engagement), whereas *ressentiment*, according to Max Scheler (2010), is the active dredging up of memories that are painful, traumatic, and self-poisoning. *Ressentiment*, thanks to repressed emotions, engages with the shameful pain so intensely that it can lead to explosive violence. Often, it is difficult to uncouple shame from *ressentiment*. One's honor is so deeply wounded—the pain of humiliation—that one commits the ultimate annihilation: murder-suicide. When Nietzsche says that there is no doer behind a deed, no independent existence of a murderer, then he suggests that all crimes are rationalizable, which I have just done, by providing a psycho-moral theory of a shame/*ressentiment* response to rejection. Importantly, Nietzsche's analysis about resisting injustice shows "how socio-political resentment can overstep the aim of righting an injustice and slide into ontological *ressentiment*" (Ure, 2015, p. 24). This insight illustrates the need for Gacaca justice to err on the side of maximizing suffering and eliminating those who benefited from the 1959 revolution. It then does not seem to matter that legitimate victims (Hutu and Tutsi) of the 1994 genocide are caught up in such deep hatred of existence.

Today's resurrection of Améry's writings is often done in the context of a reckoning with transitional justice practices such as South Africa's TRC and Rwanda's Gacaca Trials. Specifically, an implicit nod of approval is given to Rwanda's informal 'African' reconciliation as Ubuntu-inflected Indigenous justice (Teleki & Kamga, 2020) and an explicit moral condemnation is given to Tutu's heavy-handed, Christian-inflected 'Ubuntu' performance of wresting forgiveness out of unwilling, sullen victims (Brudholm, 2006). Didier Fasson (2013) argues that *ressentiment* was the prevailing affect in the TRC of South Africa, yet he pins this sweeping indictment on the testimony of a single witness, who prefers that her family's tormentor be tried in court and jailed. In the context that he provides, it seems more to be an emotion of righteous indignation or resentment.

Tutu provides an easy target since he explicitly endorses Ubuntu ethics, of overcoming differences between those who commit harm (and injustice) and those who are harmed and celebrate shared humanity. Such advocacy of forgiveness and reconciliation cannot only be found in Christian agape but also in traditional Southern African practices that focus on restitution to gain social harmony (cf. Oruka, 1976). These social critics often overlook the profound work of a female psychologist who counseled victims' families. Pumla Modikizela-Gobodo's (2008) care-ethics approach which she has called a *witnessing dance* is also part and parcel of the deep commitment toward Ubuntu ethics. It is akin to Western forms of mediation, where a mediator meets separately with the parties (i.e., survivor or their family versus harmer), often for several weeks, before a common meeting is acceptable to both. In cases where common ground was also achieved, forgiveness was a beneficial outcome, bringing closure to victims' families.

When the opportunity for a witnessing dance is missed, it can foreclose expressions of forgiveness, as portrayed in the documentary *Between Joyce and Remembrance* (Kaplan, 2003). Gideon Nieuwoudt, a white security police colonel, testified in the TRC and asked that his name not be released to the victim's family. Years later, he showed up at their doorsteps and asked for forgiveness for the torture and murder of Siphiwo Mtimkulu. His mother Joyce Mtimkulu listens politely to his account, of being only an accomplice, not a killer, and she tells Nieuwoudt that his request comes too late. Joyce says: "I have no idea what reconciliation is." During the strained dialogue with the parents, all of the sudden, their grandchild Sikhumbuzo Mtimkulu, the son of Siphiwo, throws a vase at Nieuwoudt, cracking his skull. Bleeding, he still pleads for forgiveness and leaves the home wounded. Rage and repressed *ressentiment* is expressed here against a person who represents the hated apartheid regime, who tormented not only Sikhumbuzo's father, but the entire family, who did not know whether Siphiwo was alive or dead. The film is framed by scenes of the reburial of the son, that is, what is left—his bushel of hair that fell out because of the poisoning which Siphiwo had survived, only to be targeted again by a colonel who specialized in the 'elimination' of apartheid foes.

In the TRC proceedings, applicants for amnesty were not required to show remorse. Penance or remorse seems to be required when one applies for parole, early release, and lenient sentences. Once an 'offender' is asked "take responsibility for your crimes!" the implicit expectation is that he shows remorse for his heinous actions. Pumla Gobodo-Madikizela explains that it is understandable that this is more shame-provoking than it would do any good:

> Some people when faced with their evil deeds, understand the moral implications of their actions, but to maintain some dignity to protect a sense of identity as respectable human beings, they cling to the belief that what they did was morally correct. One can get a sense that they are struggling with their denial of the truth.
>
> (2003, p. 23)

James Gilligan clarifies:

> The family of painful feelings called shame and humiliation, which, when they become overwhelming because a person has no basis for self-respect, can be intolerable, and so devastating as to bring about the collapse of self-esteem and thus the death of the self.
>
> (1996, p. 64)

Sometimes, the exhortation to let go of vengeful thinking, i.e., to practice unconditional forgiveness, may sometimes come from surprising influences: the ancestors. A relational ethical model such as ludic Ubuntu ethics is mindful of ancestors being part of the life cycle. Marleen Ramsey (2009) interviews a white former police officer who applied for amnesty at the TRC and tried to seek forgiveness from members of the Black community he harmed by murdering his loved ones.

> Brian Mitchell revealed that upon receiving amnesty he requested the opportunity to return to Trust Feed to ask forgiveness from survivors and family members of his victims. However, the people of Trust Feed rejected his request for forgiveness. Brian spent a year in limbo, deeply depressed and mentally running away from who he was and what he had done. The turning point came when he received a telephone call asking him to return once again to the village and join the community in a day of reconciliation and forgiveness. The son of a woman who had died in the massacre revealed to Brian that in a dream his mother told him, "you must forgive my killer and not seek revenge." This message brought Brian comfort and led him to a place where he could forgive himself:
>
> One can pray and ask God to forgive you for what you have done. You can understand why you did certain things, but it seems to haunt you all the time until the stage where the other party comes and accepts your wish for forgiveness. If there is no acceptance from the offended party, forgiveness, self-forgiveness isn't a reality.
>
> (Mitchell, 2002, cited in Ramsey, 2009, p. 142)

Nepi revealed that without the forgiveness of Linda and Peter Biehl, he could not have forgiven himself. He stated:

> I've always wanted to be myself, but just couldn't get there. Linda and Peter were sort of a bridge over the trauma that I, not the militant, killed this lady and ended her life. I somehow have come to forgive myself because I have been forgiven for what I did and I can go on.
>
> (Nepi, 2002; cited in Ramsey, 2009, p. 142)

Many criticize transitional justice processes such as the TRC for being too forgiving in order to achieve therapeutic justice outcomes. Brandon Hamber identifies such a "justice gap" within transition processes: He wants the gap narrowed by (1) centering victims' rights, (2) reopening the ethical debates around amnesty, (3) empowering victims and hear their righteous anger vis-à-vis shortsighted peace processes, and (4) requiring more from perpetrators (or society) (2015, p. 15). I have no trouble with demanding more from society, but I would like to see a more nuanced approach toward the accused while Hamber demands that "perpetrators should not benefit from their actions …" (*Ibid.*), echoed by Thaddeus Metz who favors "burdensome compensation and burdensome rehabilitation" (2019, p. 125). So, for example, it seems that Amy Biehl's parents did everything wrong to honor her victim status: they "adopted" two of the young men who participated in the killing of their daughter and even gave them land, housing, and jobs. Arguably, under Hamber's disciplining gaze, the young men benefited from the Biehls' generosity instead of paying what they "owe" and suffer for their crime. Hamber's generalized moralizing stance, castigating perpetrators who benefit from their misdeeds, seems unhelpful, because he discounts victims' agency and the complex stances they may take. Centering victims' rights is a double-edged demand, because it may not lead to restorative justice, but rather to more punitive, vindictive sentencing. Such ideological framing reveals that psychologists (or criminologists) interested in the pursuit of restorative justice advocate retributive (and therefore, violent) principles toward a 'non-violent' end, namely, of securing peace for the victims. They have little to say about victims' families who seek peace by being-in-relation with those who have harmed their loved ones.

The Trouble with Collective Responsibility

In 1995, German historians curated an exhibition about the magnitude of the Nazi Wehrmacht (army)'s atrocities, and it caused a vehement reaction of denial and moral outrage among politicians including former chancellor Helmut Schmidt, who refused to participate in the viewing. He, along with other former soldiers, including my own father, denied having heard of execution orders against Soviet officers and a systematic coordination of atrocities against civilians, all violating the international convention of warfare and treatment of prisoners of war. The Soviet Union paid the heaviest toll with over 30 million people killed. Neo-Nazis protested in front of the exhibition which was shown in dozens of German and Austrian cities to over a million visitors (Staas & Ullrich, 2015).

The question remains: is there a radical evil that is unforgiveable? Hannah Arendt (1998) certainly postulates this in the aftermath of the Shoah. The very act of contemplating forgiving a murderous regime that unleashed its terror through all of its institutions is unethical. But is it really the case asks Pumla Gobodo-Madikizela (2008), or is there another lesson to be drawn from the Nürnberg Trials, the Frankfurt Auschwitz Trials of the 1960s, the Wehrmacht exhibition of 1995, or the TRC of South Africa? Gobodo-Madikizela, who served as psychologist for victims at the TRC, gives a pragmatic response. She argues that if not ethically, but psychologically, there is no other option but to practice forgiveness when perpetrators and victims live in proximity, which was not the case in postwar Germany because surviving Jews had fled elsewhere and few returned (2008, p. 170–1). In her book *A Human Being Died That Night: A South African Story of Forgiveness* (2003), Gobode-Madikizela describes the encounters between victims' families with Eugene de Kock, who was responsible for over 100 murders and notorious for torturing his victims to death. He was one of the few security force officers who came forward during the TRC proceedings and outed his superiors. Several victims' family members have made peace with de Kock, as was mentioned in news of his release from prison in January 2015. Despite getting amnesty for many murders, he still received several life sentences and ended up serving over 20 years in prison.

> Sandra Mama, widow of Glenack Mama, who was killed in 1992, [...] backed the government's decision. "I think it will actually close a chapter in our history because we've come a long way, and I think his release will just once again help with the reconciliation process because there's still a lot of things that we need to do as a country," she told the BBC.
>
> (Smith, 2015)

Surprisingly, other families also approved parole for de Kock:

> In 2012, he met Marcia Khoza, the daughter of ANC activist Portia Shabangu, whom De Kock executed after an ambush in Swaziland in 1989. She said after the meeting: "We greeted each other and shook hands. His handshake was firm."
>
> During the meeting, De Kock described how he shot Khoza's mother twice in the head before pushing the vehicle in which she was travelling down a slope. She added: "I thought I would cry but strangely enough had the courage to continue to listen to him. I was not jolted because I had long forgiven him."
>
> (Smith, 2015)

Such demonstrations of genuine forgiveness are rare in any circumstances. But as for a system that was putatively set up to produce an outcome of justice and reconciliation, Gacaca was not able to achieve justice nor reconciliation for all who were impacted by the 1994 atrocities and reconciliation. While supporters of Gacaca say that it represents an innovative way of traditional justice and is about reconciliation, I would hold that it is an opportunistic use of 'tradition' in the worst possible way. Geraghty speaks of an invented tradition, and I want to add that it is an inverted tradition, as it stands on its head the original meaning of resolving conflict and reestablish harmonious relations. Kagame's Gacaca court system amounts to a persecution of an entire group that is criminalized precisely because of their ethnic status and *not* because of the crimes that they are accused of committing in 1994 or afterward (e.g., returning Hutu who are accused of propagating 'genocide ideology'). Gacaca represents a masquerading (deadly) game of *ressentiment* that accounts for the humiliating loss of power in 1959. Tutsi chosen to preside over Gacaca court proceedings assumed the mantle of neutrality, but all too often, they served as high priests who were overcome by *ressentiment* of decades of political impotence and conducted vengeful proceedings to punish their Hutu neighbors, who had gained status and economic opportunities since 1959. It was irrelevant, then, that some of these defendants like Gahatu's family or Mitterrand had saved Tutsi children and adults. Yet, given the overarching script of shame and humiliation, it is problematic to describe their innocence as irrelevant. It was highly relevant and an embarrassment for the state that these Hutu saviors did not fit the script of evil *genocidaires*. Their righteous, courageous acts made them self-righteous in their own advocacy and, worse, when they also achieved recruiting Tutsi witnesses to support their innocence. The Manichean game could not sustain itself, i.e., castigating all Hutu as evil, and therefore, no effort was spared to unleash the power of the state to imprison these saviors. Such demonization extends to women survivors. The plight of women who were sexually humiliated also has no place in the annual genocide commemorations. A Hutu woman gets no recognition nor restitution. Worse, she is ostracized for 'choosing' to be a sex slave of a Hutu commander while keeping her Tutsi husband alive in a hideout during the genocide. For standing her ground, even demanding reparations, she would face the ultimate penalty, genocide denial (i.e., genocide ideology), and punished to life in prison.

Instead of being a paradigm case of restorative justice and reconciliation, the Gacaca courts have all the markings of juridical terrorism, showcasing a worst-case scenario of negative Ubuntu. This 'indigenous' system was accompanied by political terrorism: smothering free speech, free press, assassinations of Tutsi defectors, some of whom resided in South Africa. Tutu's book (1999) proclaims that there is no future without forgiveness, and he has extolled the virtues of Gacaca as a conduit toward forgiveness. I contend that his superficial assessment of Gacaca does not match reality. With festering *ressentiment*, Rwanda-style, there is no hope for peaceful coexistence unless Hutu are recognized and accepted as humans. Escaping their current subjugated status is a precondition for building relationships, including intermarriages, in the next generation. Future generations will have to reckon with the historical amnesia regarding the atrocities and genocide committed by Kagame's troops in Rwanda and the Congo (DRC).

Conclusion: Lessons for Penal Abolitionists

Tutu implored his audience, especially victims' families, to forgive and thus used his moral stature and position as chairman to exert undue pressure, possibly further traumatizing victims. However, those who testified were free to critique him and the goals of the commission. None of that can be said of Rwanda. There is no free press; witnesses are coerced to be silent or speak against the defense (when their inclination is to defend their Hutu protectors), and Tutsi who were truly victimized by Hutu are coerced to accept their enemies' apologies while receiving little, if anything, in compensation. In the traditional, precolonial Gacaca system, there would have been a focus on just compensation. Now, offenders receive prison terms and are thus unable to make payments. Unlike the South African government's compensation gesture toward all victims' families who participated in the TRC, the Rwandan government's commitment has been mostly symbolic.

It is telling that Paul Rusesabagina, the savior of over 1,000 Tutsi, should 'choose' to live in exile, before being captured and sentenced to 25 years for terrorism charges; another savior received life imprisonment. A Hutu woman who 'chooses' to be a sex slave during the genocide receives no recognition. Indeed, Gacaca neither constituted reconciliation nor a robust truth-finding process. It represented a juridical coercive system and showcased a worst-case scenario of negative Ubuntu ideology. It was accompanied by intimidation of international human right observers, reporters, and researchers.

Tutu's book (1999) proclaims that there is no future without forgiveness, and it is tempting to praise Gacaca as a pathway toward forgiveness. There is no hope for peaceful coexistence unless Hutu are recognized and accepted as humans. Essential for all successful and meaningful abolitionist practices are a commitment toward building relationships between those who have harmed and those who have been harmed. Across the continent, there has been a focus by elders to mediate with a forward-looking ethics in mind. Harmony between conflicting parties must be reestablished in order to forge new kinship ties, marriages, and a shared subsistence living into the next generations, which are all markers of positive Ubuntu ethics.

What Gacaca enthusiasts fail to understand is (1) the necessity to be fluent in Kinyarwanda in order to follow the informal court proceedings fully (i.e., without the assistance of a translator, since all translation is political) and (2) the pervasiveness of the lack of procedural order, which so often rendered Gacaca into a kangaroo court: witness intimidation by the prosecution and judges; disappearance of evidence brought by the defense from the national archives; badgering of the defendant; badgering of the judges if they were perceived as too lenient on the defendant; and the lack of payment, making judges vulnerable to bribes. Spectators were forced to witness the proceedings and could not tend to their homes and farms (cf. Geraghty, 2016).

Outsiders, who view Gacaca as fantastic tool of reconciliation, commit the conceptual error of describing Gacaca in isolation from the geopolitical context, that is, extant land claims and Tutsi elite entitlement. Thus, outsiders will miss in completely the underlying politics of *ressentiment*, of legal and political terrorism, and will continue to be beholden to the government's singular story of what counts as reliable testimonial and which kinds need to be quietened or smothered—with the one-size-fits-all label of genocide denial. Such outsiders learn that Gacaca refers to 'grass'; to them grassy areas might conjure up a bucolic image of an African village, which solves communal conflict remediation in harmonious ways, as outlined by Nils Christie's famous essay "Conflict as Property" (1977).

Penal abolitionists should refrain from calling the Gacaca process restorative or abolitionist. Gacaca trials were designed as an instrument of repression and thus ill equipped to foster a spirit of apologies and forgiveness beyond the formulaic response that was extracted from those who had to stand trial. By contrast, the TRC represents a mixed success model, and importantly, there was a possibility for justice or even a sense of closure that seemed therapeutic to some participants. Abolitionists should study the TRC experiment and Tutu's appeal to an Ubuntu ethics that crosses racial and colonial boundaries. As a caveat, the TRC heard only a fraction of cases brought by victims' families; it was a shining example of democratization and educating the world about the evils of apartheid. However, it was not able to bring about a decolonization process and settle the land question for the majority who yearn for the return of their ancestral lands addressing the ills of centuries of colonial oppression. Furthermore, white applicants were unwilling to apologize and did not hide their disdain while pleading for amnesty. For all these reasons, reconciliation cannot be attained between oppressed groups and the state; it is only possible between members of groups (cf. Rautenbach, 2015). But the commission was no place for vengeful or victors' justice; *au contraire*, it was open to expressive therapeutic justice. African National Congress (ANC) soldiers were not excluded from the process and also appealed for amnesty for their political crimes. In Rwanda, Kagame's soldiers who committed atrocities and indiscriminate killing were exempted from the Gacaca process. Furthermore, they were not subjected to criminal proceedings. Rwanda's case is clearly one of negative Ubuntu ideology, and the Gacaca trials represent a ruse of reconciliation; retributive prison sentences were not uncommon. For abolitionists, it is important to review the facts on the ground carefully without resorting to a romantic attachment to precolonial practices.

Chapter 5 delves into a differentiation between restorative and transformative justice claims and practices. It outlines Indigenous, abolitionist, heart-based justice as it is already practiced and how it can be a blueprint for novel approaches to positive peace and harmlessness.

Note

1 For Tutsi survivors, proper family burial was precluded; actually, they were pressured to dig up the corpses and surrender them to the authorities for public display. Thousands of skulls (and in some cases entire bodies), are on display at the national memorial sites. Undoubtedly, families are resentful for being denied proper burial customary practices (Geraghty, 2014, personal communication).

5 A Transformative Justice Paradigm

A Call for Ludic Ubuntu Justice[1]

In this chapter, I discuss two issues that some penal abolitionists wrestle with:

1 What to do with the 'worst of the worst' if sanctions or punishment are obsolete?
2 How to acknowledge Indigenous justice and avoid romanticizing such approach? This presents as a challenge until it is also recognized that the Western criminal legal system is enamored with ideal theory and romanticizes this ideology of safety and security, without anyone looking at it as such.

Both issues will be reviewed comparing restorative with transformative justice.

Games We Play

As I walked to the city's public library, it occurred to me that it is situated across the street from the city courthouse. And as I approached the building, I ran into the community police officer who shared with me that he was on his way to Drug Court. I knew it was pre-conferencing time at 1pm, before the judge would render her verdict on the hapless audience at 2pm, sending some to jail for a dirty urine sample. In my messianic zeal, I shared with the cop that I would be going to the other site to meet children (and college students) to prepare them for a life of the mind, teaching children philosophy through picture books and other forms of storytelling. The idea of our Sophia's Garden project is very simple—create curiosity and mindfulness in young children and teenagers, so that they can develop critical thinking skills and a love for learning—to stay engaged till their high school diploma. If they succeed to receive that piece of paper, their likelihood of going to jail (ever) evaporates. Sharing this space with kids in a library can also be a sanctuary, as Kevin Powell (2015) evocatively describes a dreamy world and temporary reprieve from racism. So, two buildings in proximity and yet, worlds apart. One can be a protective, loving space, with caring parents, guardians, and kind librarians, and the other, foreboding, a dark,

DOI: 10.4324/9781003055327-6

> *fearful, despairing place where everybody has given up on you. No fun colorful children's books welcome you there. And the massive county courthouse, jail, and sheriff's office are also across the street.*

However, public spaces are also racialized spaces. One of the founders of Cortland's Black Lives Matter chapter shared that her three-year-old son had a traumatic experience at the library. He had cried, and a white patron called the police on the child. Public space is white property and white space, and Black toddlers need to be disciplined by police. Such children do not live within the (colonial) pale whose child-like behavior can be excused. Such racist assumption is what Black families must abide by, and they must teach children obedience games with white authority figures to stay alive. These protective parents call it: "the talk." In Spring 2021, a nine-year-old girl screamed when she was handcuffed by Rochester, New York, police (wearing body cameras) and pushed into the car; the white cop accosted her with the command: "Don't behave like a child!" The whaling girl retorted: "But I am a child!"

But whites know the comforting side of public libraries. In the colorful, warm, and fuzzy space of the children's section of the library, philosophy students from SUNY Cortland where I teach engage children with picture story books. Many of them are morality lessons about being kind to outsiders who are ostracized by other children. *The Invisible Boy* (Ludwig & Barton, 2013) is a story of a boy who is shunned by all, till a new child shows up in his class and literally reaches out to sit with him at the dreaded lunch time. At that moment, the boy literally changes from black and white pencil contours to being fully immersed in all kinds of colors. And he is at peace. He has one friend who makes life bearable. Not only that, all the sudden, the rules of the (exclusion) game change, and the other children start noticing him in a good way. When we read this picture book in a forest school, I asked the children about win-win games. Surprisingly, one ten-year-old told me that that's a communist idea! It seems so ingrained that we must have 'winner-take-all' games which are inherently violent—at least they seem violent to many Indigenous cultures who would abhor such games.

Indigenous cultures prize win-win games and instill in children that prideful attitude leads to dominance and lack of compassion—humility, generosity, and fortitude are all virtues to be cultivated in young children, strengthening a feeling of belonging and sharing (cf. Marshall, 2001). Adopting a ludic Ubuntu ethic that honors all my relations, as Lakota people invoke in their greetings, is truly eco-centric. Westerners are starting to realize the paucity of ego-centrism. Fifty years ago, activist scholar Vine Deloria noted this shift:

> American society is unconsciously going Indian. Moods, attitudes, and values are changing. People are becoming more aware of their isolation even while they continue to worship the rugged individualist who needs no one. The self-sufficient man is casting about for a community to call

> his own. The glittering generalities and mythologies of American society no longer satisfy *the need and desire to belong*.
>
> (Deloria, 1970, p. 11, emphasis mine)

No doubt, Deloria cautions whites about the path of conscientization. The task is how does this urge to belong *not* dwell in self-serving melancholia of white elite privilege that can afford to "go native." Working with Indigenous knowledge and worldviews, I want to probe how an eco-centric perspective could help us rethinking the need for punishment, specifically questioning the persistence of individualized punishment. Insights from play theory and playworkers will also help us understand better how some people spiral downward into the depth of (self)destruction and how various ludic empowerment strategies create avenues for transformation.

It seems to me that a key reason for violent interpersonal transgressions can be traced to the problem of separation. First and foremost—it is a reactive agonistic game: we hurt others to punish them—out of revenge and severe feelings of humiliation and rejection. When teachers do so ('the punishment game'), it is really another form of revenge: 'I show you how to have respect for me as authority person!' And it is not only about individual slights. We also settle score on behalf of our loved ones. What the state calls 'gangs' is really another form of family and preserving family honor. If my family member is violated (hurt, verbally disrespected, etc.), then it is my duty to go after the harmer. I think it is misguided of Western anthropologists labeling certain eastern cultures as "honor culture," because it seems to be part of the human condition: to have difficulty in tolerating disrespect of our own clan, family, and friends. In *Outliers*, Malcolm Gladwell (2008) makes a salient point about "Scotch-Irish" honor culture; he notes that this European tradition took roots among the settlers across Appalachia (in the eastern region of the United States); a curse or bullying remark becomes shameful to the point that men must fight to death and their mothers scolding them if they whimper in pain and don't die like men (pp. 164–7). The notorious borderland lawless mentality traveled to the United States. One feud ended up in court, only for the defendant to order the judge dismissed. The judge obeyed and fled, but sometime later, the court was reconvened and protected by some 60 militiamen. However, the defendant had already been killed (pp. 165–6). In other cases, jury nullification signaled to state actors (sheriff, prosecutors, and judges) that indicting white men for shooting to death others over personal slights was futile (p. 170). Gladwell continues to make some generalizations about southern (white) vs. northern (New England) mentality. Studies that involve intentional bullying of subjects show that southern men are not able or willing to laugh it off, unlike their northern counterparts (pp. 171–3). Other studies trace the problem of US violent masculinity to child-rearing and lack of nested emotional support. Health experts recommend breastfeeding for six months, whereas Indigenous wisdom advise over two years (Prescott, 1997;

Narvaez, 2021). The prosocial practice of co-sleeping with the baby may be used against parents by the family regulation system.

To rethink the justice paradigm is nothing new. Even in the United States, a holistic analysis of crime prevention was promulgated over a century ago:

> In the journal *The Medical News*, Dr. George Frank Lydston of Chicago, Illinois argued criminality could best be treated as a preventive disease by addressing the social causes that lead to juveniles becoming adult criminals. "Like all other diseases the disease of crime is one which is more rationally treated by prevention than by curative methods. Will not the law-maker join hands with the medical practitioner and endeavor, even at the sacrifice of his own interests, to prevent the diseases he treats?" Lydston was probably ahead of his time. He wrote the article in 1896. Unfortunately, it appears he is still ahead of his time today.
>
> (Singer, 2017)

Such abolitionist sentiments were also current in criminal justice circles in Germany at the turn of the 19th century. The pioneering legal reformer Franz Ritter von Liszt even appealed to letting go of errant youth instead of teaching them a lesson replete with carceral structures. "When a youth commits a crime *and we let him get away with it*, then the risk of relapse in crime is lower than the risk we face after having punished him" (1905, p. 346, cited in Albrecht, 2002, p. 172, emphasis added). The intrepid reformer did not talk about the necessity of accountability work, of soft punishment, of net widening of supervision, etc. But this is precisely what many activist organizations demand today, the topic of this chapter, focusing on healing beyond accountability and reckoning with "offenders."

Reforming 'Justice'

It seems that Transformative Justice is being invoked by everybody. What used to be called prison reform or "right on crime" in the era of the indefinite war on drugs (or the New Jim Crow) has now got a more life-affirming ring. From the streets, we hear "defund the police"—less so "defund the sheriffs, jail and prison structures," let alone the military-industrial complex. The policing apparatus is something tangible, especially when young Black cis and trans lives are at stake. As Black trans activists never tire to point out, Black trans lives still do not matter, especially when Black trans women die at alarming rates. But policy makers, philanthropic enterprises that praise their calling as "transformative" on radio waves and social media, are usually a far cry from doing just that.

New York's reform act, "Raise the Age," was supposed to be a decarceration strategy. 'Kids prisons' billions of dollars' worth were constructed instead of letting go of children (Martin, 2018; Martin & Kurti, 2020). The children under the state's intense watch must be disciplined, sanctioned, supervised instead of being loved, nurtured, mentored, and educated. Kalief Browder, whose suicide triggered the reform act, would not have got relief under this new act (Martin & Kurti, 2020). Even electronic monitoring isn't the panacea reformers hoped for. These devices have traumatic effects, especially on youth; they are harmful to the body in haunting similarity to the chains that bound enslaved human beings and those imprisoned under the convict lease system. E-chaining is a practice that leads to net widening of the carceral system and often create conditions for a debtor's prison, because the daily fees of the chains accumulate (Kilgore, 2022). We have moved from carceral reforms to a carceral devolution: federal and state prisons may realize a modicum of carceral reform, but local jailing is booming. Mass incarceration has mutated to mass supervision, as the prison-industrial complex's tentacles ever increase their reach (Price, 2015, p. 79). The family regulation system (discussed in Chapter 2) is another instance of this growth industry, absorbing many nonprofit service providers, including anti-poverty agencies, that are under the spell of publicly organized disciplinary and punitive social welfare. Abolitionists need to continuously be vigilant about the ever-expanding surveillance and electronic curtailment of basic civil liberties, especially where these are instituted under the guise of reform and decarceration.

The security industry's advertisement strategy is especially seductive, when they appeal to the health and safety advantages of electronic monitoring that now has two-way radio, made popular during the Covid-19 pandemic. Probation officers can check virtually on the detainees at any time of the day or night, listening in to conversations of unsuspecting people punished to house arrest and total surveillance. This kind of "transformation" is novel only in so far as it produces net-widening circles of supervision, which is exactly the opposite of what penal abolitionists envision in a jail-free society. The total institution has become enmeshed in all life circuits of the supervised and not-yet ensnared. William Staples' *Everyday Surveillance: Vigilance and Visibility in Postmodern Life* (2014) maps it out very well what is at stake. The global pandemic has become a useful playground in advancing face-recognition technology, temperature checks, and in touting these tools as serving the interest of public health. This is not what transformative justice (and democracy) look like.

The Need for Transformative Justice Considerations

In a previous chapter, I critiqued Hobbes' ideology of vengeance and scarcity which is embedded in psychological egoism. In this chapter, we pivot away from retributive justifications of judgment and punishment in order to develop a language of empathy and solidarity. It seems then fitting to share the lessons of the *Tao Te Ching*:

> Throw away holiness and wisdom,
> and people will be a hundred times happier.
> Throw away morality and justice,
> and people will do the right thing.
> Throw away industry and profit,
> and there won't be any thieves.
>
> If these three aren't enough,
> just stay at the center of the circle
> and let all things take their course.
> (Mitchell, trans., 2006, chapter 19)

When the great *Dao* (the way) is lost, humans create conflicts artificially. Doing the right thing is valuing harmony and compassion and loving all there is. Even affirming transformative justice seems to be a paradox—if one lives the way of the Dao, there is no need for justice. Understanding these ancient pearls of wisdom may lead us to rethink the need for youth transgressions, but abolitionists do not stop there.

How then do we get back on the right path? Hobbes' paranoid imagination of securitization had it backward; it imagined a brutish state of nature which needed to be destroyed through artificial government surveillance structures to keep all subjects in check. What if the 'natural' way were harmonious and the ideology of scarcity coupled with sanctions a particular social invention? What if the adversarial criminal justice system is a conjuring trick of 'benevolence and justice'? In fact, such system obstructs the way of Ubuntu ethics and consensual agreements and long-term peace-building practices (Murithi, 2006b).

I draw on Indigenous peace practices to make a case for *transformative* justice. In a way, this concept 'transformative justice' is puzzling, especially in a ludic Ubuntu model. Taken to its logical conclusion, in a phase or sphere where all there is love, no appeal to *justice* is necessary. All there is, *just is*. In human terms, there is always something exacting in 'wanting justice.' There is a tinge of retribution sentiments, even in restorative justice (RJ). After all, the wronged party wants to be made whole, and some repair, be it symbolic, monetary, or another form of exchange, is demanded. One can imagine a different world of social connections in terms of *individualized responses to harm.*

Transformative justice is both backward- and forward-looking concerning systems of control and violence: the criminal injustice system, settler colonialism and the iron fist of the military-industrial complex, racial capitalism, and heteropatriarchal institutions, including the Catholic church, Boy Scouts of America, etc., need to be defunded or held accountable. All is *not* forgotten or forgiven, and governments, parastatals, and multinational corporations backed by imperial armies are liable for massive wrongdoing, including ecocide. Restitution must be paid to current survivors and future generations. The rainforests of the world need global investment and protection, and Indigenous peoples need to be the agents driving the agendas of ecological reparation, reforestation, etc., including in the Sahel. Nuclear armament, drone warfare, and land mining cause terror and devastation to humans and ecosystems. Currently, Black and Indigenous peoples drive a global social justice movement that demands more than symbolic apology. Should Georgetown University, in Washington, DC, pay full tuition to the descendants of enslaved persons, who toiled on their grounds 200 years ago? Should the great grandchildren of Indian peoples who survived the cultural genocide of the mission and schooling system of the US and Canadian assimilationist ideology be paid, be given free education, and/or have legal title to federal and state lands, stolen from their nations? In 2021, mass graves have been discovered in former Black towns in the United States, decimated by systemic white supremacist terror and at the former 'residential schools'—[*sic*] in Canada harboring the remains of First Nation children. In 2022, the Canadian government announced the biggest settlement in its history, compensating First Nation communities with some 20 billion dollars for the trauma caused by the family regulation system within two decades beginning in 1991 (Indigenous Services Canada, Jan. 4, 2022). Surely, hundreds of billions of reparations must follow reckoning with their murderous settler colonial 'schooling' policies and practices.

Transformative justice must also be concerned with such systemic injustice to oppressed and marginalized peoples. Some of its precepts are the following:

1 Making amends and making whole; having empathy and focusing on healing forces; prizing harmony by participating in goodwill practices in the community, especially working with those who are socially displaced. Being concerned with a politics of recognition and solidarity, i.e., challenging racism, sexism, state violence, etc. Simply put, such nonideal justice draws our collective attention away from individualized culpable actors to specific harmful practices, which deny personhood and bodily, emotional, and spiritual integrity. Here, I will provide examples of Indigenous approaches to transformative justice, the Hawai'ian concept of Ho'oponopono, as well as Lakota models of healing circles (Marshall, 2001; (Brendtro *et al.*, 2019). I also center African reconciliation practices and consider how they have adapted to the colonial and postcolonial context (Murithi, 2002; 2006b; Nagel, 2007). I explore the complexities of rituals and whether they are open to non-shaming ways of resolving interpersonal conflict and violence. How might they appreciate an interspecies ethics (Willett, 2014)? I want to argue for a shift from human rights to ecologically based interspecies perspectives, which is also supported by a ludic Ubuntu justice worldview.
2 Specifically, I wish to connect transformative justice to healing practices which transcend shaming and even trauma-informed care. Is that

possible? Several US-based organizations and Indigenous nations highlight the importance of community accountability. How is it possible to overcome harming without resorting to punitive practices? This leads to the next sticking issue.

3 How do penal abolitionists deal with the objection of retributive abolitionism? Most abolitionists praise community accountability work, which often includes some types of sanction, which, in part, are backward-looking and desert-like punishment: 'you did such harm, now we will exile you, so that you reflect on your harm.'

Penal abolitionism is not a state of being, but it is a sketch or a process (e.g., Mathiesen, 2014). More forcefully, Liat Ben-Moshe, who foregrounds intersectional struggles of disabilities and queer anti-racism, calls for three ways of rethinking abolition: as radical form of activism, as a strategy beyond resistance, as a worldview that contests the status quo (Ben-Moshe, 2018, p. 353). She cautions against expert planning, prescription, and certainty (Ben-Moshe, 2020, p. 126). By contrast, Michael C. Coyle (2018) brilliantly argues that penal abolition visions should not be concerned with futurity, uncertainty, or dwelling in the utopian moment. Rather, he advocates that penal abolitionism is a realist position, and, *au contraire*, it is the defenders of 'criminal justice' who are mired in utopia, never able to fulfill their high-minded moralistic defense of the 'justice' system providing just punishment and safe-guarding society. And who counts as expert? Black feminist standpoint theory invites us to think of those who are directly impacted by incarceration as the knowers and visionaries for change (Hill Collins, 2000). Imprisoned intellectual Tiyo Attallah Salah-El famously notes that prisons must turn into healing and caring centers (2007, p. 205). Indeed, in recent years, several closed prisons have reopened as yoga studios or fitness arenas; some serve as spaces for film productions; some as shelters for unhoused people leaving prison.

Those fighting the abolition of slavery were not fretting about utopias. The main contestation was between abolitionists who favored the British model, gradual manumission, and radical activists who demanded immediate destruction of chattel slavery and its heinous laws of subjugation. Black radicals also demanded land and full enfranchisement, in other words, *bona fide* citizenship. W.E.B. Du Bois' (1935) prophetic call for abolition democracy, i.e., the creation of new institutions embraced by an anti-racist society, is still a demand US abolitionists attend to (cf. Davis, 2005; Ben-Moshe, 2020). I am certainly sympathetic to dismantling institutions, but I am less inclined to favor a statist rebuilding of 'just' institutions.

So, in what follows, I propose a novel way of exiting the game of 'tarrying with the negative.' At this fifth stage in my model, ludic justice adopts a trickster approach to envision abolitionist spaces and states of being. In that spirit, accountability politics will be reconsidered by comparing restorative to transformative approaches.

In the West, where the criminalizing system, buttressed by social contract theory, is so naturalized that we have forgotten how we sorted out interpersonal conflict before the birth of the modern police and modern jails. Yet, across Africa, these precolonial memories are still strong, as they are elsewhere among Indigenous peoples. Learning Africa's lessons, Lucien Lombardo (1984) invites us to replace the police with neighbors to keep the peace, court houses with a council of elders for dispute resolutions, and criminal law with tort law (p. 79). What is remarkable is that there is still a fair amount of resistance to the colonial imposition of Justitia's law-and-order ruse. In Mali, in every interview with judges, gendarmerie, and even warden, I was told that the prison is a colonial imposition by the French. And there was a lot of lamentation that the current laws are still a legacy of the former colonial power. Imprisonment is frowned upon by society, and tough judges may face community ostracism as already mentioned. Prison is a last resort of punishment for people, usually reserved for those who are socially displaced. This means that people who have migrated from another African country or who have left their rural home for the city where they live without their protective networks are vulnerable to prison terms.

We must ask ourselves, what ought to be learned from Indigenous justice worldviews and practices? What could be done to focus on forward-looking solutions without worrying if they truly lead to deterrence? If the conflict is interpersonal, what might need to be accomplished that the warring parties intermarry in the next generation? This is a pressing task for griots and griottes among the Bamana (in Mali) and the kinship institution of 'joking relatives.' These mediators or *jeliws* are tasked with keeping peace in the community. They intervene on any level, from spousal disputes to those between heads of state, to solve disputes and issue solutions for redress, if an offense or harm is committed. The main objective is to find a solution quickly, to minimize the damage, and to assure that future generations of the feuding parties and families may continue to intermarry. *Jeliws* enjoy great authority and power among the Bamana. Joking relatives also serve to keep the peace among people of different families and clans. My appeal to a ludic expression of justice takes inspiration from this great Bamana traditional practice.

In one case, a radio thief was confronted. The theft was reported to the police who told the aggrieved to sort it out 'the traditional way.' In the end, the thief had to go to his family and kin to collect bags of beans. It is indeed shameful to look your relative in the eye and ask them to contribute to a restorative fund. In the end, dozens of pounds of beans were collected and cooked in the commons. The parties in conflict and their kin all attended and enjoyed eating the beans. Many people have bodily reactions to eating beans which gave way to jokes and laughter. In the end, the customary practice teaches us that laughing it off is the best remedy; transmuting resentment and anger into joyful eating together also ensures that no feuding kinship relations emerge, and families can intermarry and forget about the harm (Kone, 1997; Kone, 2023 forthcoming).

Forgiveness Stories—Transforming *Ressentiment* into Hope

Victor Frankl's autobiography *Man's Search for Meaning* (1946/2006) is considered one of the greatest prison memoirs, and it continues to be a bestseller. It gives insights into the harrowing world of death camps as if it were written by a detached bystander and not a survivor. This is all the more important, as it was written shortly after the 1945 allied forces' liberation, and Frankl had first contemplated writing under a pseudonym. He did not showcase his own actions as noble, even though we know that he could have escaped the Holocaust by emigrating to the US. Frankl called himself a tragic optimist and took the unusual step to return to his home city Vienna where he resumed his medical practice. He adamantly refused to cast the stone of collective guilt onto Germans and led a successful public intellectual's life. By contrast, Jean Améry's existential philosophy does not cherish optimism and writes that *ressentiment* is an important emotion for Holocaust survivors, like him.

Frankl argues that society can be separated into decent and indecent people. Obviously, he was treated to many indecent men, sadistic Nazis, in the death camps. It is noteworthy that he does not label his tormentors. Frankl mentions a particular sadistic Nazi who was delivered to the Soviets; languishing in a gulag, he turned out to be one of the most caring and compassionate fellow prisoners one could ever hope for. Frankl's dyadic model gives no clear-cut recipe in "sorting out" humans. He even mentioned the actions of a friend who survived the death march with him. During the early moments of liberation, he saw his friend trample a wheat field. Seeing this "indecent" behavior, he asked if his friend could take better care. In rage, the friend continued destroying the plants. Considering Améry, Frankl's friend acted out his authentic *ressentiment*. However, Frankl does not resort to judgment; he simply observes the behavior and leaves it to the reader to grasp why people take different paths while giving meaning to their lives. His book also makes clear that there is no predictability in who will turn out to be unapologetically sadistic.

With that said, one could make perhaps some sense with Frankl's insights on the unpredictability of moral behavior, reviewing the following case. A white South African police officer, Eugene de Kock, earned the label "prime evil." He was a vicious and zealous defender of the apartheid regime torturing and murdering many political activists. Yet, surprisingly, he was ready to tell it all—and he was one of few whites who testified at the Truth and Reconciliation Commission (TRC). It gave families a first opportunity to find the remains, if there were any, of their loved ones. He didn't receive amnesty, but instead an excessive prison term of 212 years. Still in prison, he met with many victims' families, and 20 years later, he was given parole after two decades. What is most peculiar is that there are photos where de Kock is posing with families, who not only forgave him but also rallied for his release. In particular, Candice Mama's testimony stands out: Mama was told by prison authorities that a woman threw saucers or other dangerous objects at de Kock when she faced him in prison. The guards stepped in to stop the woman from committing further harm, but de Kock just waved them off. He was resigned to face her and her rage because there was nothing redeeming about him having killing her loved one. When Mama was told this story, she felt that de Kock's behavior was genuine, and she was ready to forgive him and even petition the court for his release.[2] She also gives credit to Pumla Gobodo-Madikizela, a former TRC commissioner whose careful counseling prepared Mama for a face-to-face meeting with de Kock.[3] Gobodo-Madikizela describes her therapeutic method as a "witnessing dance" which has helped many families who lost loved ones to the apartheid regime come to terms with accusers, including Black police officers. In her autobiography, *Forgiveness Redefined*, Mama also reflects on her own encounter with de Kock and her complex feelings in this profound way:

> With every question asked and every answer given, my empathy grew for this complete stranger who spoke so sincerely that I couldn't help but let my defenses down. I looked on in awe as I witnessed myself crying not because of who I had lost, but because I saw a man who was created by a regime and who took a fall for a government. A man who lost so much more than I would bear had I been in the same situation.
>
> (2019, pp. 192–3)

Even more surprising for anyone who studies forgiveness in real-life encounters, Mama reveals this compelling, compassionate reflection:

> I left having felt like I had just been lucky enough to meet one of the most brilliant thinkers of my time and someone who was also a victim to a system of indoctrination. I had forgiven him before, but having met him, I can say I have been changed by this encounter forever.
>
> (*Ibid.*, p. 193)

Mama writes movingly about her long journey toward forgiveness and self-love, which, of course, hit the key emotions of blind rage, anger, and denial as a teenager. At the same time, she also let herself indulge in popular music, singing, and dancing with great abandon and could not figure out how to hold these two aspects of her personality together (pp. 92–5). In school, she had learned (and challenged at great personal cost) the whitewashed version of apartheid, which did not reflect the brutality of her father's murder, who was caught up in Eugene de Kock's surveillance and extermination program as late as 1992. Her father and the apartheid police officer "had become interlinked in my mind like a virus that was impossible to shake" (p. 96). Coming of age in the post-TRC era, Mama, her family, and her generation had no blueprint, no guidance on how to engage in a grieving process. She could not allow herself to mourn her father's death, and post-traumatic stress disorder (PTSD) turned into *persistent* traumatic stress disorder. Her rage ultimately contributed to a life-threatening ulcer at 16 years, and it was the turning point for Mama's personal journey to find out "why." Why was her father singled out by the regime? She was minorized in a white elite school that created a fictional account of apartheid as one unfortunate but non-violent event [sic]. This white supremacist revisionism catapulted her into doing independent research, even going through the voluminous TRC tomes, documenting systemic state violence and violence against Indigenous Black humanity. In that process, she also turned inward and started a slow healing process, without psychological counseling, but with gentle assistance from a Buddhist monk and sitting in meditation at the sanctuary. A chapter also addresses the skeptics and devotes careful exploration of the myths about facile forgiveness rituals. In Mama's case, there is a lot of soul-searching exploration of guilt. If she forgave the assailant, would that mean incurring the wrath of her ancestor (her dad), her family, and community? Indeed, such wrath was not hypothetical. Mama penned her encounter with de Kock in prison, sharing her vulnerabilities on Facebook. She even mentioned that she hugged him compassionately after learning that he was unable to forgive himself. The response to her public reflection was twofold: many responded in kind and were supportive, even feeling encouraged to start their own forgiveness journey. However, a few were rageful and even hurled death threats. How dare she forgive a racist. Mama remains unapologetic for doing what felt true and liberating for herself. Her journey was one of healing-informed self-care rather than trauma-informed care given by others.

In the following, I sketch comparisons that draw inspiration from the Safe OUTside the System (SOS) collective in Brooklyn, New York, and also from individuals such as Candice Mama and others who refuse to accept themselves as victims. These two models are schematic, and transformative justice is somewhat idealized (cf. Tables 5.1 and 5.2). It is difficult to find Indigenous practices that address all topics listed under transformative ludic Ubuntu justice. And yet, Ubuntu ethics is not simply an add-on to a theory of conflict resolution. But it is a central feature of: How do I do by my community? It is not wedded to a liberal rights discourse.

Is it possible to imagine a victimized person (and, even more so, a responsible person) could release the memory of harm (and harming) through specific healing and meditation playwork, which centers self-care, self-forgiveness, and forgetting? To many forgetting seems problematic. Others stress forgiveness as being vital for one who has been harmed, but few also address the importance of forgiving the self. Would it not be helpful to "reprogram," to heal at the cellular memory level assisted by a healer? When the trauma cannot be transmuted, it will continue to trigger a self-harming emotional response and add to daily toxic stress. A common complaint about community accountability is that the process can be very long, even taking years to complete. Leah Lakshmi Piepzna-Samarasinha writes in "Cripping TJ" that many folks engaged in transformative justice work are also disabled and

Table 5.1 Restorative Justice vs. Transformative Ludic Ubuntu Justice

Restorative Justice	*Transformative Ludic Ubuntu Justice*
Wedded to punishment paradigm—backwards-facing	Non-punitive paradigm—forward-facing
Conditionally forgive harmer, but won't forget	Forgive self and others and let go; focus on healing, wrap-around programs for all involved, including transforming the past through ludic performances)
Moral blameworthiness; individualist ideology	Ubuntu ethics; relational worldview
Work within structures of oppression	Dismantle systemic oppression, Safe OUTside the System
Liberal "feel-good," charity approach	Intersectional, anti-oppressive social justice
Creation of law-abiding individual (non-recidivism)	Abolitionist practice is process and goal
Decarceration and legal reforms as goal	Excarceration and law abolition as goal
Linked to Prison-Industrial Complex ("carrot-and-stick" approach)	De-linked from PIC (there are no penalties for non-compliance)
Carceral feminism, retributive abolitionism	Pod-mapping, abolitionist feminism; revolutionary love
Laws must be corrected	Most laws will be abolished (or just fade away, become irrelevant, won't be enforced); law abolitionism
Community-policing; police must be corrected (police as guardians, not just warriors)	Abolish police and prosecution; violence disruptors (transform policing into community care work; provide de-escalation communicative education)
Sentencing circles	Healing circles, community conferencing
Discerning from "free will" (necessitates sanction)	No backward-facing sanctions, punishment
Trauma-informed care (backward focused)	Healing-informed care (forward looking)
Reparation	Reconciliation, transmutation of past energies
Rehabilitation	(Re)claiming and building new relations
Individualist focus	Communal, relationship-building focus
Holding somebody accountable	Holding somebody in loving perception
(Community) accountability work	Abolitionist play/holistic family constellations
Individual is held accountable	State/institutions are held accountable
How did person fail us?	How did we fail as a community (as caregivers)?
Reckoning with individual failures	Seeing all as interconnected, interwoven
Individual must be corrected	Loving what is; being responsive and in-tune
Harmer must take responsibility	Meaningful mutual aid: committed self-care, the pod

Table 5.1 Cont.

Restorative Justice	*Transformative Ludic Ubuntu Justice*
Being ostracized, shamed in "reintegrative way"	Love and Compassion transmutes shaming
Victim in charge of process	All are equally listened to and have a stake in the process
Linear time, efficiency	Circular time, Crip time
Restricted to mostly non-violent transgressions	Dialogue inclusive of all harm committed
Prosecutor or mediating judge (vertical structure)	Circle structure: power-sharing, consensual (horizontal structure)
Expert-driven mediation	In healing circles, elders are community mediators and violence disrupters

If we go a step further, then

Table 5.2 Newtonian physics (RJ) meets quantum physics (TJ)

RJ	*TJ*
Particle	Wave
Individual responsiveness	Interconnectedness
Harmer vs harmed	No victim, no perpetrators
I am a drop in the ocean	The drop of ocean is in me (Rumi)

discloses that coping with panic attacks and PTSD makes this work quite challenging (Dixon & Piepzna-Samarasinha, 2020, p. 235). Importantly, disability "is a part of many stories of abuse" (p. 241). Accountability processes must be "accessible to our disabilities and neurodivergence" and not discredit the survivor's stories (p. 244). A better way to approach the process is to insist that it occurs on "crip time," a concept borrowed from Ellen Samuels. Transformative justice has been described as the longest process in the world, and if one used the flexible approach as normative rather than rigid deadlines, the process would be allowed to take its course without anyone panicking and making hasty judgment calls (pp. 244–5). Might the process include, besides self-care, a nod to building consensus on what needs to be accomplished to attain healing of self and community? Sanctions tend to be unilateral, top-down, and one has to look very carefully whether the sanctions are happily accepted or lead to further resentment and shame response to rejection.

Demanding accountability/apology/recognition of harm, and emotional alignment ("proper" facial/bodily expression of contriteness) assumes a rational, self-interested, emotionally engaged, or resilient subjectivity. Emotional and cognitive intelligence may just be unattainable in what is called living among people who all have had their share of childhood trauma, major woundedness, and unresolved, deep-seated anger. But this utopian ideal is what is daily demanded from toddlers to adults in kindergarten as well as in the theater of the courthouse. What does it mean to a four-year-old 'to be responsible' when the key responsible way to be is to play and try out playful ways of being social? 'Time out' is a frustrated adult's maximum punishment along with public shaming and hitting the child. The legacy of settler colonial child raising turns up in different guises (Narvaez, 2021) as will be discussed below. For now, I want to trouble the universally accepted strategy of community accountability among penal abolitionists. What if we endorse responsiveness and being-in-tune with others, exploring positive ludic Ubuntu transformative approaches? They would consider accountability as a means to an end (which is harmony as public good). But accountability is not an end in itself. It is shored up by nervous penal abolitionists who want to address the objection of a 'sanction-free' world replete with Hobbesian pessimism about the human condition. What if we dare to *excuse* the behavior, how heinous it may be, and take a Daoist perspective of vanishing moral agonistic games and ritual-bound institutions? If this seems scandalous, then reconsider corporate criminality and golden parachutes. Even a public employee may be handsomely paid off for bullying behavior unbecoming of his office. The former chancellor of the State University of New York was forced to resign and received a year-long paid leave (over $400,000) plus a guaranteed professorship in one of the 64 SUNY Political Science departments. He will be collecting about three times the annual salary of a tenured professor.

In Praise of Accountability?

Acclaimed RJ proponent Danielle Sered describes the mission of Common Justice, a New York City-based organization in the following way:

> Accountability requires five key elements: (1) acknowledging responsibility for one's actions; (2) acknowledging the impact of one's actions on others; (3) expressing genuine remorse; (4) taking actions to repair the harm to the degree possible, and guided when feasible by the people harmed, or "doing sorry"; and (5) no longer committing similar harm.
>
> (2017, p. 17)

Sered's five steps of accountability work are plausible, especially given her proven record working with young people. Doing accountability work has become the credo of many organizations that own the label abolitionism or transformative justice. Mariame Kaba, a leader in the transformative justice and abolition movement in the United States, hails Sered's approach and her book as a blueprint for our time. Indeed, *Until We Reckon: Violence, Mass Incarceration, and a Road to Repair* (Sered, 2018) presents a compelling approach to alternative dispute resolution mechanism. Sered initiated the Common Justice project which tackles the underlying causes of violent behavior among young people and is highly critical of the criminalizing penal system. As such, Danielle Sered presents RJ as being firmly rooted *outside* the system. In practice, the organization is a court diversion service. I mention Sered's work in this chapter (rather than in the previous one), because it points to the difficulty of separating RJ praxis from abolitionist, transformative justice ideals (cf. Harris, 2007). Moreover, Sered articulates accountability principles which are common to RJ groups, and, increasingly, in queer people of color abolitionist circles (Magnani & Wray, 2006; Brazzell 2018; Dixon & Piepzna-Samarasinha, 2020). Yet, I find that her five-step program is an *individualist* one, putting the complete burden upon the 'responsible person.'

The road to repair between court-involved persons and the harmed involves a lengthy accountability process. In addition, her organization provides wraparound services for survivors (p. 134). Interestingly, Sered briefly references Elizabeth Kübler-Ross' five stages of grief with respect to those who harmed having to do their own healing work (p. 125). And there is even a brief gesture toward Ubuntu promising relationship-building and communal support (p. 105). Throughout the book, she presents a passionate critique of the prison system from a utilitarian perspective: a prison sentence takes a person out of their community and eliminates any hope for the 'responsible party' of actually taking responsibility. Her organization Common Justice received start-up funding from the Vera Institute, a New York City-based prison reform nongovernmental organization (NGO). Working within the establishment has brought Sered national recognition and an award by then-US attorney general Eric Holder.

Common Justice provides a model for meaningful decarceration work in its intervention and wraparound service for youth. For this diversion, the youth have to stay with the program within a 15-month period. Sered's organization works with young people who committed acts of (street) violence but does not provide programming for those accused of sexual or intimate partner violence (pp. 133–4). In one case, a young man accused of several hate crimes was also not eligible for support and got a prison sentence instead (p. 115). It is also unclear if the organization accepts participants who have substance use challenges. What if celebrated youth-centered organizations did not differentiate and invited all to apply, including those accused of committing sexual or gender-based transgressions? In a way, it means that abolitionist work is deferred because these young people are deemed too risky (to funders? to staff? to the courts?) and incorrigible or disposable—best served by the dungeons that the criminal legal system always supplies.

Common Justice prides itself for focusing on survivors' needs. For instance, in one case, a young man, Pablo, received their assistance for over one year and one day asked Sered how many cops work in New York City? She replied that there are 35,000. He then asked how many staff work at her organization Common Justice. Six people. "Pablo said, *That's hilarious.* I asked why. And he said, *Well, because it was y'all who could keep me safe*" (p. 82). Six people could promise enduring safety for an adolescent, where a protective order *and*

35,000 people sworn "to protect and serve" failed Pablo. Pablo's 'mistake' was to call the police on Alberto and his friends, and they reacted by beating up his brother, when they did not find Pablo at home. Committed to RJ, Sered showcases Pablo's victimization to argue that survivors receive emotional and material support from her organization rather than through the courts.

In another case, Sered profiles Donnell, one of its star clients, who now works as youth coordinator for the organization. She outlined his tailored, *mandatory* program which included some 30 action items. Some of them focused on doing repair work with the person whom he harmed such as an apology letter and group sessions, while many others were dedicated to personal emotional support and growth—writing a resume, keeping a journal (p. 144). Several of these items are geared toward self-empowerment and about navigating white supremacist, elitist public spaces, e.g., where young people such as Donnell are trained to dress professionally for court appearances. But what happens with those who do not comply with the mandated program? We learn that only 6% of the court-referred cases are terminated because of new criminal convictions (p. 134). But we do not learn how many get terminated by the organization for noncompliance with the negotiated accountability work, which is centered on the victimized party and is very emotionally demanding as well as time intensive, since the mandatory programming involves a violence intervention program in addition to the RJ process (*Ibid.*).

In the case of Trish, such threat of termination is hinted at parenthetically. Her sanction entailed using inconvenient public transport for over a year, because she caused harm to Ana on the subway. If Trish had violated the terms of the agreement that Ana requested, she would have been sent to youth prison. Ana rationalized this sanction because she, too, had to stay off the train because of acute PTSD. In addition, Trish was asked to complete programming, school, hold a job and she had to write in a daily journal what Ana must have felt in the aftermath of the attack. All ends well for both parties, because Ana's PTSD symptoms subside as soon as she begins to dialogue with Trish, and Trish is "living a healthy, productive, law-abiding life" (pp. 116–7). Successful completion of Common Justice's dual justice program means that felony charges are removed (p. 134), so, arguably, it serves as an incentive program for young people who want a 'second chance.' Is it also a kinder and gentler probation office?

Sered presents a critique of the criminal legal system, and yet her organization is bound by its regulatory system. She notes that she views transgressions as a moral issue, while the system focuses merely on crime as a legal infraction (p. 138). When young people are remanded to her organization by the courts, will they also disclose voluntarily all other kinds of harmful transgressions, in addition to the specific charge? Will those harmed parties also be invited into the circle, or would the voluntary disclosure be relayed back to the court and draw additional charges? It is unclear how the court system retains jurisdiction over the court case unless staff members are deputized as probation officers.

The organization and Sered are committed to the principles of racial equity and also note the shortcomings of RJ within a racist, misogynoir system (pp. 206). However, her disposition is neither entirely abolitionist nor wedded to a transformative justice approach. Sered famously writes a parable about a hamburger stand that sells the worst type of food within 200 miles and yet there's a line of customers who are hungry—the crux is that there is no alternative on this desolate road. Sered notes that this stand signifies the prison system and all its toxic failures it offers to a disillusioned public. Many still drive by and stay hungry (p. 46). In fact, not all serious harm is even reported as is well known about sexual assault cases, but survivors often do not even report other physical assault to the police. Common Justice tries to reach those who stand at the hamburger shop and convince them that an alternative path is possible, even while still collaborating with the shop owners (i.e., the courts, policing, and other violence workers). This is the crux of RJ approaches—still working within the system and using the system's problematic language of 'law-abiding' success stories and other terms that are wedded to the illusion that committing transgression is something that can be overcome (cf. Coyle, 2018; Coyle & Piché, 2021).

Sered argues that "[a]ccountability is the corollary to grief for those of us who are responsible for harm, and it is as essential as a grieving process is in restoring us to our best selves" (p. 128). Furthermore, she recently noted that "at Common Justice we think of accountability as an act of love. We think of accountability as a pathway to dignity" (Rice & Smith, 2019). How is accountability a corollary to *grief*? It seems a sensible proposal, especially if the accountability work comes from within. From a healing, relational perspective, grieving would be accompanied by nurturing self-forgiveness, and experienced elders, shamanic practitioners would also attend to the primary wound inflicted—lashing out is very much also a lashing out against myself.[4] Furthermore, what gets lost in Sered's account is that participation in alternatives to incarceration is not necessarily a choice, and folks submitting to the process have to "own" the shaming process: accountability's corollary may be guilt, mostly. Diversity studies experts know very well that anti-racist work gets derailed when whites participate unconsciously out of guilt. Much appraisal of community accountability does not interrogate the dimension of volition or intentionality, even though it is always assumed that participants come to the process voluntarily. Sered's justice model appeals to *mercy* cum accountability. Mercy *cannot* be granted without submission to an accountability process (p. 95). The process may even involve lifelong repair work to mend relationships. Mercy is thus given on a conditional basis, as it is granted only when the responsible party shows authentic remorse and goes through the arduous process of making amends. Mercy is also selectively granted, as the organization does not accept all cases. What if the harmed person simply short circuits the elaborate public process and grants forgiveness without demanding anything in return? Is this then a case of unsuccessful accountability work? To account for, to reckon also gets perilously close to a (risk) assessment approach, using the one metric that criminal justice experts assess and validate: a low recidivism rate, lowering school dropout and suspension rates. On the other side of the scale (of reckoning), the moral force of "doing sorry," i.e., repairing the harm—involves working through precise steps toward redemption in order to receive recognition rewards or feeling loved and dignified by the professional staff who are invested in soft retribution and trauma-informed care. From a Buddhist perspective, there is another possibility, which decouples the self from the need for soft retribution. I must find a way to still love the person who tortures me, unless I'd be guilty of dehumanizing them. Indeed, a Tibetan monk was concerned that he would adopt hateful feelings toward his Chinese captors and torturers. Meditation trains to cultivate compassion even for those who presently harm the body (Begley, 2009).

While love can be withheld, dignity is not something to be granted or restored, it is an inalienable good. However, this has little value in US jurisprudence, as human dignity is not even enshrined as a value in the federal or state constitutions, except in Montana (cf. Jackson, 2004). As Evelin Lindner advocates:

> A future of dignity, a future beyond systemic humiliation, is within our reach. Equal dignity in loving solidarity—what I call *dignism*—can become reality. It may sound like utopia and it is utopia. Global dignism, however, is a necessary utopia, a *eutopia*, and it remains necessary even if the probability of its realisation is small. Humankind's survival depends on this eutopia. The alternative is environmental collapse and a militarised world that ends in mutual destruction.
>
> (2022, p. 427)

The case of Trish's legal requirements seems to be at the crossroads of vindictiveness and teaching a lesson—toward what end? Perhaps to earn dignity points? Sered (and Kaba, 2021) may think that accountability work which includes sanctions is not considered punishment, but in Trish's case, during that one year on 'probation,' if she had slipped even once (say, taking the subway to get to work on time), she would have faced a prison term. Accountability work is supposed to be voluntary, and it is unclear how it can be counted as such. Secondly, it seems to be an illustration of Braithwaite's model of reintegrative shaming and arguably retributive. Trish had to mimic Ana who refrained from taking subways because of the harm she had endured; furthermore, Trish had to keep a diary about her introspective work, which was read by the staff and evaluated for signs of progress (i.e., moving from denial, anger, to acceptance of responsibility) (pp. 114–8). Sered recognizes that shame is a driver of violence and says that the only way out of shame is accountability (p. 126). Her reintegrative shame model is questionable as it may lead to more humiliation. On the other hand, John Braithwaite (2011) holds that acts of apologies and forgiveness are gifts that cannot be demanded.

They are "emerging values" that may come about through the restorative process (p. 349). Such values differ from "constraining values" such as respectful listening, non-domination, empowerment, equal concern for all stakeholders, appealability, accountability, and freedom from racist and sexist oppression (p. 348).

Is it the case that both those who are harmed and have harmed and their respective advocates and pod members could get equal play, equal compassion, and that care is taken to minimize shaming practices and rituals? In the spirit of ludic transformative justice, I argue that another path be a practice of a humble acknowledgment of a plethora of reasons for the harm and focus on forward-looking practices such as acceptance, unconditional forgiveness, love, and healing.

Demanding apologies and accountability replete with encouraging remorseful emotions are still tethered to a backward-looking retributive justice model which also depends on the illusionary free will which determines culpability. When we understand the reasons of the act, then we may literally excuse the actor for their wrongdoing. Perhaps we might want to muse with Joshua Greene and Jonathan Cohen that neuroscience "will change these moral intuitions [regarding retribution and desert] by undermining the intuitive, libertarian conceptions of free will on which retributivism depends" (2004, p. 1783). They use neuroscience as a proxy for a spiritual all-knowing point of view that renders all judgment into a compassionate forgiveness (*Ibid.*). Love (*agape*), according to Martin Luther King, imbued with power, implements "the demands of justice, and justice at its best is love correcting everything that stands against love." King, who called himself an extremist for love, urges his audience to realize that "power without love is reckless and abusive, and love without power is sentimental and anemic" (1986, pp. 246–7). For those who critiqued the Black Power Movement as destructive, King answers that such protest is justified where it maintains its moral compass, directed at the needs of the beloved community. In its contemporary expression, from Moral Mondays which engendered a national poor people's campaign (2013) to Black Lives Matter protests of police brutality (2014), King's words ring true as righteous indignation against systemic violence and using peaceful protests to imagine a more just and loving society. A moving example of poetic indignation is by an artist who sports a t-shirt with the emblazoned motto "love terrorist" in a flash mob protest in New York City's Times Square facing police headquarters. In his spoken word requiem for the slain African American Eric Garner, Daniel J. Watts voices despair and hope for a better world for Black men like him. In the background, a choir of mostly Black artists from Broadway hum rhythmically to support his cries for change (Watts *et al.*, 2014). As King's letter to the white clergy from a Birmingham jail cell reveals, his extremism for love faced condemnation and continues to be a revolutionary stance. And, of course, King became an early target of Federal Bureau of Investigation (FBI) surveillance and smear campaigns.

As has been amply pointed out by critics, restorative programs do not deal with structural injustice—they offer solutions within an unjust world and calls it justice. The focus is on individuals who do harm and *not* excuse the situations that brought about the harm. Special attention is paid to those categorized as victims and what their needs and wants are, so that RJ is foremost about centering victims' voices. Thus, RJ, at least in the Western and European context, is about correcting the wrong of silencing the victim in the court room where the prosecution 'impersonates' the will of the victim and demands harsh retribution. Yet, such reactive measure might be shortsightedly punitive since the courts overly empower victims. After all, they are afforded impact statements at sentencing, on the witness stand, and at parole hearings, they may present petitions against release and even speak about their safety needs, etc., often affecting the outcome.

What might be some other drawbacks of community accountability? Kai Cheng Thom notes how a community accountability process may backfire on all involved:

> Having been witness to many community accountability processes that have seemed to create more harm for those involved, I must emphasize that survivor-led does not mean that those who identify as survivors are necessarily experts in transformative justice, not that the identified survivor in a dynamic of abuse should get to dictate what happens to the identified abuser.
>
> (cited in Dixon & Piepzna-Samarasinha, 2020, p. 74)

The INCITE! Collective uncovers oppressive communicative tools that maintain power and control in progressive accountability groups. Building on their analysis, the Respons Kollektiv in Germany provides corrective guidelines for successful dialogues that avoid denial, minimizing, manipulation, or victim-blaming (Brazzell, 2018, pp. 130–40). These are important steps to take to foreclose a cycle of humiliation. Indigenous justice reminds us that we are all related and interconnected.

Most transformative justice organizations invoke a "call-out" culture to address individual wrongdoing by a community member. The person committing the harm needs to be educated about such harm and show that they will resolve not to commit any such harm in the future. They call it accountability work. How is it different, affectively and content-wise, from RJ that demands apology coupled with restitution instead of imprisonment?

If it is the case that proponents of the accountability paradigm have a multilevel sanctions process involving shunning and public shaming, in addition to demanding redress, might it not be dangerously close to an "abolitionist retribution paradigm" that Reznik (2019) favors? In fact, in a lot of cases that illustrate community accountability processes, we see 'small t' transformations that resemble RJ practices, rather than bringing significant healing to a community and contributing to systemic changes (cf. Harris, 2007, p. 565).

Three approaches to consider:

1 Accountability demand to tackle institutional forms of oppression such as policing, medical neglect, corporate criminality such as wage theft and union busting.
2 At the individual, interpersonal level, abolishing harm is not possible. At best, one can train disrupters of violence to minimize harm. Community accountability is touted among penal abolitionists, but such process can take years, meanwhile an individual's integrity is tested daily, and they are confronted with daily slights, rejections, and triggering events that release toxic shame reactions. Transgressions continue to occur, never mind the success stories of RJ; these behaviors may be of a different kind or are eventually decriminalized (e.g., loitering, being unhoused, street work, requesting change, sex work, smoking cannabis).
3 In a postsecular world, other modalities to dealing with interpersonal harm are possible. Shamanic intervention and a healing approach to harm or even an artistic and humorous approach of ludic Ubuntu can bring novel dimension to transformative justice. Here, the scapegoat is a heuristic device to deposit known transgressions and be cleansed of them (see Figure 5.1). Indigenous examples include the Hawai'ian justice concept of Ho'oponopono, the Lakota Circle of Life, and the Acholi's model of Mato Oput.

Ruth Morris notes that accountability work often reverts to RJ demands that an "offense" is time-stamped and dealt with in isolation. All the examples given in Sered's book speak to this singular isolated 'treatment.' Morris (2000) argues that RJ "still accepts the idea that one event now defines all that matters of right and wrong—it leaves out the past, and the social causes of all events" (p. 4).

Shifting from Trauma-Informed Care to Healing-Informed Care

Thus, I want to propose that transformative justice makes no demands to parties to come together to exert specific sanction, a playbook of counting up dozens of 'payback' activities—even though they may be hugely valuable for the participants as illustrated in Sered's narratives, for the potential of personal reflection, introspection, and growth. Transformative justice is in the service of *healing* dimensions and thus stands outside the "clinical" framework of enumerating deeds, misdeeds, errant behavior, and serious harm.

Praising an accountability process forecloses a deeper 'reckoning' with abolitionist philosophy associated with truly transformative and ludic justice praxis. The former is stuck in an individualist ideology that is backward-looking, finding fault with decisions that have a 'time-stamp,' usually focusing on a specific transgression in space and time. It is troubling that most abolitionist theorists and organizations have bought into this linear framework of personal responsibility while denying that accountability work is anything like sanctions or punishment. What has been left behind is a recognition that environmental causes play a huge role; at the same time, it is interesting that defense attorneys might use psychologists' evaluation referencing Adverse Childhood Experiences (ACE) scores to negotiate more lenient sentences, given that the accused witnessed violence (cf. Levenson *et al.*, 2017; 2016). Is this a moment of squaring the circle? Is it not contradictory to employ ACE scores to buttress the role of the environment and minimize the role of individual culpability while, nevertheless, demanding that the harmer undergo a self-scrutiny on why they acted in a harmful way and how they will pay it forward?

Trauma-informed care resonates with the backward-looking project of accountability work. Asked about racial progress in the United States, Malcolm X famously mentioned that if you stick a nine-inch knife into a person's back and pull it out some six inches, it is not a sign of progress. It is not even progress to pull out the knife completely since a festering wound needs to be attended to. Only when the wound is closed, progress has a chance. His prognosis also resonates with Indigenous people in settler colonial countries (e.g., New Zealand, Australia, United States, and Canada). They have the highest rate of incarceration of Black and Indigenous peoples, and excarceration (i.e., pulling out the knife) has not happened anywhere, let alone land reclamation. ACEs from an anti-racist perspective are imperfect in giving a complete diagnosis of the intergenerational trauma which affects "bodies of culture," as Resmaa Menakem lovingly describes Black people. He appeals to somatic abolitionism which is an "embodied anti-racist practice and process of culture building." All bodies, practically,

> are infected by the virus of white-body supremacy [WBS]. This virus was created by human beings in a laboratory—the Virginia Assembly, in 1691—then let loose upon our continent. It quickly infected people of all colors, backgrounds, and economic circumstances. Today, the WBS virus remains with us—in the air we breathe, the water we drink, the foods we eat, the institutions that govern us, and the social contracts under which we live. Most of all, though, it lives in our bodies.

Somatic Abolitionism gives us the "wisdom of human bodies respecting, honoring, and resonating with other human bodies" (Menakem, n.d.) Menakem addresses the need for healing in an Ubuntu, relational way. ACEs do not tackle the daily interaction with WBS unleashed upon bodies of culture in the form of microaggressions (insults, assaults, and invalidations). ACEs do not address what it feels like when a cop flags you down, invades your home, and stops your car.

The collective SOS, affiliated with the Audre Lorde Project, Brooklyn, New York, devised a protocol for taking safety measures when hosting parties. The collective empowers queer Black folks to train members in violence intervention and prevention; they have alternative emergency phone numbers, so that if people are harmed, they can call the number to get taken to the hospital, etc. At all costs, police contact is avoided, and if police show up, there are folks who will be able to engage with them, so that nobody gets arrested (Rodriguez, 2021). Penal abolition is envisioned as "ridding the community not only of institutions of violence and corrections but also of the perpetual punishment of African bodies in the United States. It means enabling life-affirming institutions and practices that rehumanize us after slavery and colonization" (Rodriguez, 2022, p. 179). S.M. Rodriguez clarifies that SOS' community-focused work focuses on self-healing (not self-loathing), and thus it does not cater to traditional forms of RJ that prizes personal accountability. Such abolitionist work also pivots toward holding state institutions accountable that cause harm. They note that "[r]etribution is not a form of justice; it is a recapitulation of violence" (Rodriguez, 2021, p. 195).

Within social work, especially court-mandated services, trauma-informed care is now becoming increasingly popular. However, it still focuses on DSM[5]-generated labeling of a person living with a mental illness. From a shamanic Indigenous perspective, this makes little sense. Such labeling is actually considered harmful and often trained experts come with implicit bias and arrogant, judging attitudes, especially when they have to work with those labeled "sex offenders." Geral Blanchard (2012; 2020) has worked in Western and Indigenous settings around the world and shares refreshing perspectives about shamanic wisdom that make his method more akin to healing-informed care. In *The Difficult Connection: The Therapeutic Relationship in Sex Offender Treatment* (2012), he even suggests that such relationship be respectful and allow for playfulness and laughter. It is important to be compassionate and humanize the relationship and not set oneself apart but tune in to the vulnerability of the other. Indigenous ways of knowing share the wisdom of reciprocity, of looking at oppressive aspects in oneself, where one has gone horribly wrong, mistreating other beings, human or nonhuman animals, or other sentient beings. Relational, community-based care takes time and is not set in a clinical office, where the stranger-expert dictates the terms of engagement in a scripted way. In fact, Indigenous healers asked Blanchard (2020), why his society cages so many patients, when it clearly makes them more aggressive but does not treat sex addiction or harmful behavior. An African shamanic healer, Malidoma Patrice Somé (1997), equally expressed horror at visiting someone in a mental hospital, and he found Western modalities quite primitive. These are wedded to a Cartesian metaphysics, Newtonian physics, and Kantian transcendental analytic; in other words, very much enmeshed in a limited three-dimensional ideology. By contrast, Somé is quite aware of what the patient, who presents as neurodiverse to the experts in white coats, actually needs. Subsequently, he brought several folks to his country and used shamanic healing to harmonize so that they would be comfortable for working in higher dimensions as well as traveling to lower dimensions. Even putting his work into English descriptors feels inadequate, but it is certainly not romanticizing the Indigenous way of healing that is common to healers across continents.

Healing-informed care is forward-looking, and as such it focuses on a caring, non-judgmental, compassionate relation in community that establishes a foundation for belonging and letting go of trauma, i.e., a backward-looking focus (Blanchard, 2022). What Blanchard does not address but certainly practices is that such healing perspectives are necessarily postsecular. His work goes beyond those of his expert peers who are still wedded to the trauma-informed care philosophy in Safer Society. Safer Society was established by Faye Honey Knopp, the lead author of *Instead of Prisons* (1976), one of the first prison abolitionist books. She made it her calling to work with those labeled as disposable people, and Safer Society is still devoted to her philosophy today. In *Instead of Prisons*, she outlines many successful excarceration programs. One of them features a couple in San Francisco, California—the husband had been caged for a sex addiction and founded a group with others—Sex Offenders Anonymous: they persuaded judges to release men to them to provide peer support (p. 153). But since then, draconian laws have been instituted to mark those stamped with the "SO" label (i.e., "sex offender") still civilly dead, as their addresses are published online along with photos. They cannot live in a certain radius of schools, and they tend to have very long parole conditions (of post-carceral penal supervision). Some get lifelong post-conviction sentences in institutions that are considered 'civil confinement,' but they are really prisons. From a shamanic perspective, this is primitive adjudication, as the person will never receive healing, and since sexual violence continues to be a serious epidemic in Western societies, vulnerable children and adults do not feel safer. Do we abolish the DSM manual, the 'Bible' of psychologists and psychiatrists, otherwise known as 'the book of insults,' and do we need to have an abolitionist lens toward psychiatric and social work? Indeed—if these disciplines continue to freeze-frame and further harm people, abolition of this clinical *modus operandi* is what is needed today. It is important to remember that court-and-prison-appointed psychologists work for institutions (such as the courts, the family regulation system) and *not* for those shamed, labeled, and medicalized with psychotropic drugs that benefit corporate pharma.

Experiencing Ludic Ubuntu Justice through Performance Art

Taking their cue from the French Situationists, Jacques Lesage de la Haye, formerly incarcerated French psychoanalyst and anarchist penal abolitionist, shares that he helped shut down a psychiatric ward in a prison where he had worked as psychologist. Later he worked for some 30 years to close the notorious asylum at Ville-Évrard which used to house over 2,000 patients and now still has some 400 beds for patients of all ages. In an interview, Lesage de la Haye explains the outlandish acts of resistance undertaken by his Asylum Information Group, in the radical tradition of Frantz Fanon. The goal was clearly an attack on psychiatry: eliminate the straitjackets, open the asylum, and stop the deadly treatments:

> That leads to the deconstruction of the asylum. We started up a whole bunch of wacky activities: we invited musicians and started bands with the patients. Crazy stuff: forty-five harpists, the drummer from Taxi Girl, hard rock, punk, pop bands, all on the grounds of Ville-Évrard. One patient, Farid …, told me, "This singer is crazy, Jacques. I'm not crazy, but him!" It was amazing, three hundred people, nurses, patients, musicians. We made a whole mess for thirty-one years up to my retirement …
>
> (Lesage de la Haye, 2021, p. 116)

A good abolitionist mess, certainly. And I ask: where does one find on harpist, let alone 45?

S. Leigh Thompson, a diversity educator who studied with Agosto Boal, brought theater of the oppressed, to SUNY Cortland in 2016. I just share one memorable example. A lead student is selected to be in the center of the circle. His hand pair up with two other people who are also paired with two others, respectively. Except for the leader, everyone else must stare into one hand of the person, they are paired up with. When the leader makes any move, it makes a ripple effect concentrically—all our bodily movements are affected. A veritable dance of a puppeteer. Every action creates a ripple reaction and shows the powerful web of oppression. Those in the outer rings see very little what goes on in the inner circle. So, they blame the person in front of them for their 'misery.' To me, it also showcases from a shamanic perspective that our words carry on in relational ways and through time and space dimensions, including the ancestors and not-yet-born. Being in this enacted web of oppression, the body feels restricted movement, and the mind erases any possibility for opting out—do I know why the caged bird sings? I react to my own limitation by picking on another, who must move their body along the way my hand commands. It feels as if we were in magnetic relation with each other, and it gives us a limited, myopic field of vision as I only see my hand interact with another, and I must pay attention where my face needs to move at the will of my 'oppressor.' This exercise also externalizes what highly sensitive empaths who have mirror-touch synesthesia or emotional contagion deal with every day.

To bring in another ludic example, envisioning Ubuntu justice, penal abolitionist artist Mikah Bazant creates cities of refuge, places of love for transformative justice (Figure 5.1).

A transgression memory exercise may be helpful reminding ourselves that it is all too human to put into sharp relief hurt and pain from humiliating

Figure 5.1 "Miklat."
Source: www.micahbazant.com/miklat-miklat/, printed with permission from Mikah Bazant.

childhood experiences, where we have faced harm. However, what of those faint memories that play up the transgressor side in us? It would be a good exercise to commit to paper, as Bazant suggests, of harmful behavior, especially that which never faced a police officer or other authority figure who threatened to turn us over. It is also a stark reminder that over 90% of humans commit serious transgressions during our life, but few of us ever face a criminal trial for these (Figure 5.2).

> The root of the modern scapegoat concept is an ancient ritual in which the community was cleansed by placing their transgressions onto a goat, which was then sacrificed or led out to die in the wilderness.
>
> Another strategy of dealing with social transgression, also described in the Torah, are the Cities of Refuge, or Arei Miklat. In theory, a person accused of a serious crime could flee to a city of refuge and live a full life, safe from violent retribution. This imperfect model of the cities of refuge was a starting point to imagine how we can create sanctuaries, transformative justice, and healing, even in a world where we are both scapegoats and participate in scapegoating.
>
> This piece was a way to create a concrete and metaphysical City of Refuge, and then to invite the goat inside the city.
>
> (Bazant, n.d.)

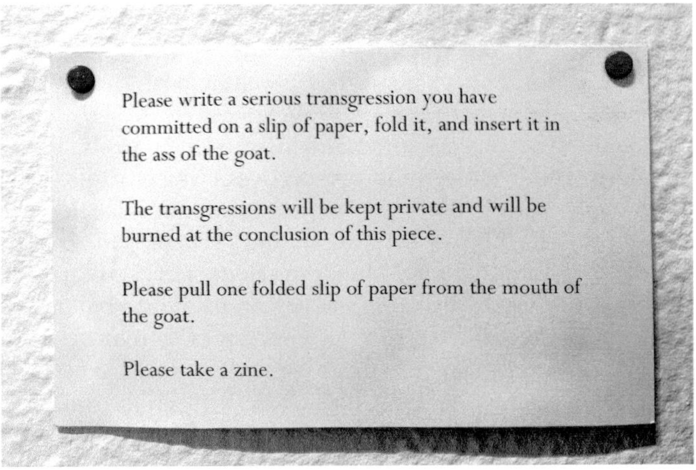

Figure 5.2 Instruction for "The Scapegoat."
Source: www.micahbazant.com/miklat-miklat/, printed with permission from Micah Bazant.

Bazant brings to light something that often gets lost in conflict mediation discussions: to scapegoat others and being scapegoated are two sides of the same coin. Many examples from organizations committed to transformative justice have processes to expel someone to a 'city of refuge.' This is especially true for those who caused harm through sexual assault or intimate partner violence. What might be powerful examples of inviting them back after a period of time?

Why is forgetting problematized by those who advocate for alternative dispute mechanisms? With a good dose of muted outrage, one exclaims: "I will forgive, but I won't forget!" There is an energetic charge or grudge hanging on to this promise, which will certainly prolong the hurt, trauma, suffering in oneself. Why prescribe punishment as a cure to a harmed person who is reacting to haunted past by harming others? As H. Odera Oruka (1976) argues Western juridical systems continue to be a resounding failure as long as there is a search for wrong origins of criminality such as culpability and responsibility. For what? And why? The right origins search would be to look for the underlying causes of criminal behavior and to eliminate the criminal forces or factors:

> People dealing with such treatment should investigate or study the psychology, physiology, economic background, heredity, the environment, etc., of the criminal. Having collected enough data from such a study, they will then be able to understand the personality or the character of their patient, the criminal.
>
> (*Ibid.*, p. 88)

At that point, the patient (note, not the criminal) will be ready for treatment. Oruka outright rejects punishment because it is a primitive solution. It gets worse when punishment means residing in a secluded cell, away from human touch and sociality. It amounts to prescribed psychological torture enforced by legal terrorism, i.e., the state (p. 108).

It is also valuable to reconsider a therapeutic model on explaining causation or culpability from Indigenous perspectives, which stress behavior rather than label. If someone had a 'psychotic' experience or is labeled 'schizophrenic,' they are prescribed heavy medication and perhaps sent to a psychiatric or forensic prison for a lifetime. Malidoma Somé (1997) offers another view that focuses on healing by bringing the person back into balance, using rituals that work with the 'afflicted' person's ancestors to remove pain and imbalances. While not endorsing rituals, even professional bodies such as the British Psychological Society have distanced themselves from the efficacy of labels (Cooke, 2004). On the other hand, labeling may serve a critical purpose to understand how traumatic bodily injuries may lead to violent expressions. Phillip Adams shot six people to death and turned the gun on himself in 2021. He played football for two decades and was denied medical treatment and settlement payment by the league. Unbeknown to his family, he developed a severe degenerative brain disease [chronic traumatic encephalopathy (CTE)], and among its symptoms are violent mood swings and memory loss (Hernandez, 2021).

Letting go of a memory could be likened to a filtering and cleansing technique. Could it not be aided in a holistic healing manner, e.g., assisting the traumatized body at the cellular level, e.g., through multimodal approaches? In Western modality, sight has primacy, while healing practices emphasize touch, sound, and smell. Some may benefit from olfactory therapy, expressing their needs through inhaling essential oils, subtly alluded to in Biblical scriptures as herbs or spices (frankincense, spikenard, cedar, etc.). It can be stressful when trauma is stuck in the body and cannot be transmuted and when it continues to trigger an emotional stress response (fear, suffering, panic) amounting to nothing less than toxic stress which the body holds in memory. Forgiving is an art of fore-gifting (with a nod to Derrida), of letting go so that I can receive a release. Releasing and cleansing is the gift to oneself.

Forgiveness and Ludic Ubuntu in the Indigenous Wisdom Traditions

The Hawai'ian Justice Concept of Ho'oponopono

Ludic Ubuntu ethics also has a contemplative and spiritual aspect, which is best illustrated by Indigenous conflict resolution practices. Rather than struggling against prison authorities, the ludic spirit may be revealed through qualities of mindful surrender, forgiveness, and compassion for the other. The Hawai'ian justice concept of Ho'oponopono illustrates what may transpire when one embraces the scapegoat. Introspection and self-reflection are prized values in Indigenous cultures. Words have power, and silences are valued. Scholar Malcolm Nāea Chun notes that pono is the most important virtue or value in Hawaii (Chun, 2006a; 2006b).

Pono is a core Hawaiian virtue, which refers to living the balanced way, doing what is right by the community writ large. Its opposite is *hewa* (concerning acts of theft, murder, and even wasting food) and both describe other-regarding actions. Pono is not only right action but also good character—a state of being: "It was pono when one's eyes saw something and one's heart desired it, but one was ho'omanawanui [patient] and did not go to take it, but quickly left forgetting about it without even touching it. This was pono" (Davida Malo, cited in Chun, 2006a, p. 10). A good leader who follows pono is one who can say at the moment before passing on: "Try as you may, you will not be able to undo the good I have done!" Such a *mensch* was King Kamehameha who uttered these last words (Chun, 2006a, p. 18).

A chief's greedy character is especially problematic on an island where food has to be carefully and generously distributed among all. Ha-la-e-a was a notorious chief who demanded the entire daily catch of fish from some of the fishermen, feasted on it, and threw away leftovers. After a while, the people's council convened and decided that all fish would be deposited into the chief's canoe and the dozen or so fishermen would all turn their back (and canoes) on him. After some five canoes emptied their load, the chief's canoe began to sink, and still more fishermen unloaded despite his protests with the words: "Here is all the fish that the chief desires!" His greedy request not only exiled him but ushered in his death sentence (Kawaharada, 2006). This may also serve as parable of settler colonialism and its ecological footprint: the catastrophic carelessness and gluttony that marks global ecocide—burning down rainforests, fossil fuel extraction, and industrial fishing, covering more than 55% of ocean surface (Gibson, 2018). Indigenous Hawai'ians did not overfish. They respected the balance, practicing ecological justice. Each clan had a connection to a specific totemic animal, say, a sea creature who they were forbidden to eat, because they believed that an ancestor's spirit inhabited it. Conservation was paramount, and a chief advised to fish only at certain times of the year. Dividing the catch also followed protocol of fairness and generosity toward all parties involved in fishing as well as hospitality toward strangers (Kawaharada, 2006). There is no great chain of being, dictating separation between species including plant beings, but all are connected in the web of life. Such sacred beliefs of interconnection of life and totemic bonds are also shared among the Bamana of the Mande world (Kone, 2023, forthcoming). What happens when transgression occurs disturbing the balance?

Ho'oponopono is an emphatic "doubling effort" of restoring *pono*; its practice is invoked to make it right again and bring conflicting parties together for a healing and reconciliation ceremony. To heal means to "give life," repairing the fractured bonds between two people, families, or a large community. It begins with "[d]eep and clear understanding, appreciation, and awareness of pono" (Chun, 2006b, pp. 19–20). Mary Kawana Pukui was instrumental in resurrecting the practice in the 1950s. and the Queen Lili'uokalani Children's Center provided the institutional support. Pukui calls it is a mental cleansing: "clearing the mind of a sick person by family discussion, examination, and prayer" (Chun, 2006b, p. 5). It is significant that the focus initially is not on a transgression, but on examining feelings of guilt, hurt, and resentment in the human being suffering of an ailment and the emotional states of their entire family. Spirits may have brought on a sickness and a traditional healer needs to understand all this in a holistic way before preparing medicine. The process also brings into relief that the focus is not about casting blame on somebody but about restoring harmonious relationships and healing; such communal process is focused on present and future (i.e., forward-looking ethics). Traditionally, ho'oponopono was not to be used in resolving violent and abusive conflict; this was the domain of the chiefs (Chun, 2006b, p. 20). Similarly, in Rwanda, as noted in Chapter 4, Gacaca practices focused on minor transgression and conflict in precolonial times, while the king would be involved in major and violent events. This is also true in the case of Inkundla/Lekgotla forum led by a council of elders and sub-chiefs. If the disputes were of a different magnitude, the king would get involved (Murithi, 2006b; Issifu, 2015).

Unique about the ho'oponopono practice in family conflicts is that one takes turns in a victim/harmer dyad, assuming the position of the other in pretend-play may lead to mutual apologies. Rendering mutual forgiveness is also a desired outcome in order to move beyond the conflict. In addition, they may perform a type of "family constellation" ritual, putting absent relatives in their rightful place, using stones as placeholders. Participants will then bow their heads in front of the stone, asking the relative for forgiveness, expressing love for them, and thanking them. German practitioners of alternative conflict resolution will recognize such practice resembling Hellinger's family constellations, where the person trying to heal from conflict chooses audience members as placeholders for an absent family member (Duprée, 2017).

What happens to the scapegoat? Through this ludic interplay, there is a deeper understanding that all are connected, including the ancestors of both parties; resolving personal conflict necessitates finding an intergenerational resolution and bringing peace to the ancestors and not-yet born.

Hawai'i has Aloha Spirit law in its Constitution (similar to Ubuntu in South Africa's Constitution), and it can be used to rein in *haole* property claims. The government must grant Indigenous people access and rights to worship on vacant land. It is worth to consider the virtue ethics embedded in the Hawai'ian Constitution:

> Akahai, meaning kindness to be expressed with tenderness;
> Lōkahi, meaning unity, to be expressed with harmony;
> 'Olu'olu, meaning agreeable, to be expressed with pleasantness;
> Ha'aha'a, meaning humility, to be expressed with modesty;
> Ahonui, meaning patience, to be expressed with perseverance.

In some spiritual, modified practices, it is also a ritual to get in touch with sorrow, grief, and reflect on hurt feelings by adopting a process of self-forgiveness and self-love. Such practice is not soul-searching for guilt; rather it is about healing and restoring balance within such that it may resonate outward and touch the hearts of others involved in hurtful encounters. The traditional ho'oponopono also acknowledges that resentment or grudge is a deep-seated hurtful emotion and a circular, repeated approach toward healing (uncovering layers upon layers) may be necessary. It occurs in some six stages, moving from entanglement, to stating the problem, removing the poison, sitting in silence, offering confession and apology, to a final release and letting go (*hihia, kukulu kumuhana, mahiki, ho'omalu, mihi, kala*) (Chun, 2006b, p. 24). Setting something right means that I get to untangle the knots (mistakes) of my fishing net and try anew to tie new robust knots, treating all relations as sacred and equally important (cf. Chun, p. 27). The fishing net remains a powerful metaphor to showcase that the web of life is a social dynamic activity and a way of being.

It resonates with Desmond Tutu's explanation of Ubuntu ethics, as seeking out what potential harming is in each of us. This may make us connect in a more compassionate manner to somebody depicted as the 'worst of the worst.' The focus is on healing-informed care for all involved in the community, rather than the Western modality of trauma-informed practice that is individualist and survivor-focused and, importantly, attended to by licensed specialists. Increasingly, ho'oponopono involves professionals (religious figures, social workers, lawyers), yet, Pukui would have rejected such professionalization, as the connection to a cultural family practice would be lost (Chun, 2006b, p. 23).

Indigenous approaches vary with respect to the need of forgiveness for setting in motion transformative justice. However, repairing relations has primacy. Among the Diné people, there is no word for apology—rather, the sorrow is expressed in a way of asking for forgiveness, because the other has the power to do so. Diné historian and elder Wally Brown says:

> Among our Diné there is a code of conduct. A code or philosophy that requires one to be kind and forgiving as well as charitable. *Jijooba'á* and *Hijooba'á*. These two words sound very similar. One means to forgive and let go of any ill will. The other means to give freely when others are seeking your help.
>
> (Brown, 2021)

From a Western perspective, it looks as if there is a great deal of burden put on the one who is victimized. Brown counsels that the Diné people treasure the circle of life, relationality, charity, harmony, and letting go of past grudges.

Sociocentric versus Ego-Centric Justice—Returning to the Relational Horizon of the Medicine Wheel

Belonging (to the cycle/circle of life) is positioned in a dynamic opposite to independence—a self-recognition that I can learn to fail and experience, so that I can master my skills and hone my talents, still being connected to the whole—through generosity, gift-giving to others. Belonging to Mother Earth (or, to a deity Ani, for the Igbo people), to one's pod or community is foundational for nurturing one's 'peace gene.' Under a watchful elder, a toddler's arduous learning of building and destroying sandcastles is an attempt of playing human, embodying individuation. There are no plastic baby walkers accelerating infant development (cf. Eddy & Moradian, 2018). In the moral sphere, elders take care to assist younger ones so that personal slights may not turn into a cycle of humiliation and (self)destruction. And it is up to the kinship network and the community to remind the group member of one's connection to the whole. Michael McCullough, author of *Beyond Revenge: The Evolution of the Forgiveness Instincts* (2008), claims that there are blueprints for both revenge and forgiveness that are expressed differently, say, in the Western box versus cycle of life. He suggests that both empathy and vengeance are hardwired. However, I want to argue that the "peace gene" is connected to a primordial and fundamental need for belonging. When that "instinct" is disrupted and the child is cut off nested care, she internalizes and magnifies feelings of fear, anger, ignorance, and greed of the Western box. So, revenge thinking develops in the social context from a profound sense of not-belonging and not-being-loved. The Lakota sociocentric cosmology and the Iroquois nations' Great Law of Peace showcase that peaceful societies prepare children for the path of harmony, for ecological balance, and for kindness toward strangers. The Western box provides ideological justification for thinking of vengeance as co-equal with empathy (at the cognitive, abstract level). But such cognition ignores that childhood is not experienced (in general) as nested. Violent games of separation teach a child that independence means adversarial positioning against a group or joining them in fear of being hurt and humiliated, which spurs the child and teenager on to fight back and overwhelm the other. Rage is the key to such games, not aligning thought and feeling to note that I am never separated from another—when they feel hurt, I am hurt. Dignity is not an abstract concept, but a relational one, when one has experienced a nested, loving childhood.

Among the Lakota, women play an important role to hold families together even during the onslaught of white supremacist genocidal policies such as the "missionary" boarding school imprisonment. The women show quiet fortitude and resistance to deeply repressive practices. When a young girl complained to her mother that she was prohibited from speaking her language, her mother's advice was: "whisper!" (Marshall, 2001, p. 172). The outlaw regime across North America was so far-reaching that all customary practices (language, religion, kinship relations, subsistence work) were criminalized, yet Indigenous peoples continued to persist with their resistant, fugitive knowledge. A mother who shielded her child from kidnapping by US or Canadian government "social welfare" forces committed a criminal act; upon discovery, her child was removed and placed into "boarding schools," and the mother also faced prison time—a stark outlaw warning to other mothers not to commit the same "offense." As Pamela Palmater (2020) puts it, one was born criminally Indigenous: people had to break each 'law' to maintain their Indian identity. This legacy of criminalization of all ways of being Indian means that genocide is not just a historical fact but is ongoing. The Western box is all-alluring, yet paradoxical: holding harmless those who criminalize *and* demanding accountability from those who face perpetual criminalization from *in utero*, prenatal alienation till their (premature) death from racism, settler colonialism, and hetero-patriarchy. How does one fight back? Patricia Monture-Angus (1995) argues that a recovery of Indigenous law is vital that centers family and diverse kinship relations, going beyond the Western patriarchal nuclear family (p. 258). The call for Indigenous nations' sovereign self-determination entails an opting out of Western adversarial punishment games and the colonial violence that such institutions (including the family regulation system) bring to bear on Indigenous bodies and nations (Holmes & Hunt, 2017, p. 53).

In addition, the Western box promises freedom (from a paternalist state) but is stern, punitive, and quite unloving. It becomes clear that it might just be absurd to demand responsibility when the "responsible" party has never experienced nested care, growing up in a loving supportive environment. From birth, Western babies are separated, put in cribs, and have to fortify themselves somehow by living in isolation. They experience the shock of alienation and lack of recognition. They lack supportive touch in a lovingly community environment, where other women would also provide extensive nurturing care to the birth mother. More neuroscientists, therapists, and social workers are beginning to understand that alienation from birth mothers is an ur-trauma that cannot be repaired, even though it is a fact that child separation through the family regulation system affects hundreds of thousands of children and their birth families and has a disproportionate impact on Black and Indigenous communities. Yet, these experts are not concerned about the perpetuation of colonial child-rearing practices of cribs, lack of support for doulas, and the lack of extended paid family leave to ensure parent–child bonding.

How is it possible to return to a life-giving/life-affirming circle with centuries of threats of intervention, genocide in myriad forms including kidnapping and forbidding the Indigenous child from speaking their language and withholding religious traditions in an outlaw manner? Racist, colonial hauntology must be overcome by ludic abolition of structural, systemic oppression and abolition of the nation-state.

The Western box is built around the figment of abandonment. The 'box' is rooted in the toxic energies of a blame game. Its anchor emotions are greed, ignorance, fear, and anger.[6] It begins with little 'boxes'—in the American parenting game, it is called 'time out!' when a toddler is sent into another room and perhaps the door is locked. As penal abolitionists and abolitionist teachers call attention to the cradle-to-prison pipeline, it also behooves us to look at each of the thousands of 'cuts' children face on the way to normalizing social death. The box signifies an encasing propagated by the fear of ostracism; from a young age, one is separated, living in racially segregate neighborhoods. Citizens are connected to each other through the abstract language of patriotism and a flag. Abstract liberty rights against the state are 'gifts' by that abstract entity, the (white, settler colonial) state. From the feeling of fear (of not belonging) externalized as anger, lacking skills that are honored and valued by others, and ignorance of what is important in life (literacy—says the state—and living to work) which turns into greed—why be generous when I never learned how to receive love through a sense of belonging? The result is self-expression in harm, which will be prosecuted by the state (on behalf of an individualized entity or corporation). The state operates in a way to maximize harm in what it considers punishment in a penal institution (i.e., exile) which provides a cage as a new home for the angry, hurt, and fearful person who is lacking skills, money, and social connections, thus magnifying social death. This is what we call the criminal justice system. Yet, as Vine Deloria suggests, the seduction of possessive individualism is no replacement for "the need and desire to belong" (Deloria, 1970, p. 11).

Lakota Circle of Courage

Its core values and representing the four directions are generosity, belonging, mastery, and independence (Brendtro, Brokenleg, & Van Bockern, 2019). The medicine wheel or wheel of courage presents a virtue ethics that validates the need for a sense of belonging as well as exploring confidently one's uniqueness. Its other opposites-in-unity illustrate the pursuit of learning skills and knowing not to boast about it—as the community encourages generous feelings and actions, akin to the Indigenous African Ubuntu ethics. Clearly, belonging is a primordial, constitutive value, and it drives Indigenous attentiveness to nested care: breastfeed babies when they demand; never allow punishment or hitting of children; allow babies to set their own schedule for sleeping and waking; bond with babies with positive touch and co-sleeping (cf. Figure 5.5). Nested care also means that the child is free to follow their own path of learning and playing (Narvaez, 2021). Western thinking immediately raises objection and warns that such a child is raised to be spoiled or willful, as illustrated by a gruesome German fairy tale (cf. Ahmed, 2014; Figure 5.4). Indigenous wisdom shares that the drive for autonomy and zealous pursuit of mastery is not decoupled from the communal sensibilities of knowing one's place in the community and generosity. Such nested cosmology strengthens social cohesion (Figure 5.3).

> The gift of self is the most meaningful anyone can give. A rich man who writes a check to a hospital to build a new research facility is certainly an epitome of generosity. Generosity is a necessary virtue, but unless that man has given away all of his money he has not performed an act of sacrifice.
>
> (Marshall, 2001, p. 106)

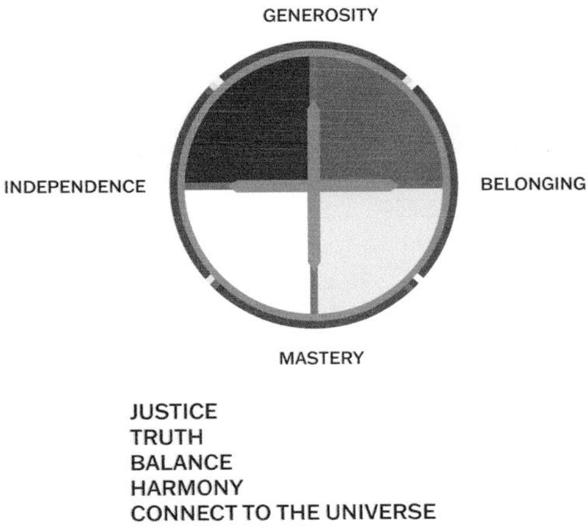

Figure 5.3 "The Circle of Courage," portrayed by Lakota artist George Bluebird.

Source: Reprinted with permission from Brendtro, Brokenleg, and Van Bockern (2019).

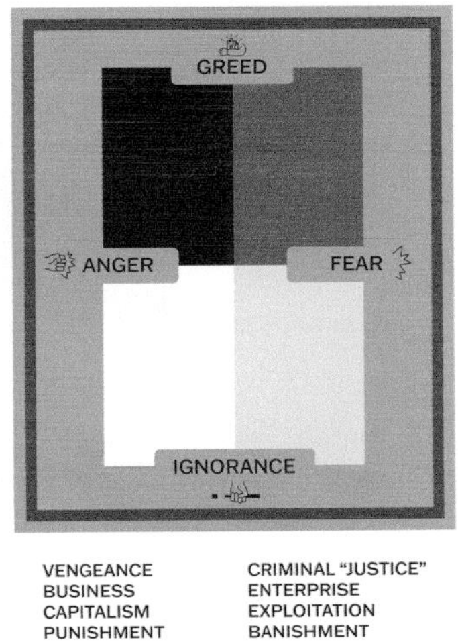

Figure 5.4 The Western Box of Punishment.

Source: Graphic design provided by Victoria Alvisi.

Since the Lakota people moved about two to three times per year, it was not a virtue lugging many possessions. The following Lakota story illustrates how generous giving, even to a fault, is honored in cultures that value social cohesiveness and prize belonging to a community (Figure 5.5).

> A certain man had many possessions because he was reluctant to part with anything he owned. His dwelling was filled with all manner of things and he had a large herd of horses to carry it all each time the village moved. Though he had all those fine things, he had no friends, and he was getting old and didn't want to spend his last days alone.
>
> He sensed that his time was drawing near and he wanted the people to think and speak well of him after he died. So he spoke to the wisest old woman in the village. "What is the answer?" he asked. "I do not want to spend my last days alone."
>
> "Be generous," the old woman replied.
>
> The old man pondered the woman's advice and then sent the camp crier among the people to announce that he would make a feast and that everyone was invited. The day of the feast came and the people gathered. True to his word the old man fed all the people. Then he gave away all of his possessions, all of his horses, and even his lodge. He left himself with only the clothes he wore—no lodge to sleep in and no horse to ride—but that night he was invited to sleep in someone's lodge, and the next night in another lodge.

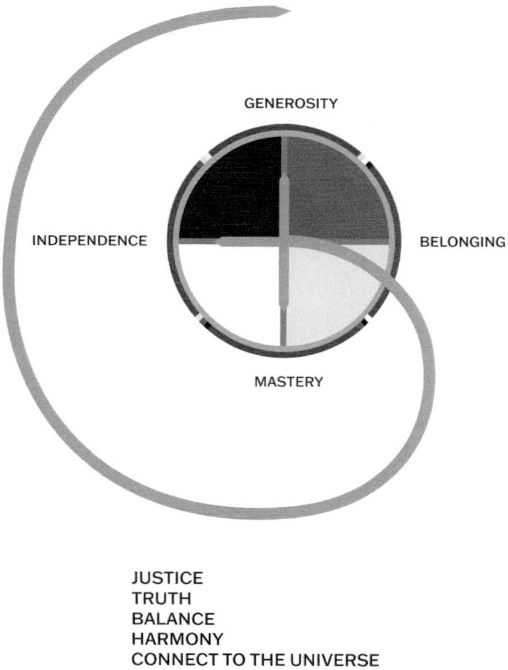

Figure 5.5 A Ludic Ubuntu Circle of Courage.
Source: Graphic design provided by Virginia Alvisi.

> And so it was until the old man died. He had no possessions, but he had many friends, and it was spoken of him that he was a generous man.
> (Marshall, 2001, pp. 194–5)

Seen from a Western 'box' context, such old man would be a poor man; he would even end up living unhoused in the streets. Those who strike riches with the lottery and are 'careless' with their giving find themselves under the opprobrium of Aristotelian foolhardiness. In an ego-centric society, hoarding (of tangible assets and stocks) or greed is considered a virtue rather than a severe character flaw. The ancient Egyptian goddess Ma'at presents a regulative virtue-based worldview with 42 principles which focus on the self being in harmonious cooperation with all their relations. Might it be worth embracing simplicity where jurisprudence was to be reduced to *one* page of code of conduct such as 'you shall not hoard possessions!'

In a ludic Ubuntu way, the Lakota engage children (and adults) with the elusive figure of the trickster Iktomi—what is the coyote for the Diné. This shape-shifting animal is the topic of many stories and highlights the free-rider problem: cunning willfulness always takes advantage of others' well-meaning spirit of hospitality, generosity, and kindness. It easily became transposed onto the settler colonial reality, where these strange newcomers had clearly forgotten the message of Mother Earth admonishing us to give back and forward generously, because we humans owe it to the earth which feeds us with unconditional love.

> The Lakota look at the land and see a relative. The white man looks at the land and sees a commodity. Neither side is wrong because ultimately all we can do is live our own truth. Sometimes, however, one truth hides another. Beware of Iktomi.
>
> (Marshall, 2001, p. 123)

Marshall is generous here in avoiding value judgment. A ludic Ubuntu ethics which generates feelings of belonging without stifling freedom of expression or learning invites interplay at the micro and macro levels (Figure 5.5). The following case study from our local Sophia's Garden project (teaching philosophy to children—from toddlers to teens) showcases what is at stake.

Applying the Circle of Life Philosophy: "You Can't Say You Can't Play!"

The field of violence prevention draws on many disciplines and practices. Teaching philosophy to young children has shown me another course of action for preventing psychopathic behavior. It also draws on educator Vivian Paley's (1993) innovative anti-bullying research and the simple play rule she introduced in a kindergarten that made its own revolution (toward sociality, developing social intelligence). In Thomas Suhs' film *Reject* (2016), Paley's philosophy was put to a test. In the treatment group, children had to commit daily to a mantra: "you can't say you can't play." This way, children modeled to each other that everybody was welcome to take turns in games and playground gym equipment. Longitudinal studies and comparison with a control group showed that the treatment children avoided clique formation and increased their friendship behavior and attitudes toward all children, whereas the control group did not. There were nay-sayers. A few parents, who exemplified the Western box model, as outlined above, complained that the children should have the choice to play with whomever they liked to play. Of course, diverse groups in terms of ability and race/ethnicity benefited from this rule, and no child was literally left behind. This study illustrates well what happens when children molded in the Western box way. They absorb the values of individual merit, autonomy, independence, at the expense of sociality, interdependence, vulnerability, and empathy. Nudging children toward taking turns playfully fosters a spirit of generosity, while appreciating each other's deep learning and attaining mastery in various games and deepening social intelligence.

In my philosophy class with six graders, I explored various philosophical themes, some basic logic, and worked with children's stories such as my favorite picture storybook *Frederick* (Lionni, 1967), a story about a poet mouse who sits on a rock during the summer and fall season, when all the fellow mice are busy with collecting seeds and nuts. In the end, the poet sings about the colors of summer and shares tales that he 'collected' while meditating on the rock. The mice are happy with the contributions because they sit in the dark cave during the long cold winter months with nothing to eat. Frederick's food for thought turns out to be a blessing, not a luxury.

In my pedagogical approach, I was careful to draw out children's creative answers and encourage them to explore the power of imagination and use of analogies (what this story reminds me of …). One of the biggest compliments I received at the end of the course was Malcolm's wondrous exclamation: "She never gave us any answers. She only asked questions." Their schooling experience is filled with tests, grades, and sitting all day—well, my course was also done in the sitting way, unfortunately. The peripatetic school had that advantage: doing philosophy while walking the busy roads of Athens. Research on children's philosophy reveals that philosophizing may even be therapeutic. (There is a Philosophical Practitioners organization which champions the approach of *Plato, Not Prozac!* (1999)—a primer for the profession.) Even two years after the end of a philosophy class, children show better learning outcomes in reading and math. During such class, as Thomas Wartenberg (in NEPM, 2014) reports, children started to take their critical thinking skills and exploration of argumentation to the playground. Instead of beating each other up, the boys decided to listen to each other's disagreement and argued philosophically with each other, being committed to finding a peaceful, dialogical path.

The kindergarteners who explored the Paley school of thought also came up with their own peaceful strategy. During lunch they invented the slogan: "You can't say you can't sit!" All children are welcome to sit with each other, nobody is at risk of being ignored or marginalized. There is hope for positive peace as children who grow up in a setting of nested care will take the path of ludic Ubuntu ethics seriously. Obviously, this would mean to rethink the educational system being guided by transformative principles as Bettina Love (2019) and Gholdy Muhammad (2020) have articulated: abolitionist teaching, exploring joy, and cultivating genius.

Healing Circles, Not Sentencing Circles

Sentencing, i.e., a pronunciation of past wrongdoing, pushes an 'offender' into shame response, being rejected and ousted from social, communal, familial relations. They feel being a burden on others who are put into a pity relationship or rage (against their family member and/or the system). It is extremely difficult upholding family or friendship ties over years with folks exiled into the prison system.

What if we focused on healing and then building trust, or do it all at once (i.e., healing and trusting)? Children are great at this game. Without adults' prompting, they release grudges and reunite with their conflict partner, laughing together hilariously as if nothing had happened. Learning to be like children, frolicking in the Now.

To re-lease, let go of past, of harm means in Nietzschean terms that the metamorphosis of spirit begins: the weighed-down camel becomes the spirited lion, free at last from burden of shame, guilt, traumatic memory, and punishment, and its final transformation into children at play is complete.

> Healing from Harm
> I, the Lord, have called you in righteousness;
> I will take hold of your hand.
> I will keep you and will make you
> ...
> to open eyes that are blind,
> to free captives from prison
> and to release from the dungeon those who sit in darkness.
> (New International Version, Isaiah, 42, 6–7)

The prophet Isaiah, whose words are reiterated in the canonical gospels of the New Testament, proclaims that the Lord will lead the chosen people out of carceral caves (or dungeons); it is only up to the Lord to play judge, prosecutor, and juror, echoed in the Egyptian goddess Ma'at's task of holding the scales, measuring the weightiness of guilt harbored in a human joining the ancestors against the weight of a feather. In a way, it is the mortal being who engages in self-punishment, as images of their lives, parade in front of them in the transitioning process. Abolitionist ideals in Christian and Jewish faith communities are used to reimagine Hebrew and Christian law which is truly nonviolent and stays away from committing further harm, which is what the punishment regime is about. Following Walter Benjamin, Daniel Loick (2018) argues that Hebrew law has pedagogical value but refuses to engage in policing, adjudication, etc. As such, this law can be envisioned as a law without violence, lacking the state's enforcement power. It is worth studying peaceful practices among Amish communities across Midwest and Northeastern states in the United States (Kraybill, 1989). A non-Amish man Charles Roberts killed five schoolgirls and then turned the weapon upon himself. The Amish immediately went to the widow's family and offered their support, even setting up a fundraiser. Their action was much publicized because victims' families are not supposed to act in such generous way of *agape* fellowship. Of course, I do not want to minimize that the parents may have been pressured by the community to act in forgiving ways, yet long-lasting friendships were built between the Amish and Roberts' parents, where Roberts' mother visited a severely insured girl every Thursday to read and sing to her (Kraybill *et al.*, 2010; Itkowitz, 2016).

James Scott (2010) shares that, historically, peaceful communities (whom he calls Zomnians) simply evaded the state's conscription and punishment by running to the hills (or other territory that is difficult to penetrate with wagons, etc.). Similarly, Indigenous people and maroon Africans fraternized and disappeared into the swamps of Virginia and Florida, where they evaded the power of the slave state for decades, sometimes fighting back (Saul, 2018).

Tao Te Ching lays out the virtue of leadership: repeatedly, the sage recommends letting go of punishment (in addition to being troubled by desires for material possessions and rituals that invoke judgment). Transformative justice is forward-looking, releasing judgment and trusting people and the process, including those who are regarded as untrustworthy (Mitchell, 2004, chapter 49). It is the opposite of a Kantian disposition (of accounting, reckoning with every slight of the past, backward-looking risk assessments, focusing on deserts). The challenge for abolitionists is then to be fully committed to peacemaking which entails no judgment of those who harm (cf. Pepinsky, 2006). Lao-tzu goes further to eschew any ethical demands. The focus is on just being, or as Mogobe Ramose (2003) says "rheomode"—the movement of being. Being in the center of a circle may look like stasis, but it is about being in harmony with all there is. Lao-tzu has stern warnings about the violence of the elites and government. Instead of bringing balance and staying centered within the Tao, they squander money on weapons instead of working towards peace (chapter 53). Chapter 60 advises: don't give evil any power. It is always there, it will not go away, but get out of the way of evil, and it won't have any power (Mitchell, 2004).

In settler colonial states, *sentencing* circles have been allowed to showcase the state's interest in RJ practices, as a nod to Indigenous practices outside the prison framework. Elders in a community are granted a modicum of authority, but if the consensus "verdict" is too lenient, the representative of the state (the Crown) will interfere and pronounce an indictment in the Western, adversarial court (cf. Proulx, 2003, p. 31). Sentencing circles are not healing circles. In New Zealand, the government usurps Mãori justice tikanga justice with Family Group Conferencing and calls it RJ, Mãori-style (Vielle, 2011, p. 213). This youth-oriented justice program invites police, social workers, and other representatives of the state, a small segment of the youth's family, and prescribes a set procedure that focuses only on legal disposition, including sentencing the young Mãori to prison. Tikanga justice, by contrast, focuses on belonging and is community centered without state actors attending. It also attends to healing of all involved and addresses spiritual dimensions. The focus is not on sentencing but on creating harmonious relations because if one member is hurt, the rest of the community is hurt such that each member will either feel some sense of harm or bearing responsibility for harm (Vielle, 2011, p. 204). In some Indigenous nations, feigning adherence to procedural (hierarchical) justice is used as ludic appeasement. Robert Yazzie, former Chief Justice of the Diné Supreme Court, puts it this way:

> [our courts] were created out of a fear of a State takeover of criminal and civil jurisdiction, and as a defense. They were designed to look like justice of the peace courts with the hope that, with the appearance of The Law Way, the state would leave us alone.
>
> (cited in Tobin, 2014, p. 67)

Indigenous nations, of course, have not experienced meaningful ways of running their own healing and conflict resolution in autonomous fashion. However, as much as possible, they refigure the US imposed juridical frame into a peacemaking, relational, horizontal model, resembling a circle "perfect, unbroken and a simile of unity and oneness" (*Ibid.*). If one must label something a crime, it is also a crime not to belong, not to be in relations with others, an insight explored by Craig Proulx in *Reclaiming Aboriginal Justice, Identity, and Community* (2003). Some First Nation folks who live in urban centers may receive holistic services that foreground the medicine wheel philosophy of healing when such organizations are run by First Nation staff who have agreements with the state for running diversion programs (Proulx, pp. 34).

Us versus Them and the Dance of Interdependence

A RJ paradigm is still wedded to an adversarial system. In Ngũgĩ wa Thiong'o's masterful decolonial novel *Petals of Blood,* the protagonist Karega gives a prison abolitionist speech nothing short of prophetic:

> For as long as there's a man in prison, I am also in prison: for as long as there is a man who goes hungry and without clothes, I am also hungry and without clothes. Why then need a victim hurl insults at another victim?
>
> (1986, p. 240)

Long-time prisoner of war Leonard Peltier's call to compassionate being-with-each-other is also based on the recognition that we are dependent on each other, precisely because we are already interdependent. In the poem titled "We Are Not Separate," he is very specific about the fluid boundaries across (human) beings, and if there is accountability work to be done, it must be a mutual dance:

> We are not separate beings, you and I.
> We are different strands of the same Being.
>
> You are me and I am you
> and we are they and they are us.
>
> This is how we're meant to be,
> each of us one,
> each of us all.

You reach out across the void of Otherness to me
and you touch your own soul!
(Peltier, 2000, p. 213)

This is not about romanticizing human relationships. It comes from a deep understanding of the wisdom of the Lakota circle of life—of feeling the interconnection with all living. Yet, he still calls out those who torture and torment other beings. In another chapter, he shows the racist, sadistic mindset of guards who taunt him so that they could send him to the hole, solitary punishment. For him, such punitive cell is no different from the one that he is caged in. Categorically, Peltier states: "All prisons, without exception, are cruel and unusual punishment. Every one of them should be declared unconstitutional" (p. 143).

If transformative justice is about loving all that is, unconditionally, how then is such prophetic sensibility not in contradiction with a fighting spirit and resisting injustice? Peltier answers that he would not get defensive or reactive and give the guards the satisfaction of becoming a victim and show his anger toward them:

> I would refuse to be their victim. I am not a victim. I am a warrior. I will accept my pain, whether inner or outer, as a warrior does, without whining, without whimpering, as we learn to do in Sun Dance. Sun Dance sends us out into the world hardened against pain the way a charred stick is hardened against fire.
>
> (p. 147)

Of course, the pen is mightier than the fist, and in his prison writings, as an organic intellectual and political prisoner, Peltier is able to influence the next generation of Indian children to follow the way of the elders. And non-Indian readers also benefit from his inspirational teachings on how to deal with the forces of reaction. At the same time, Peltier's poem seems to allude to the fact that guards are also prisoners, and if all are interconnected, then the state of being a prisoner is intertwined with those who are guards, police, prosecutors, judges, jurors, and all, who are bystanders to the behemoth of the world's largest imprisonment experiment ever witnessed. Indeed, all lives are imbued with dignity. To contextualize this political frame is to say, all lives matter *because* Black and Indigenous lives matter; all lives matter *when* Black and Indigenous peoples are being humanized globally, when there is great compassion with prisoners who are locked away in US total institutions: state and private (supermax) prisons, jails, shock or boot camps and military lockup units, civic-confinement prisons, immigrant detention centers, global Central Intelligence Agency (CIA) secret prisons and Guantánomo Bay's gulag, psychiatric locked units and civil confinement centers, youth secure centers, to name a few.

The recent pandemic affords a glimpse into the reason why we are literally all interconnected. It may have been one infected person who exhaled and thus transmitted viral particles that eventually spanned the globe, and the prisons, along with refugee camps and nursing homes, of course, became the epicenter of infection rates. This is a sobering and unsurprising reality because social distancing and personal protective equipment are not guaranteed nor enforceable. Since guards, for the most part, do not reside within prison structures, they became the main vectors for transmission. The crisis also provided an excellent opportunity to accelerate decarceration efforts, but the US prison system slowed its response so that activists resorted to shaming slogans: "a prison sentence should not be a death sentence!" US epidemiological data show (again) that Black and Indigenous lives do not (yet) matter, since they experienced heightened mortality rates, whether they reside in certain boroughs of New York City or on Diné Nation territory. Why might that be? Rupa Marya and Raj Patel have a surprising theory about it, as discussed in *Inflamed* (2021). It has a long history, roughly 600 years, and has to do with outlaw imperial behavior: genocide, enslavement, and racial extractive capital. Mehta and Patel argue that were Indigenous peoples able to enjoy food sovereignty, their microbiomes would be their protective shield against pandemics of any modern pharmacological kind. I share an historical example of a living shield from transnational encounters on a Caribbean island. One weapon that captive Central African peoples brought along to Haiti was the mosquito. And in their epic revolutionary overthrow of the colonial forces, headed by the French, they waited out the Europeans, because sure enough, they would succumb to malaria during the rainy season. In the end, the French liked to blame the loss of their crown trophy imperial possession on the insect, rather than on the superior fighting force of the insurgent maroon Africans, who abolished slavery and colonialism upon declaring itself free from imperialism in 1804. The web of life is not appreciated in Western social ontology, but once it is understood, it can no longer be unseen. 'All my relations' include the visible (mosquito) and the invisible (virus).

Unity Consciousness

InterBeing—my existence is interwoven with yours, even with ancestors. This is Ubuntu's spiritual dimension, which also resonates with Buddhist philosophy. It differs from the Kantian deontological impetus that requires recognition of reciprocity—to put myself in another person's shoes, purely from a *rational (white) man's* perspective. So often prisoners ponder if judges, prosecutors, and jurors could just spend a week in jail—would they still give in to draconian sentences, 10, 20, life, or even death? Famously, a Colorado warden endured a night in solitary and decided to empty out the solitary row right after that sobering experience (see Chapter 1).

In Tutu's memorable words, my fate is inextricably tied to yours, even if I am the prisoner and you are the torturer. What part of myself do I judge harshly? So I argue that Hobbes' *Leviathan* has it strangely upside down. The leviathan is cast as the body (politic) of the king or sovereign who is made up of all of his subjects, as miniature figurines/composites of the super body. In settler colonial criminal law that means that when the king's charges (prosecutor and judge) indict the commoner, who harmed another commoner, the king gets to pose as victim, in effect silencing and disappearing the actual harmed party. The relic of that leviathan is the prosecutor representing 'the people.' Actual restitution has become irrelevant in this game of retribution and reaffirmation of 'law and order,' and the machinery of the carceral where the convicted and condemned 'do time' is its logical modern consequence. *Leviathan*'s book cover can be recast. What if we took that image literally? If the sovereign punishes a subject, does he not punish his own life and limb, in his own body? That others need to be seen as an extension of myself, not as self-isolatable automatons? If we accomplish this metaphysical feat, then in the end, we must recognize that all punishment is futile and obsolete, and at least, irrational. If I punish, I literally punish myself, or a part of myself.

Sacred texts emphasize that only the creator or divine serves as judge. As criminal laws are abolished, prisons become obsolete. When prisons are eliminated, so does "crime" vanish. Progressive educators have long held that the key to transforming discipline and punishment vis-à-vis children means two things: (1) culpability becomes an obsolete term when the full weight of the trauma of childhood is taken into consideration by those who are in the business of judging adolescents and adults; (2) when a paradigm shift in educational institutions occurs along with a different approach to parenting, harming, or violating another's body and subjecting them to emotional abuse would be unthinkable.

A good indicator for a society's 'peace index' is studying any society's attitudes of girls and women, or, even, of their founding myths and origin stories. Many Indigenous peaceful societies do not have a word for rape, because it is an unthinkable violation (Peaceful Societies n.d.). Among the Buid, any gender-based violence (assault, rape, physical harm) is abhorred, and women are free to marry and get divorced as they please. Violence in general is viewed as a form of insanity, as if a violent spirit takes possession over the harmer. Verbal confrontation and shaming are shunned, and disputes (mostly related to divorce and property claims) are settled by consensus in a *tultulan* meeting space, where community members do not face each other, avoiding eye contact (Gibson, 1989).

When humiliation and shaming practices are turned into humility education and practices that grow the capacity for empathy and reciprocity, any urge to engage in raging, hurtful, harmful, and otherwise inconsiderate action is in need of healing. Specifically, with a ludic Ubuntu perspective that teaches that we are all interconnected, the need for punishment and revenge thinking simply vanishes. Once one has reached a higher dimension of complete acceptance and loving what is, one would also recognize all others' intention immediately. Deception would become a futile game. Here is where a turn toward Indigenous metaphysics is helpful.

Reintegration without Shame and Punishment

Luis J. Rodríguez paints a rich tapestry of hope and redemption in his autobiographical book *Hearts and Hands: Creating Community in Violent Times* (2001). Drawing on Mexika Indigenous knowledge and his own perilous path joining a street organization, sniffing glue, and other toxic substances as an adolescent in Los Angeles, he comes to terms with his calling as elder, parent, and grandparent to mentor and counsel youth who exit the prison system. Where others see young disposable bodies, he sees tortured children crying out for love and support. Rodríguez builds on the insight that violence is "organized in childhood and *acted out* in adolescence" (p. 296). To address such trauma and ACE,[7] he says it cannot just be dismissed but needs to be patiently worked through with rituals in a sacred setting. "Rituals geared to this process can help take the punch out of any hate and violence than can arise from such traumas" (p. 296). In 1996, he gathered 70 young people, most of them being of Mexican Indigenous descent, from four different Chicago gangs along with adults from mainline Christian churches in a secluded camp in Woodstock, Illinois, to conduct a sweat lodge ceremony. He engaged Julio Revolorío, a Guatemalan Mayan and Sundancer, taught by Lakota elders to teach the young people building their own sweat lodges. By the end, transformation in attitudes helped shift the energy, mending their hearts, and some young members of one group apologized to members of another group whom they had challenged prior to the ritual taking place. Such apology was organic and not prompted by any adults in the room (pp. 296–7).

Seeking Safety, Not Punishment—Insights from Polyvagal Theory

Numerous abolition toolkits now focus on safety, not just harm repair and reduction (Brazell, 2018; SOS, n.d.). The TJ Curriculum Kit, developed by Mariame Kaba, is a step in the right direction (Project NIA, 2013). Kaba notes correctly the root of violence stemming from systemic oppression and specifically names the criminal injustice system as an originator and perpetrator of state-organized violence. And it focuses on healing for survivors and accountability processes for those who are responsible for harm. The vignettes also reveal that those who are accused of the harmful action are incarcerated or driven away. Kaba (2021) clarifies that her attention goes to survivors. It is indeed valuable work to pivot the attention away from calling the police and seeking a community response to do violence-interruption-and-prevention work. However, exiling or incapacitating a person gives an incomplete vision of what transformative justice practices are able to accomplish (cf. Dixon & Piepzna-Samarasinha, 2020). Often, those who favor transformative justice pass over in silence of what healing could mean for all those involved. What does it truly mean to embrace those scapegoated?

What keeps us genuinely safe? I will now turn to insights gleaned from polyvagal theory to understand how the complex neurological response system to trauma is mobilized to create a sense of safety. Stephen Porges (2017) argues that humans qua mammals need social interaction and play, which at its best is interactive, not solitary. Even playing computer games with others does not count as a social activity, since mammals need facial cues to look for guarantees for safe interaction (p. 80). Social engagement includes listening to different voices and intonations and one's sense of body and breathing ability—all connect to the self's sense of safety (pp. 25–6). Porges adds a new dimension to the conventional theory on vagal response to fear—flight or fight. His new dimension denotes immobilization, which will be familiar to feminist anti-violence advocates. Specifically, a common response to a traumatic event is freezing or fainting, a human version of playing dead (p. 103). He laments the Cartesian cognitive turn in the Cogito—what if Descartes had uttered "I feel (myself), therefore I am" (p. 217)? Porges finds current US education policies of children on the Autism spectrum woefully incapable of adapting to the specific needs, especially of children with auditory sensitivity. A child who puts their fingers in their ears does not engage in disruptive behavior; instead, they signal that their body is in pain and cannot handle the sensory overload (p. 209). Porges' polyvagal theory and treatment plan for highly traumatized children or adults also may resonate with therapists who use pretend-play and a version of family constellation in traumatized play therapy (Gil, 2017). Of course, this guided play is very serious and is supposed to ease children into building trust with adults and expanding their horizons to create joy and even laughter in their play and daily activities.

Porges also finds hospital spaces traumatizing for many and argues that mammals do not enjoy constraint or confinement—this clarion call for transformative change can be easily extended to another coercive institution, the prison, specifically, solitary caging. The neural pathways for social interaction and for healing are the same (p. 100). "When we are in a defensive state, then we are using metabolic resources to defend. It's not merely that we can't be creative or loving when we're scared; we can't heal" (p. 101). How terrifying then, to be sick with Covid and be isolated in a hospital, when restoration of health depends on social support and interaction. Worse, getting sick in prison is life-altering and even life-threatening, since caring sociality is proscribed. In US prisons, a gentle touch is forbidden and draws extra punishment, including solitary confinement. Porges' response to nuanced trauma treatment is particularly urgent for those who leave prison and cannot get prison out of their mind, what is now being called post-traumatic incarceration syndrome.

Perhaps Porges is dwelling in biological determinism, but so is recent social science research that pays attention to ACE and even develops a rating system for psychological intervention (or prediction of future incarceration). Former warden Thomas Galli's (2017) portrait of a white boy of an upper-class German family is telling. He writes that this boy got bullied at school and received no safety outlet, social support such as emotional care, a hug, or talk therapy from his parents who are jurists who did not want to be bothered with his school problems. He ended up fighting a bully at school who almost died. In prison, he finally receives 'respect' and is encouraged to play a toxic manipulation game with his scandalized parents. As Galli insinuates, the adolescent taunts his father who had abandoned him to visit, only to give him a lesson of shaming. The son hits the father in the face, a revenge for being an unwanted child and enduring a loveless childhood.

For women and gender nonbinary folks, a common shame response to rejection may not result in outward violent rage as Herbert Thomas (2006) postulates, who worked as psychiatrist in men's prisons. I argue that his theory should be reframed as a shame response to *violation*, and here I am cognizant of the Latin roots of rape. Using insights from polyvagal theory, traumatic responses may reflect guilt and immobilization including developing agoraphobia, a body's safety response to a hostile world. Such withdrawal from the world should be celebrated, not pathologized because it shows a survival strategy. A harmed and traumatized person needs validation to begin the slow healing process of down regulation of the vagal system to relearn what safety and attachment feel like. Affirming and validating immobilization due to fear is also an insight gleaned from feminist therapy for survivors of sexual assault who feel guilty for not fighting back.

So, neuroscience seems to support the strong environmental thesis buttressed by neurobiological decision-making circuits that show volition plays a very minor role in transgressive behavior/acting-out these impulses. Mainstream criminologists and forensic psychologists argue that "criminality" wanes when the prefrontal cortex has fully claimed its executive function role (at around 25 years), so that impulse control is fully "online." What of parents and caregivers all over the world who are fully committed to corporal punishment? Is that not also a question of impulse control or the lack thereof?

Role of Laughter and Forgiveness in Healing Relations—Surprising Redemption Stories

In the following, I want to showcase examples that illustrate that a penal abolitionist stance is a necessary but not sufficient condition to engender ludic transformative justice. By this, I mean that there are moments that rise out of a spiritual awakening, compassionate encounters between strangers who refuse to be enemies, and acts of kindness that go beyond conventional understandings of reparation and reconciliation work.

Here, I want to shift to the example that Angela Y Davis foregrounds in her concluding remarks in her book on the obsolescence of prisons (2003). She briefly shares the remarkable story of Amy Biehl's family engaging in reconciliation work with some of those held responsible for taking Biehl's life in 1990. I agree with Davis that this is an exemplary case for international transformative justice possibilities, even though the teenagers who were found guilty spent four years in prison. The TRC commission granted political amnesty to the young men, and to the surprise of the applicants, the parents not only did not oppose amnesty but also expressed their unwavering support for the society's forgiveness process and their solidarity with the South African people. They knew in their hearts that Amy Biehl would have supported that decision. The parents said it was not for them to forgive the applicants but for South African people to do so. Amy was a white, upper-class Fulbright student who worked against Apartheid and admired African National Congress (ANC) leader Chris Hani who was gunned down by a white supremacist just shortly before her own death (MonicoABHS, 2018.).

Two of the amnesty applicants, Easy Nofemela and Ntobeko Peni, asked the Biehl parents to forgive them. And they also wanted to show the Biehls their youth program they had started in Guguletho Township where Amy had been killed. The young men had started their own process of accountability, and there is no record of any demands made by the white American couple. In fact, the parents were intently focused on the future, on seeking nonviolent self-sustaining projects, and they did not wish to know what role Nofemela and Peni assumed in the circumstances of Amy's death. As they moved forward with their plans to invest in South African youth in townships, the parents were guided by the burning question: "What would Amy ask us to do?" And they were motivated by putting Desmond Tutu's Ubuntu message into practice. In a way, they did adopt the young men: they offered the young men jobs in the Amy Foundation (formerly Amy Biehl Foundation), and Amy's mother Linda Biehl gave them plots of land in honor of her late husband, so that they could build their own homes (Davis, 2003). Linda Biehl says: "I've grown fond of these young men. They're like my own kids. It may sound strange, but I tend to think there's a little bit of Amy's spirit in them." Responding to skeptics who wonder why he works for the foundation, Nofemela shares that "I now passionately believe that things will only change through dialogue" and that he is committed to forgiveness (The Forgiveness Project, 2021). Over the past decades, thousands of township children have been supported in afterschool programs, apprenticeship opportunities, and much more.

There's a photo of Linda Biehl sharing a tender laughter with Easy Nofemela—on the day of the 20th anniversary of commemorating her daughter's death at the gas station in Gugulethu. Another photo depicts Nofemela's daughter engaging Biehl in a playful activity and addresses her as her grandmother (OCR, 8/27/2013). Redress and reconciliation can have many faces, and in this case, the US-based family decided to continue the passionate work of the daughter leaving a legacy that includes those who directly harmed and now serve as community leaders and role model. In a small but quite significant way, it is also to recognize that forging transcontinental interracial friendships may also include opportunities for reparations: It is quite clear to the Biehl family that these young men who witnessed apartheid police murder and brutality and grew up to hate any white person would have chosen a path of peace under different circumstances, i.e., without the vicissitudes of settler colonialism. The journey toward reconciliation was initiated with an anthropologist Nancy Schaper-Hughes who shared with Amy's parents that the two young men wanted to meet them personally. Intermediaries play an important role, doing shuttle diplomacy between the parties, vetting expectations, and helping to mediate. For Peni and Nofemela, moving forward in their self-forgiveness journey meant that they needed to reach out and ask for forgiveness. Receiving jobs and land to build their homes in addition to a lifelong friendship were the gifts granted *beyond* forgiveness, and their life stories show it is possible to reach a ludic ubuntu phase of acceptance and personal transformation even across unlikely dyads and continents. Furthermore, accountability work may show up in different guises; when all is forgiven, moving forward together without any need of extra sanctions imposed on the 'responsible' party is also an aspect of 'doing the work.' With new precious ties that bind, restitution and reparation take on new dimensions not discussed in conventional community accountability work.

What could be learned from spiritual considerations in a postsecular Western context?

Consider the life story of Willie, known affectionally as the Bible smoker. Wilhelm Buntz (2018), a white German man who appeared on Germany's "Most Wanted" list of dangerous men, was found guilty of some of the 150 offenses including manslaughter he committed and Ernst Bloch, a German philosopher, prophesized that he would die in prison, labeling Buntz as incorrigible. Yet, he left prison at 32 years in the 1980s. Buntz got early parole after an epiphany reading (and smoking) the Bible.

Convicted of dozens of violent transgressions and bank robberies, Buntz was often thrown into the solitary cage, because he could not control his rage. Prison management would only allow him to have the Bible. So Buntz schemed an ingenious plan. He asked the prison pastor for the biggest tome, which he used to smuggle tobacco and matches. Then he started a peculiar ritual. A nonbeliever, he read one page from the Bible each day and cut it into four segments because the thin pages worked well as wrapping paper for his hand-rolled cigarettes. Nothing affected him until he read the New Testament passage of the Sermon of the Mountain and God's proclamation: "you are the salt of the earth, you are the light of the world." At this point, he stopped tearing out the pages and had a philosophical introspection, reflecting on his past life.

Buntz was an unwanted, unloved child, and his mother literally abandoned him in a field. He was nursed back to a modicum of physical health during a seven months' stay in a hospital. After a brief reunion with his violent, abusive father, Buntz was institutionalized in group homes and youth prison. He had a speech impediment and discovered that earning respect meant bullying and taunting his peers. Only once, he felt tenderness, when his mother visited him in a group home, and he thought she would reunite with him. After she ended the brief visitation, he vowed never to let anyone make him feel vulnerable again. During a field trip in Austria, Buntz stole his counselor's car key, and during the brief joyride, he collided with a police car. The officer died at the scene, and Buntz spent years in a brutal Austrian youth prison where guards beat up all teenagers on Thursdays.

Eventually, after his spiritual conversion in prison, Buntz wrote to the prosecutor confessing to all 150 offenses, which he had recorded as tattoos on his body. He was weeks away from release. The prosecutor promptly wrote back enclosing pages of indictments totaling another 20 years; the last page included a simple letter addressed to "brother Buntz" and concluded that all these other 100 plus offenses were of lesser nature than the ones he was found guilty of and wished him a good new life in Christ.

Re-entry proved very challenging, as he had to learn to adjust to a noninstitutionalized environment and learn how to use nonviolentist language. He also owed some 500,000 dollars. Buntz took it upon himself to visit all those whom he had harmed in order to apologize and ask for forgiveness. His last visit was the most challenging: finding the Austrian widow and her children. When they finally met, she did not know who he was, and Buntz insisted that all her children be present as well. What he learned from her was profound. The officer's wife gave birth on that same day of the fatal accident over a decade earlier (in 1971). She heard the news of the accident when she had just given birth to her fifth child. Only then, Buntz disclosed to her that he had killed her husband. The widow did the unexpected. She gave him a huge hug and shared that since that accident, she and her children prayed daily for the boy who took the life of her beloved husband and children's father. She also said that now her deepest prayer had been answered and that Jesus provides a new life and wipes out the past. At this moment, Buntz began to cry for the first time in his life—at 32. It was as if his heart opened for the first time, that he felt understood and resonated with others' sorrow, expressing compassion—an emotion that he buried after his fateful encounter with his mother—a veritable spiritual deliverance from the path of destruction he had known.

To this day, Buntz is very close friends with the family; he is married and raises his two sons in a loving way. In fact, he discloses that he has never quarreled with his wife. Buntz no longer stutters and with his televised life story (2020) attracting a huge following of diverse people, many of whom disclosing their own violence-and-neglect-filled childhood and turning their lives around with just one loving anchor or mentor, who unconditionally believed them. Buntz peppers his storytelling with humor and compassion and shares that he now enjoys laughing a lot, while walking the spiritual path (2021). I need to emphasize that Buntz transformed his life in the prison, being labeled 'the worst of the worst,' not because of prison, but in spite of it. It is perhaps noteworthy that Buntz shares the trauma of maternal rejection with the Norwegian Anders Behring Breivik who killed 77 people in 2011. Former prison warden Galli notes that extreme cases such as Breivik show that "evil" actions almost never come out of nowhere (Galli, 2017, p. 162).

Buntz was not required to walk the path of accountability by the courts. He took it upon himself. In the 'Lakota way,' it is said that a woman who spread rumors about others and drove them into despair was shunned by all, including her husband who left and returned to his family's village. All alone, she finally consulted with a wise elder who gave this woman feathers. She was supposed to put a feather in front of the door of every person she gossiped about. The shunned woman obeyed. The wise elder then asked the young woman to return all feathers to her. The latter began to weep and complain that the wind had blown them away. The elder's counseled that, indeed, like feathers, hurtful words can never be brought back again. "There is only one thing you can do: Never say such hurtful words again. But first take a gift to everyone you have hurt and shamed with your words as a sign that you will change your ways." The woman followed the advice and ended up giving away everything she owned because she had spoken hurtful words about so many. She remained with one dress, and people forgave her because they noticed that she had changed her behavior. Living a long life as a quiet woman, she was known as One Dress (Marshall, 2001, pp. 198–9). With organic introspection a kind elder guides and shares community values which may align with the younger woman's own need for connection; when there is dissonance, then adjustment through acts of repair and changed behavior in the long term will benefit all involved. Is an apology always important? There is no set formula for transforming a situation and hurt feelings—the Diné do not even have a word for apology.

A Prayer for Laughter

Candice Mama also refuses to let herself be defined by the past and the person who took the life of her father. She enjoys laughter, dancing, and spreading joy, as she did in our encounter at a dignity studies conference in New York City in 2017. However, it was not always so. In her autobiography (2020), she makes clear that this shift toward healing only occurred after she was confronted with a life-threatening ulcer at age 16. And the recognition of self-forgiveness and the need to forgive her dad's assassin took time. It is far apart from a perspective that Jean Améry takes, a survivor himself. He proposes (contra Nietzsche) that *ressentiment* is necessary and what is owed to the forgotten victims of the Shoah. Reconciliation itself is totalitarian and Améry assumes the role of what Sara Ahmed calls "killjoy" (Ahmed, 2010;

Van Tuinen, 2021). Self-righteous Germans (and for that matter, white South Africans) must not revel in reconciliation talk; Améry brings to bear testimonial injustice, as his testimony sits uneasily with those who sponsored or benefited from genocidal atrocities. A killjoy's message cannot be received, and it is not of the kind of Frankl's tragic optimism which focuses on forward-looking healing and a steadfast refusal to allow ressentiment to take hold of him.

What might be even more scandalous is humorous laughter that another survivor of the Shoah defends. Edith Erbrich makes it her calling that the Nazis would not take that human expression away from her. She shares in her memoirs, *I Never Forgot How to Laugh*, as a seven-year-old child, she was deported from Frankfurt to Theresienstadt and was supposed to be transported to Auschwitz on the day after her liberation. Tellingly, saying "yes" to life means that "I will not turn my heart into a murderous pit" (p. 83).[8]

Sometimes, laughter is an emotional release that often is expressed with tears of joy and mingled with tears, weeping for dignity.

There is a different kind of laughter, not quite reeking of *Schadenfreude* but still ominous. It is the kind of laughter that James Baldwin finds chilling in a certain French courtroom, when he is finally acquitted from the offense of using a hotel's bedsheet in his humble abode in Paris. "This laughter is the laughter of those who consider themselves to be at a safe remove from all the wretched, for whom the pain of the living is not real" (1984, p. 158). It is the kind that haunted Baldwin in the United States only to be triggered by the French courtroom frolicking and mocking him. He received an acquittal and not a stiff sentence for misappropriating property after spending almost a week in Paris' own dungeons.

Unconditional Forgiveness

Psychologist Victor Frankl is famous for frowning on castigating all Germans as already guilty for Nazi crimes against humanity. He vehemently argued against the concept of collective guilt. He even returned to Vienna, without his wife or parents who were killed in Auschwitz. Frankl propounded a theory of tragic optimism, making use of Nietzschean insights and adding his own aesthetic-moral counterweight to Freudian psychoanalysis by focusing on the patient's future self.

There is an opening for self-healing and self-love when a witnessing dance succeeds. Those who are participating, even unwittingly, also realize that it brings about self-forgiveness. Albie Sachs' books *The Soft Vengeance of a Freedom Fighter* (1990, 2000) and *The Strange Alchemy of Life and Law* (2009) circle around the incessant desire finding out the truth who ordered his assassination. "Henri" finally appeared in an amnesty hearing of the TRC and demanded a personal session with Justice Sachs, a commissioner and constitutional court member. At this meeting, Sachs felt defiant and did not extend his hand to greet Henri, who in turn left dejected, because he did not receive a forgiveness gesture he hoped for. (Instead, Henri was sent away with some 'repair' homework to do, namely, to follow up with all the folks he victimized.) Years later, they met inadvertently at a party in Johannesburg, where Henri's demeanor had changed. Henri shared that he did meet with Sachs' friends who were all victimized by Henri's terror actions in Mozambique, where Sachs almost lost his life due to the car bomb Henri's men had planted. Using the victims' first names with "great affection and enthusiasm," Sachs could see that he spoke the truth. Decades earlier, one of the victims, Bobby, had sent a note to his friend Albie in a hospital in London that the bombing will be avenged. Soft vengeance turned toward Ubuntu: Sachs now extended his hand to Henri in appreciation for keeping his word to talk to the anti-apartheid freedom fighters Henri had victimized.

> [Henri] went away elated. I moved away and almost fainted into the arms of a friend of mine. I heard later from the puzzled organizers of the party that he had left suddenly and gone home and cried for two weeks.
>
> (Sachs, 2009, p. 94)

Sachs' action speaks to interpreting Ubuntu-botho as a RJ ethic, involving a dialogical encounter, reparation, reintegration, and participation of other people who are close to parties (p. 101). In his interpersonal encounters with folks like Henri, Sachs is not interested in material reparation. As justice, he interprets Ubuntu-botho as a dignitarian ethic, which encompasses not only liberty principles but basic socioeconomic ones, linking "the right to freedom with the right to bread" (*Ibid.*, p. 173).

Pumla Gobodo-Madikizela (2003) also shares an encounter of families who reconciled with a state agent who killed their beloved child. It was again in dialogical format outside the courtroom which provided the conditions of possibility for such ways of restoring the humanity of the person who aggrieved them bitterly. Looking directly at the responsible person, a mother said with quiet conviction: "now I believe you, as I see it in your eyes!" It is the gut feeling that "knows" when someone speaks the truth that encompasses deep remorse so that forgiveness could be possible. This conditional forgiveness is built into RJ processes. Transformative justice suggests that even the thought of forgiveness may hold back aggrieved parties and get in the way of transmuting conflict energies.

Beyond Forgiveness

In the final analysis of reflecting on interpersonal relationships, one may want to heed the sage's advice: do not insist on the practice of forgiveness. It is not for you to forgive somebody, and it is actually healthier not to entertain the thought of forgiveness, because it establishes a causal entanglement in your mind: you must have engaged in the conscious act of criminalizing another person in order to forgive them afterward. It pollutes the mind with judgments due to unrealistic expectations of another person which linger on beyond the performative forgiveness statement (Sadhguru, 2020). This insight stems from the compassionate and realistic insight that I also commit transgressions and why should I have higher expectations of others than of myself? Letting go of the need to forgive helps one avoid the need to criminalize others. Furthermore, two lessons are learned: (1) I am no better than the other person; (2) others (as do I) act out of ignorance, so there is no need to forgive when they didn't know how to comport themselves; it seems nonsensical to forgive that which could not have done differently. As Plato says, to know the Good is to do the Good—no exceptions. Lao-tzu frames the blame game in this way:

> Failure is an opportunity.
> If you blame someone else
> there is no end to the blame.
>
> Therefore the Master
> fulfills her own obligations
> and corrects her own mistakes.
> She does what she needs to do
> and *demands nothing of others*.
> (Mitchell, 2004, chapter 79, emphasis mine)

In his commentary, Stephen Mitchell reminds us of Confucius' illustration: "In the archer there is a resemblance to the mature person. When he misses the mark, he turns and seeks the reason for his failure in himself" (p. 113). Thus, the insight is that blaming, criminalizing, and forgiving are rationalizations born of the same vindictive, fear-based emotion that seeks to sow division rather than compassion, harmony, and a unity consciousness that we are all interconnected.

Nietzsche brings in an additional frame of a critique of sin-laden guilt and seeks to trouble the *Tat/Täter* dyad discussed above. Abolitionists are keen on disrupting this dyad as well, as the transgression committed 30 years ago does not define me who I am today. Letting go of the need to blame and the need to forgive bring us back into a life-affirming dance of life, of playfulness without grudges and burdens, where the sage meets the child. In fact, in Indigenous worldviews, life is not linear but imagined as a circle.

In *The Lakota Way* (2001), Joseph Marshall, a Lakota scholar, describes the medicine wheel as encompassing the four directions, four seasons, four colors (red, yellow, black, and white), and elements of life (earth, wind, fire, and water). Marshall emphasizes the significance of the circle as a nonhierarchical depiction of life: all life is sacred and has equal value (p. 225). It is expressed in the prayer "all my relations" (*mitakuye oyasin*), spoken when entering the circular sweat lodge, which represents the womb (p. 227). These words are repeated when leaving the lodge, symbolizing each participant's rebirth (p. 228).

> We don't arrange our dwellings in circles any longer. Our villages are now housing projects and our houses are square. ... Interestingly, I've noticed that anytime a group of Lakota gather together, they naturally form a circle. Perhaps there is a grain of genetic memory that compels us to subconsciously reconnect with a part of ourselves that has been trampled by [...], paternalism, racism, indifference, and other challenges wrought by four generations of cultural upheaval. Though the circle is not as common in everyday life as it once was, it is still a prominent part of our ceremonial lives. ... Fortunately, the circle is a never-ending flow, and more young people from each generation are reconnecting with traditions and values.
>
> (Marshall, p. 226)

Medicine Wheel Meets the Western Box

From Heraclites to Rousseau and Nietzsche, Western play aesthetics centers around the romantic notion of the solitary male child and the trope of *homo ludens*. What if this care-free play is actually always already embedded in an unacknowledged social imaginary, in the circle of a supportive family and fictive kin structure, as exemplified by the Lakota wheel, where children play with age mates and others, who could also be ancestors, imaginary friends, elves, dragons, and other magical beings that children envision. Yet, in the Western disciplinary imagination, adults get to label games and play-acting, determining what is proper play. Their children face opprobrium and ridicule, when they face the materialist, ego-centric, binary-gendered norms and constraints of the Western box. Carefree playfulness faces disruption in the Western paradigm, a display of Ubuntu in the negative, a game of separation and traumatic memories that get re-imprinted in the collective unconscious every generation.

It is the child who exclaims in protest 'how can I hate another human when I am myself a human!'[9] That child feels understood by the elder who smiles in recognition of such profound wisdom that we are all one, we are all interconnected. It is the inverse of the modernist opera *The Magic Flute*, dwelling in metaphysics of light and anti-Black racism, which proclaims that nobody who cannot entertain love deserves to be called a human being. And those of a darker hue cannot possibly be at the same level of a white male enlightened philosopher, as Kant opines. Circles radiate love and nonhierarchy of humans, and they work with the contrast of light and darkness, as exemplified in Yin and Yang symbolism.

Yet, the lessons from traditional Lakota ways also involve ostracism, as a form of punishment. A young woman who hurt others with gossip was eventually shunned, to teach her a lesson, becoming 'the loneliest person in the village.' Being committed to social death was a crisis point. So, she turns to the oldest woman, renowned for her wisdom and kindness, who counsels the young woman to put a white feather in front of the door of each person she had gossiped about. After that act was completed, the wise woman instructs the young woman to return all the feathers to her. However, the wind had blown away all of them. The elder admonished that words wound and can never be brought back. The only solution is to stop shaming others with words and present a gift to everyone who was harmed by the gossip to show that she will not do it again. In the end, the community forgave her because she never spoke unkindly about anyone again (Marshall, pp.198–9). I would argue that the public shaming was minimized as the young woman sought out a personal, private counsel, and it was left to her whether to follow the advice of the elder sage. The prized goods to attain were reintegration and forgiveness by the community through making individual amends (repair work). Another way of looking at the harm of gossip or bullying is to do a community introspective—how do we enable such behavior and what is our joint responsibility to undo the harm through reintegrative play-acting and other healing performances.

Transitional justice mechanisms such as Gacaca ritualistic condemnation of Hutus, innocent or guilty of perpetration of war crimes, might do well adopting a holistic perspective. The impetus here is to avoid any future blood shedding. Reviewing the Mato Oput practice among the Acholi of Northern Uganda is instructive. As there are several versions of it, I will mention just two of them. One is emphasizing a communal aspect of shared burdens, between responsible parties and those who were victimized. The former brings a sheep, the latter a goat for communal slaughter, where each animal is given to the other party; then both parties drink a potion of Oput, a bitter herb, to signify that conflict and strife are bitter, and both parties agree never to engage in such bitterness again. In addition, the party harmed is compensated with lifestock as a way of restoring the peace in the community (Tom, 2006).

Sultan Somjee, a founder of community peace museums in Kenya and South Sudan, reports another version of Mato Oput that describes more humiliating features. Since a person has harmed using a weapon, the arms are bound behind the back

> to show submission; his/her arrogant head is forcefully lowered as a gesture of humiliation and made to drink like an animal. The mouth that abused and spoke foul language, is filled with the bitter stuff of a specially prepared mixture.
>
> (Somjeen, 2018, p. 4)

The physical cleansing may be provoked through a feeling of nausea, as the drink is revolting. Meanwhile, the rite requires the elders to pronounce their reprimand as well as extolling the principle of Utu to all onlookers so that they accept the responsible person back into the community and to ask them to restore trust and relationship bonds. Utu is the Swahili word for humanity and resonates with the Southern African word 'Ubuntu.' Utu is here used to invoke peace, well-being of the community, and reconciliation (*Ibid.*, p. 2). Committing violent harm in warfare cuts off a soldier from the community, the ancestors, the spirit world, and such a person has literally lost their Mtu (their humanness and dignity). In another rite, former soldiers step in freshly cracked eggs with their right feet. Eggs represent life, and they are reminded of its innocent nature. Afterward, the former fighters brush up against a pobo tree branch, to cleanse them. Finally, they step over a pole, ask for forgiveness, and are welcomed back into the community by village elders and chief. While the ritualistic cleanse is a public encounter, the responsible parties may still be shunned, especially if the warfare continues and no compensation is given (Tom, 2006).

From Peltier's unity appeal to Ramose's rheomode of Ubuntu, transformative justice is not a utopian ideal; it is a human expression whose time has come. I reside in the center of the Iroquois Confederacy, on unceded Onondaga territory. This oldest confederation on earth wove democratic, consensus-building political framework with a Great Law of Peace of the confederation of the five nations (Gibson, 1992). It is often said that consensus is possible only in small intentional communities. How should it be possible in a space that is as large as Germany today? Imagine a community that bases its values on liberty, dignity, and equality. This is exactly what happened over 1,000 years ago or earlier in the territory where I live. The oldest living democratic praxis among five nations who all speak different languages, the people of the longhouse: Haudenosaunee or Iroquois people, where women are empowered serving in the Council of Matrons, which served as the executive branch of government (Gunn Allen, 1986). Ludic Ubuntu peace practices centering on the ideals of generosity and sustainability, welcoming strangers, and housing displaced refugees, adopting even whites, who refuse to leave, when "discovered" by white colonial intruders, adopting even a sixth nation. Such enduring peace was only possible by endowing women with social and political decision-making, in societies organized through matrilineal descent and matrilocal place-making. Women speak freely their mind including in any discussion of warfare, select the male leadership according to ideals of humility, extreme generosity, and fairness. Traditionally, a new chief is the poorest among them because he'd rather give items away than hold on to extra possessions.

It was only upon the colonial genocidal conquest that women were disempowered and made aware about how backward the English unity law is—unity that works solely in favor of the married (white) man. And the Indian women's way of life and their relaxed dressing, too, gave rise to the angry manifesto penned by Elizabeth Cady Stanton in 1848. An elite, well-educated white woman, she was outraged about the blatant sexist constraints she faced in the abolition movement that wouldn't allow women to comingle with men, let alone speak (in the London convention of 1840). Stanton noticed the discrimination that women faced, being prohibited access to all higher education, work, and political office. In short, she was outraged about the endurance of the Aristotelian ideal of public man—private woman. However, nowhere are the "red roots of white feminism" (in the famous words of Paula Gunn Allen, 1986) acknowledged in her manifesto. This racist amnesia follows the well-rehearsed cultural imperial erasure of the red roots of American democracy by the white elite slavers two generations earlier (1776). Colonial British law and subsequent American common law meant that Indian women lost their property rights—it is often said, by white chroniclers and generals, no less, that sexual assault and rape were unknown in precolonial times. Those white women captured by Indian men refused to return to the allures of the "civilized" ways, because these whites were quite aware that it meant instant civil death and living with the uncertainty whether their body or psyche would take a beating—or worse (Roesch Wagner, 1992).

Redressing Structural and Systemic Violence and Injustice

Are we in an "age of reconciliation" (Yamamoto & Ayabe, 2011)? Some 40 truth commissions have been convened since 1979, yet have they also brought peace and transformative justice? From his prison cell, political prisoner/prisoner of war Indigenous activist Leonard Peltier shares poignant insights about abolitionist futures:

> Today in South Africa men and women from both sides are being allowed to come forward in public Truth and Reconciliation tribunals to confess their misdeeds and be given political absolution. That, I think, won't be necessary here. Besides, the trials would take centuries. We need not courtrooms but schoolrooms, not jails and prisons but decent homes and jobs for the millions of every color—including many, many white people—who are being denied their human and civil rights every day of every week by the special interests that are trying to steal America. ....
>
> If building more prisons for those of us who are unlike yourselves is to be your strategy, then, I promise you, you cannot build enough prisons to hold us all. I ask America, as one familiar with your darkest side as well as with your shining possibilities, rethink this current craze for building ever more prisons for ever more of those of us born different than you. We don't need more prisons. *We need more compassion.* That compassion is our highest possibility.
>
> (Peltier, 2000, p. 207, emphasis mine)

There is much wisdom in Peltier's call for a spiritual pivot. Peltier was not able to watch the TRC proceedings from his prison cell—the televised testimonials certainly riveted a nation. Yet, there is no need for symbolic cleansing of state actors' collective crimes. He argues for a real economic justice investment in all poor communities across the United States, including poor whites. Arguably, reconciliation cannot happen between states and individuals; it is possible at an interpersonal level, whether it is between Amish and non-Amish, or white US parents and "adopted" South African young people.

So far, this chapter has focused on interpersonal conflict transformation, which is what most authors and activists who favor community accountability and transformative justice focus on. How is it possible to scale up these efforts and what are the elements of transformative justice at the societal level? In Chapter 4, I discussed these large-scale justice efforts comparing Gacaca in Rwanda with the TRC of South Africa. Neither transitional justice experiment took on the long view on history, specifically, of the legacy of the European colonial violent conquest and its divide-and-conquer tactics. And, as the TRC commissioners readily noted, reconciliation is an empty word when it is not accompanied by a serious commitment to addressing "the land question," in addition to creating investment in jobs, education, health, etc.

Since the emergence of the Black Lives Matter movement, born out of protest against police brutality and outlaw lynching of Black Americans in 2014, we have seen a rise of intensified calls for scrutiny of settler colonial states' crimes against humanity from occupied Hawai'i to the neocolonial nation-states of South Africa and Namibia.

To put it bluntly, nobody in the Jefferson clan is going to jail for their ancestor's crime of enslavement of human beings for generations. No descendants of military officers, Dole's CEO, nor the US president's family who ordered and executed the capture and imprisonment of the last Queen of Hawai'i are answering to charges of wrongful invasion, kidnapping, and occupation of the entire territory up to this day.

Pretend-play may have to be taken to another level for abolitionist and ludic insights. There is a lot of negative pretend-play in the prison industries. The prison warden (Thomas Galli) is lectured by the circus director, who is his prisoner. In the circus arena, everyone knows it is a show, and magic tricks are being played. Similarly, in prison, the convicted are wild animals who are transformed into docile bodies. But contrary to the circus, very few know that the prison warden is the true magician. The director continues:

> I have met more people outside in the free world who I would label as evil or bad than among the fellow men inside this prison. But we all pretend as if real danger, resocialization, and evil people exist inside this arena. And we pretend as if the prison were no circus arena but reality, the real life.
>
> (Galli, 2017, pp. 58–9)

The prison as a total institution is built on this noble lie, specifically, that it exists to promote resocialization or rehabilitation. Nothing is further from the truth. If the circus director is right, then it makes sense to go against the grain and argue that the penal abolition is already in place, not a utopian deferment. And as Coyle (2018) and Coyle and Piché (2021) show so convincingly, there are already penal abolition frameworks that play a role not only for those committing high crimes and misdemeanors in state office (working under the color of law) and corporate criminal and felonious acts that smack of genocidal and ecocidal practices. Furthermore, they show that few of the harms (on the street) reported to the policing apparatus get prosecuted and fewer still get conviction. Marginalized, oppressed people already know that the penal system *is* the violent box that does not repair harmers nor restore the harmed (Kaba, 2021). It is clear to them that the 'usual suspects' (i.e., disposable populations) continue to be arrested and convicted to uphold the frail logic of the circus of incarceration.

Taking transformative justice seriously at the meso and macro levels entails a different approach to undoing the massive wrongs of the past. It is the season of reparations demands, accelerated with a reinvigorated global Black Lives Matter movement in 2020. During the summer of 2021, Germany has finally acknowledged that the mass murder of Herero and Nama peoples must be named as genocide but short of apologizing only offered a mere 1 billion euros in redressing the first genocide of the 20th century, committed by officers of the German Reich. Politicians reached a deal, or so they thought, with the Namibian state, at the exclusion of the Indigenous groups, descendants of the survivors. The deal avoids language of reparation and promises "development aid," of one billion euros over a period of three decades which is supposed to benefit the Herero and Nama communities (Ossenbrink, 2021). And Australia again has its moment of reckoning. It was clearly not enough to apologize for the genocidal practices of child kidnapping, and reparations offered to survivors (75,000 Australian dollars per person). Cumulative effects of this intergenerational trauma are that Aboriginal and Torres Strait Islanders face shorter life expectancy, higher incarceration rates, and 11 times higher child removal by the family regulation system than non-Indigenous people. Thus, the trauma continues as the settler colonial child-removal policy reproduces another face of "the stolen generations" (Al Jazeera, 8/5/2021).

Black Americans, too, are now calling for a national reckoning of over 400 years of enslavement and perpetuation of servitude under new guises (Jim Crow, convict lease system, COINTELPRO, war on drugs, red-lining, wage theft, lynch terror, medical brutality, etc.). The US government's theft of the very modest reparative measure of a Black homestead act of 40 acres awarded to Black Americans after 1865 is worth at least 11 trillion dollars, and this reparative measure would mostly focus on eliminating a huge wealth gap and what is owned to the descendants of enslaved Africans (Darity, 2021).

Another expression of reparative justice involves community-based trauma across the United States. From Tulsa, Oklahoma to Rosewood, Florida, and Wilmington, North Carolina, dozens of Black free towns were torched or submerged. Fania Davis (7/8/2016) drew inspiration from the South African TRC proceedings to raise consciousness about re-memory projects and calls for reparations.

Unity consciousness requires an equity mindset and a critical review and devolution of structural oppression. The union's slogan "an injury to one is an injury to all" exemplifies this collective conscientization. Hence, it is even more egregious that unions historically have manifested a sexist, racist, and even imperialist mindset. Here, too, a deep introspection into umbrella organizations such as the AFL-CIO must prompt an accountability process and reparative measures to the descendants of harmed groups.

Eric Yamamoto and Sara Ayabe (2011) propose a robust legal framework that offers "social healing through justice" in this age of reconciliation anchoring four principles: recognition, responsibility, reconstruction, and reparation (p. 510) which involve Indigenous healing practices drawing on ho'oponopono and ubuntu (p. 522). These are necessary guidelines for a redress framework in order to move closer to reconciliation. They warn that this framework must go beyond empty symbolism and involve stakeholders (e.g., Native Hawaiians and all three branches of government) to bring about reparative measures at the societal and individual levels. Only then is it possible to achieve a modicum of peaceful coexisting in the postcolony (*Ibid.*).

It is worth mentioning that the Black Panther's Ten Point Action Program gave Black people a communal/socialist blueprint for ludic Ubuntu justice and a liberation program that was utopian, and at the same time, it laid the foundation of the realms of the possible. If there must be a nation-state, the just path forward involves a defunding of the Pentagon and the policing system and an investment in a Department of Peace and Compassion that focuses on repair and reparations abroad and within; part of the reparative measures must be assisting those who have been harmed by US criminal intervention in their nation-states with speedy immigration to the United States. Part of the immigrant's cry for justice is "we are here because you were there!" What if that rallying cry is performed in spectacular ways?

Since their uprising, a protest of the North American Free Trade Agreement and the Mexican government, the Zapatistas are always an inspiration for doing things in the positive, ludic Ubuntu way. In summer of 2021, a delegation decided to sail back to Europe, to reconquer Spain in their own ways.

Their delegation is commemorating the destruction of Tenochtitlán, capital of the Aztec Empire, 500 years ago, retracing the route of the ruthless Spanish conquistador. In 1521, in a typical manner of colonial European military warfare, the means were guns and bioweapons: the invaders' gift to the Indigenous people was smallpox, which only exacerbated mass deaths among the Aztecs (Hudson, 2021). In their statement, the visitors noted: "we are going to tell the people of Spain two simple things. One, they did not conquer us; we are still here resisting, in rebellion. Second, they do not have to ask that we forgive them for anything." Ironically, the Zapatistas had to wait before entering to get Covid clearance, lest they intentionally infect Spaniards (Wilkins, 2021).

Who Is Invited to Participate in Ludic Ubuntu Justice Principles?

If we ask a Lakota elder who intones 'all my relations,' does that automatically mean any outsider has an invitation to participate in educational, spiritual, or healing circles? If a Zulu invokes "*umuntu ngumuntu ngabanye bantu*" (a human is a human through other humans), does this mean that whites are welcome to share in Indigenous ceremonies that center on hospitality and overcoming differences? A circle signifies the womb, an egg, the unborn life that struggles from within to break the shell. If Indigenous circular practices celebrate an eco-centered life, then settler colonialism stands for natal alienation: breaking the egg from without, which means instant death. Why would anyone wish to invite death (or coyote) within a sacred circle? Pumla Gobodo-Madikizela's (2003) witnessing dance may serve as a metaphor for bridge-building here. Obviously, transformative justice from a macroscopic lens involves a complete transformation of all institutions besides law and a redistribution of wealth. Is there a temporal limitation? Not if the Zapatistas' 500-year-long memory serves as a moral compass of what needs to be done.

Nothing but systematic atonement for the legacy of land theft and genocide is necessary before white settlers (*abelungu*) can dream of being called *Abantu* (becoming a human). Reflecting on the passing of Archbishop Desmond Tutu, Panashe Chigumadzi (December 31, 2021) calls for reparations which the TRC under Tutu's leadership failed to achieve:

> Today, we Black people, 79% of South Africa's population, own 4% of agricultural land, while white South Africans, 9% of the population, own 72% of agricultural land. In 2014, Oxfam reported, two white men—Johann Rupert and Nicky Oppenheimer—owned as much wealth as the bottom half of the population. The 74% youth unemployment rate—concentrated among Black "born frees"—is the world's highest. It is unsurprising then, that in their statement to the South African Human Rights Commission's 2015 hearings, Abahlali baseMjondolo, a Durban

shack dwellers' movement whose members have faced arrest, assault and assassination in their struggle for post-apartheid liberation, cried out that poor Black people "are not counted as human beings."

Abolition democracy must extend worldwide producing egalitarian systems. These are the demands of a sacred web of life. A ludic Ubuntu ethics must be deeply embedded in social justice considerations which call for transformation of all of societies' institutions because there are none that are not affected by the faces of oppression, specifically of settler colonialist outlaw regimes, predatory capitalism, and heteropatriarchy.

Living on Iroquois Nations' land, I have always found their prayer of gratitude which extends to all species inspirational for a new way of connecting. It has been thought that trees compete for sunshine, typical of anthropocentric thinking. Now science tells us that there is no competition but only cooperation. What if we started to emulate the tree beings who connect far and wide? Through their root systems, they offer nutrients to other species. Trees for peace, reforest to create peace for trees, honoring Wangari Maathai's legacy. Reforesting cities and creating community spaces are no longer radical ideas. We are not (yet) like trees. In the meantime: Zomnians of the world, unite—we have nothing to lose but our fear!

Accountability, ultimately, is about counting those made disposable and dispossessed as human beings. Ludic Ubuntu as transformative justice provides one way that another world is already alive, especially where there is a respectful turn toward Indigeneity, of remembering or adopting ways that have once been framed as primitive by those who did the looting and orchestrating genocide. A global reckoning is imminent, and penal abolitionism is at the center of what is doable and possible.

Notes

1 This chapter draws in part from previous work: "An Ubuntu Ethic of Punishment." *The End of Prisons* (M. Nagel & A. Nocella, eds.), 2013, pp. 177–86.
2 Candice Mama, presentation, Dignity and Humiliation Studies conference, Columbia University, December 1, 2017, New York City.
3 Personal email, December 10, 2017.
4 Experts studying trauma-informed care of those who commit sexual transgression note that many have had such harm done to them as children (Levenson *et al.*, 2016; 2017).
5 DSM stands for *Diagnostic and Statistical Manual of Mental Disorders*, now in its fifth edition.
6 Thanks to Tony Gaskew for naming these emotions.
7 The Center for Disease Control and Prevention and the health organization Kaiser Permanente developed a diagnosis in the 1990s and made changes to the categories in 2007 (www.cdc.gov/violenceprevention/aces/about.html). For a discussion, see Fitz-Gibbon and Hall Fitz-Gibbon (2019, pp. 14–5).

8 Erbrich (2014) reflects:

> Ich mache aus meinem Herzen aber keine Mördergrube. Ich sage die Wahrheit und spreche aber auch unangenehme Dinge, aus, auch wenn das für mich Konsequenzen hat. Das gefällt vielen nicht, und es ist nicht immer einfach. Aber ich kann gut damit leben. ... Wenn ich mir etwas in den Kopf gesetzt habe, dann führe ich das auch durch. Meine Schwester sagt, dass ich immer schon einen Dickkopf hatte, der muss mir wohl in die Wiege gelegt worden sein. Ich will mich nicht verbiegen.
>
> (pp. 82–3)

9 My niece Mareike Griemsmann (personal communication, 2014).

Bibliography

Abadi, M. (2018). A police officer who went to jail undercover quit the force after he got out. *Business Insider*. Retrieved April 28, 2022, from www.businessinsider.com/60-days-in-season-4-drugs-violence-2018-4#:~:text=A%20police%20officer%20from%20Texas,and%20became%20a%20car%20salesman

Abidor, M. (2010). *Communards: The story of the Paris Commune of 1871, as told by those who fought for it*. Pacifica: Marxists Internet Archive Publications.

Abramson, L., & Moore, D. B. (2002). The psychology of community conferencing. In J. Perry (Ed.), *Restorative justice: Repairing communities through restorative justice* (pp. 123–140). Lanham: American Correctional Association.

Abu-Jamal, M. (2009). *Jailhouse lawyers: Prisoners defending prisoners v. the USA*. San Francisco: City Lights Books.

ACA. (n.d.). *The history of standards and accreditation*. Retrieved April 21, 2022, from www.aca.org/ACA_Member/Standards___Accreditation/About_Us/ACA/ACA_Member/Standards_and_Accreditation/SAC_AboutUs.aspx?hkey=bdf577fe-be9e-4c22-aa60-dc30dfa3adcb

ACES Too High News. (n.d). *What ACEs/PCEs do you have?* Retrieved April 23, 2022, from https://acestoohigh.com/got-your-ace-score/

Achebe, C. (1959). *Things fall apart.* New York: Doubleday.

Agbakoba, J. C. A. (2019). *Development and modernity in Africa: An intercultural philosophical perspective*. Köln: Rüdiger Köppe Verlag.

Aggarval, U. (2016). The ideological architecture of whiteness as property in educational policy. *Educational Policy*, *30*(1), 128–152.

Agozino, B. (2003). *Counter-colonial criminology: A critique of imperialist reason.* London: Pluto Press.

Ahmed, S. (2010). *The cultural politics of emotions*. New York: Routledge.

Ahmed, S. (2014). *Willful subjects*. Durham: Duke University Press.

Albrecht, H.-J. (2002). Juvenile crime and juvenile law in the Federal Republic of Germany. In J. Winterdyk (Ed.), *Juvenile justice systems: International perspectives* (pp.171–206). Toronto: Canadian Scholars' Press.

Alcoff, L. M. (1991/1992). The problem of speaking for others. *Cultural Critique*, *20*: 5–32.

Alexander, M. (2010). *The new Jim Crow: Mass incarceration in the era of colorblindness*. New York: The New Press.

Alexander, L. (2022). *Fear of a black republic: Haiti and the birth of black internationalism in the United States*. Urbana: University of Illinois Press.

Al Jazeera. (August 5, 2021). Australia to pay reparations fund to "stolen generations.". Retrieved from www.aljazeera.com/news/2021/8/5/australia-to-create-reparations-fund-for-stolen-generation

Allan, A. (2000). Truth and reconciliation. *Ethnicity and Health*, *5*(3–4): 191–204.

Allan, A., & Allan, M. (2000). The South African Truth and Reconciliation Commission as a therapeutic tool. *Behavioral Sciences and the Law*, *18*(4): 459–477.

Améry, J. (1986). *At the mind's limits*. New York: Schocken.

Amnesty International. (February 17, 2000). USA: A life in the balance—The case of Mumia Abu-Jamal. Retrieved April 27, 2022, from www.amnesty.org/en/documents/amr51/001/2000/en/

Amnesty International. (2007). *Rwanda: Fear for safety/legal concern: François- Xavier Byuma*. Retrieved April 15, 2015, from www.amnesty.org/en/documents/afr47/007/2007/en/

Annett, K. D. (2016). *Murder by decree: The crime of genocide in Canada. A counter report to the "Truth and Reconciliation Commission."* Toronto and Brussels: International Tribunal for the Disappeared of Canada.

Arendt, H. (1998). *The human condition*. Chicago: The University of Chicago Press.

Ashforth, A. (2005). *Witchcraft, violence, and democracy in South Africa*. Chicago: University of Chicago Press.

Asquith, N., Barkowsky-Théron, I., & Roberts, R. (Eds.). (2017). *Policing encounters with vulnerability*. Cham: Palgrave MacMillan.

Asumah, S. N. (2007). Development crisis, predatory regimes, and prisons in Africa: An impedance-facilitation perspective. In M. Nagel, & S. N. Asumah (Eds.), *Prisons and punishment: Reconsidering global penalty* (pp. 139–146). Trenton: Africa World Press.

Babbitt, S. (July 17, 2017). The bell tolls, or should, for Ana Belén Montes. *Counterpunch*. Retrieved April 14, 2022, from www.counterpunch.org/2017/07/17/the-bell-tolls-or-should-for-ana-belen-montes/#_edn1

Baldwin, J. (1984). *Notes of a native son*. Boston: Beacon.

Bandes, S. (2017). Compassion and the rule of law. *International Journal of Law in Context*, *13*(2): 184–196.

Bazant, M. (n.d.). *Miklat miklat*. Retrieved from www.micahbazant.com/miklat-miklat/

BBC. (2014). *Rwanda's untold story*. Retrieved from https://vimeo.com/107867605

BBC. (1999). Police plan Sting protest. Retrieved from http://news.bbc.co.uk/2/hi/entertainment/502859.stm

Beauchamp, K. (Dir.), (2005). *The untold story of Emmett Till*. ThinkFilm.

Begley, S. (May 4, 2009). Adventures in good and evil. *Newsweek*: 46–48.

Bellamy, J. (1973). *Crime and public order in England in the later Middle Ages*. London: Routledge and Kegan Paul.

Ben-Moshe, L. (2013). The tension between abolition and reform. In M. Nagel, & A. Nocella (Eds.), *The end of prisons: Reflections from the decarceration movement* (pp. 83–92). Amsterdam: Rodopi.

Ben-Moshe, L. (2018). Dis-epistemologies of abolition. *Critical Criminology*, *26*: 341–355.

Ben-Moshe, L. (2020). *Decarcerating disability: Deinstitutionalization and prison abolition*. Minneapolis: University of Minnesota Press.

Benson, S. M. (2017). Democracy and unfreedom: Revisiting Tocqueville and Beaumont in America. *Political Theory*, *45*(4): 466–494.

Bernstein, E. (2010). Militarized humanitarianism meets carceral feminism: The politics of sex, rights, and freedom in contemporary antitrafficking campaigns. *Signs*, *36*(1): 45–71.

Bernstein, E. (2012). Carceral politics as gender justice? The "traffic in women" and neoliberal circuits of crime, sex, and rights. *Theory and Society*, *41*(3): 233–259.

Bernstein, N. (2005). *All alone in the world: Children of the incarcerated.* New York: The New Press.

Bernstein, N. (2014). *Burning down the house: The end of juvenile prison.* New York: The New Press.

Bhengu, M. J. (2006). *Ubuntu: The global philosophy of humankind.* Cape Town: Lotsha Publications.

Bilchitz, D., Metz, T., & Oyowe, O. (2017). *Jurisprudence in an African context.* Cape Town: Oxford University Press.

Bills, K. (November 3, 2017). White supremacists assaulted dozens of us in Charlottesville. Almost none have been punished. *Time Magazine*. Retrieved March 29, 2022, from https://time.com/5009452/charlottesville-white-supremacy-dennis-mothersbaugh/

Blanchard, G. (2012). *The difficult connection: The therapeutic relationship in sex offender treatment* (2nd ed.). Brandon, Vt: Safer Society Press.

Blanchard, G. (2020). *Awaking the healing soul: Indigenous wisdom for today's world.* Center for Peace Research.

Blanchard, G. (January 18, 2022). *Ancient ways and modern times: A conversation with Geral Blanchard.* Webinar. Brandon, Vt: Safer Society.

Blinder, A., & Fernandez, M. (April 9, 2015). South Carolina police shooting seen as crime strategy gone awry. *The New York Times*. Retrieved 15 April, 2015, from www.nytimes.com/2015/04/10/us/south-carolina-police-shooting-seen-as-crime-fighting-gone-awry.html?ref=topics

Bloom, P. (2013). *Just babies: The origins of good and evil.* New York: Crown Publishing.

Boonin, D. (2008). *The problem of punishment.* Cambridge: Cambridge University Press.

Bowers, W. J., & Pierce, G. L. (1980). Deterrence or brutalization: What is the effect of executions? *Crime & Delinquency 26*(4): 453–484.

Bowlby, J. (1988). *A secure base: Parent-child attachment and healthy human development.* London: Routledge.

Braithwaite, J. (1989). *Crime, shame, and reintegration.* Cambridge: Cambridge University Press.

Braithwaite, J. (2011). In search of restorative jurisprudence. In M. Tonry (Ed.), *Why punish? How much? A reader on punishment* (pp. 337–352). New York: Oxford University Press.

Brazzell, M. (Ed.). (2018). *Was macht uns wirklich sicher?* Münster: Edition Assemblage.

Brendtro, L., Brokenleg, M., & van Bockern, S. (2019). *Reclaiming our youth: Our hope for the future* (3rd ed.). Bloomington: Solution Tree.

Briggs, L. (2021). Twentieth century black and native activism against the child taking system: Lessons for the present. *Columbia Journal of Race and Law*, *11*(3): 611–638.

Brown, W. (July 5, 2021). Navajo teachings: Do this for a peaceful life. *Navajo Traditional Teachings*. Retrieved from www.youtube.com/watch?v=8fKyCfh-LlI

Brudholm, T. (2006). Revisiting resentments: Jean Améry and the dark side of forgiveness and reconciliation. *Journal of Human Rights*, *5*(1): 7–26.

Buntz, W. (2018). *Der Bibelraucher: Die knallharte Lebensgeschichte eines Ex-Knackis.* Holzgerlingen: SCM Verlag.

Buntz, W. (June 4, 2020). Wilhelm Buntz über die lebensverändernde Kraft Gottes. Königskinder. *Idea.de.* Retrieved from www.youtube.com/watch?v=mFZGYw4GHAE

Burnet, J. E. (2009). Whose genocide? Whose truth? Representations of victim and perpetrator in Rwanda. In A. Hinton, & K. O'Neill (Eds.), *Genocide: Truth, memory, and representation* (pp. 80–100). Durham: Duke University Press.

Butler, P. (2017). *The chokehold.* New York: The New Press.

Casella, J., & Ridgeway, J. (March 23, 2013). Visiting Billy Blake after 25 years in solitary. *Solitary Watch.* Retrieved May 12, 2022, from https://solitarywatch.org/2013/03/23/a-visit-to-billy-blake-still-a-consummate-dreamer-after-25-years-in-solitary/

Chappell, B. (June 6, 2019). Former German nurse guilty of killing 85 patients in serial murder case. *National Public Radio.* Retrieved April 25, 2022, from www.npr.org/2019/06/06/730281642/german-serial-murderer-nurse-is-found-guilty-of-killing-85-patients

Cheliotis, L. K. (2014). Decorative justice: Deconstructing the relationship between the arts and imprisonment. *International Journal for Crime, Justice and Social Democracy, 3*(1): 16–34.

Chicago Defender. (December 13, 2013). *Blame it on 'Affluenza,' Rich kid syndrome.* Retrieved from https://chicagodefender.com/2013/12/13/blame-it-on-affluenza-rich-kid-syndrome/

Chigumadzi, P. (December 31, 2021). Can white South Africa live up to ubuntu, the African philosophy Tutu globalized? *The Guardian.* Retrieved from www.theguardian.com/commentisfree/2021/dec/31/white-south-africa-ubuntu-african-tutu?fbclid=IwAR3FSxwyGE2J7QRw3epCCZbDtm2qMoQvOY20bJ0jcwmuI9Lt3-Mqv8nEy_s

Children's Bureau. (2016). *AFCARS Report #23.* Retrieved November 25, 2016, from www.acf.hhs.gov/cb/resource/afcars-report-23

Christie, N. (1977). Conflict as property. *The British Journal of Criminology, 17*(1): 1–15.

Chun, M. N. (2006a). *Pono: The way of living.* Honolulu: University of Hawai'i.

Chun, M. N. (2006b). *Ho'oponopono: Traditional ways of healing to make things right.* Honolulu: University of Hawai'i.

Churchill, W. (2004). *Kill the Indian, save the man.* San Francisco: City Lights Publishers.

Clark-Pujara, C., & Cox, A.-L. (August 27, 2020). How the myth of a liberal North erases a long history of white violence. *Smithsonian Magazine.* Retrieved March 14, 2022, from www.smithsonianmag.com/smithsonian-institution/how-myth-liberal-north-erases-long-history-white-violence-180975661/

Cohen, S., & Taylor, L. (1973). *Psychological survival: The experience of long-term imprisonment.* Middlesex: Penguin.

Coletta, A. (2022). Canada reaches $31.5 billion deal over indigenous children put in foster care unnecessarily. *The Washington Post.* Retrieved April 10, 2022, from www.washingtonpost.com/world/2022/01/04/canada-indigenous-foster-care-settlement/

Comaroff, J. L., & Comaroff, J. (2004). Criminal justice, cultural justice. *American Ethnologist, 31*(2): 188–204.

Cooke, A. (Ed.). (2004). (2004). Understanding psychosis and schizophrenia. A report by the Division of Clinical Psychology. *The British Psychological Society.* Retrieved from www.bps.org.uk/what-psychology/understanding-psychosis-and-schizophrenia

Cooper, Stephen. (1/9/18). Call the death penalty the vile torture it is. Retrieved 1/15/18 from: www.counterpunch.org/2018/01/09/call-lethal-injection-the-vile-torture-it-is/

Cornell, D. (2014). *Law and revolution in South Africa: uBuntu, dignity, and the struggle for constitutional transformation*. New York: Fordham University Press.

Cornell, D., & Muvangua, N. (2012). *uBuntu and the law: African ideals and postapartheid African jurisprudence*. New York: Fordham University Press.

Cover, R. (1983/1984). Foreword: Nomos and narrative. *Harvard Law Review*, *97*(4): 4–68.

Cover, R. (1986). Violence and the word. *The Yale Law Journal*, *95*(8): 1601–1629.

Coyle, M. J. (2013). *Talking criminal justice: Language and the just society*. New York: Routledge.

Coyle, M. J. (2018). Who is mired in utopia? The logics of criminal justice and penal abolition. *Social Justice*, *4*(154): 79–116.

Coyle, M. J., & Nagel, M. (Eds.). (2022). *Contesting carceral logic: Towards abolitionist futures*. New York: Routledge.

Coyle, M. J., & Piché, J. (2021). The "dark matter" of justice: Penal abolition practices in everyday life. In M. J. Coyle, & D. Scott (Eds.), *The Routledge international handbook of penal abolition* (pp. 343–353). New York: Routledge.

Coyle, M. J., & Scott, D. (Eds.). (2021). *Routledge handbook on penal abolition*. New York: Routledge.

Coyle, M. J., & Young, S. (2022). The rhetoric of dehumanization: Japanese American concentration camps and the US criminalizing system. In M. J. Coyle, & M. Nagel (Eds.), *Contesting carceral logic: Toward abolitionist futures* (pp. 132–146). New York: Routledge.

Culp-Ressler, T. (2015). Is this the beginning of the end of the death penalty? *ThinkProgress*, March 31, 2015. Retrieved April 9, 2022, from https://archive.thinkprogress.org/is-this-the-beginning-of-the-end-of-the-death-penalty-ff2d9d036dab/

Dante, A. (1995). *The divine comedy: Inferno – purgatory – paradise*. New York: Berkley Books.

Danzinger, S., Levay, J., & Avnaim-Pesso, L. (2011). Extraneous factors in judicial decisions. *PNAS*, *108*(17): 6889–6892. Retrieved April 25, 2022, from www.pnas.org/doi/full/10.1073/pnas.1018033108

Darity, W. (April 30, 2021). The true cost of closing the racial wealth gap. *The New York Times*. Retrieved from: https://www.nytimes.com/2021/04/30/business/racial-wealth-gap.html

David Walker Memorial Project. (n.d.). *David Walker: Unsung hero in the struggle against slavery*. Retrieved May 1, 2022, from www.davidwalkermemorial.org/david-walker

Davis, A. Y. (1981). *Women, race, and class*. New York: Random House.

Davis, A. Y. (2003). *Are prisons obsolete?* New York: Seven Stories Book.

Davis, A. Y. (2005). *Abolition democracy*. New York: Seven Stories Press.

Davis, A. Y. (2012). *The meaning of freedom: And other difficult dialogues*. San Francisco: City Light Books.

Davis, A. Y. (November 1, 2014). From Michael Brown to Assata Shakur, the racist state of America persists. *The Guardian*. Retrieved December 28, 2014, from www.theguardian.com/commentisfree/2014/nov/01/michael-brown-assata-shakur-racist-state-of-america

Davis, A. Y., Meiners, E., Dent, G., & Richie, B. (2022). *Abolition. Feminism. Now*. Chicago: Haymarket Press.

Davis, F. (July 8, 2016). This country needs a truth and reconciliation process on violence against African Americans-right now. *Yes! Magazine*. Retrieved from www.yesmagazine.org/social-justice/2016/07/08/this-country-needs-a-truth-and-reconciliation-process-on-violence-against-african-americans

Decker, A. (2015). The social services to prison pipeline. *The Indigenous Criminologist (blog)*. Retrieved February 25, 2017, from http://juantauri.blogspot.com/2015/11/the-social-services-to-prison-pipeline.html

Deloria, V. (1970). *We talk, you listen: New tribes, new turf*. New York: The Macmillan Company.

Deonna, J. A., Rodogno, R., & Teroni, F. (2012). *In defense of shame: The faces of an emotion*. Oxford: Oxford University Press.

deQuattro, P. (2015). Representing a parent in dependency court who also has a parallel (related) criminal case. *NACC Law Manual*, 218–224. Retrieved November 25, 2016, from https://c.ymcdn.com/sites/www.naccchildlaw.org/resource/resmgr/2015_Conference/Children's_Law_Manual_2015.pdf

Desmond, M. (August 14, 2019). In order to understand the brutality of American capitalism, you have to start on the plantation, The 1619 Project. *New York Times Magazine*. Retrieved January 1, 2020, from www.nytimes.com/interactive/2019/08/14/magazine/slavery-capitalism.html

Dhawan, N. (2014). Affirmative sabotage of the master's tools: The paradox of postcolonial enlightenment. In N. Dhawan (Ed.), *Decolonizing enlightenment: Transnational justice, human rights, and democracy in a postcolonial world* (pp.19–78). Leverkusen: Verlag Barbara Budrich.

Diabate, N. (2020). *Naked agency: Genital cursing and biopolitics in Africa.* Durham: Duke University Press.

Dierckxsens, G. (2015). The ambiguity of justice: Paul Ricoer on universalism and evil. *Etudes Ricoeriennes/Ricoeur Studies*, *6*(2): 32–49.

Dixon. E., & Piepzna-Samarasinha, L. L (Eds.). (2020). *Beyond survival: Strategies and stories from the transformative justice movement*. Chico: AK Press.

Dotson, K. (2011). Tracking epistemic violence, tracking practices of silence. *Hypatia*, *26*(2): 236–57.

Doughty, K. (2015). Law and the architecture of social repair: Gacaca days in post-genocide Rwanda. *Journal of the Royal Anthropological Institute*, *2*: 419–437.

Douglass, F. (1855). *My bondage and my freedom*. London: Partridge and Oakey.

Douglass, F. (1999). *Selected speeches and writings*, Chicago: Lawrence Hill.

DPIC. (2022). South Carolina death-row prisoners file suit to block firing-squad executions until courts address challenges to executions methods. *Death Penalty Information Center*. Retrieved April 10, 2022, from https://deathpenaltyinfo.org/news/south-carolina-death-row-prisoners-file-suit-to-block-firing-squad-executions-until-courts-address-challenges-to-execution-methods

Drucker, E. (2013). *A plague of prisons: The epidemiology of mass incarceration in America.* New York: The New Press.

Dübgen, F. (2020). Rethinking the Law: Taking clues from ubuntu. In L. Mattutat, R. Nigro, N. Schiel, & H. Stubenrauch (Eds.), *What's legit? Critiques of law and strategies of rights* (pp. 157–175). Zurich: Diaphanes.

Du Bois, W. E. B. (1935). *Black reconstruction*. New York: Harcourt Brace.

Dunbar-Ortiz, R. (2014). *An indigenous peoples' history of the United States*, Boston: Beacon Press.

Duprée, U. (2017). *Ho'oponopono and family constellations.* Baden-Baden: Earthdancer Books.

Dyer, J. (2000). *The perpetual prisoner machine: How America profits from crime.* Boulder: Westview.

Eddy, M. H., & Moradian, A. L. (2018). Childhood nature in motion: The ground for learning. In A. Cuter-Mackenzie, et al. (Eds.), *Research handbook on childhood nature* (pp. 1–24). New York: Springer International Handbooks of Education.

Edelman, M. W. (May 22, 2015). Child watch column: Overmedicating children in foster Care. *Children's Defense Fund.* Retrieved May 20, 2017, from www.childrensdefense.org/newsroom/child-watch-columns/child-watch-documents/OvermedicatingChildrenInFosterCare.html

Education for Liberation Network & Critical Resistance Editorial Collective. (2021). *Lessons in liberation: An abolitionist toolkit for educators.* Chico: AK Press.

Eligon, J. (July 1, 2011). Strauss-Kahn released as case teeters. *The New York Times.* Retrieved August 6, 2022, from https://www.nytimes.com/2011/07/02/nyregion/new-yorkers-and-french-await-latest-dominique-strauss-kahn-legal-turn.html

End Violence Against Children. (March 17, 2022). Wales has prohibited all forms of corporal punishment: Here's how they did it. Retrieved March 25, 2022, from www.end-violence.org/articles/wales-has-prohibited-all-forms-corporal-punishment-heres-how-they-did-it

Equal Justice Initiative. (2017). Lynching in America: Confronting the legacy of racial terror. Retrieved February 8, 2020, from https://lynchinginamerica.eji.org/report/

Eubanks, V. (2018). *Automating inequality: How high tech tools profile, police, and punish the poor.* New York: St Martin's Press.

Estreicher, S. (November 13, 2017). How to stop the next Harvey Weinstein. *Benefits Pro.* Retrieved April 26, 2022, from www.benefitspro.com/2017/11/13/how-to-stop-the-next-harvey-weinstein/?slreturn=20220326094045

Eze, E. C. (2001). *Achieving our humanity: The idea of the postracial future.* New York: Routledge.

Eze, M. O. (2010). *Intellectual history in contemporary South Africa.* New York: Palgrave-Macmillan.

Fasson, D. (2013). On resentment and ressentiment: The politics and ethics of emotions. *Current Anthropology*, *54*(3): 249–69.

Fitz-Gibbon, A., & Hall Fitz-Gibbon, J. (2019). *Nurturing strangers: Strategies for nonviolent re-parenting of children in foster care.* New York: Routledge.

Fluellen, R., & Trone, T. (2000). Do drug courts save jail and prison beds? *Vera Institute.* Retrieved April 26, 2022, from www.vera.org/publications/do-drug-courts-save-jail-and-prison-bed-space

Foucault, M. *Discipline and punish.* New York: Pantheon, 1977.

Frankl, V. (2006). *Man's search for meaning.* Boston: Beacon Press.

Franklin, K., & Werner, S. (April 16, 2020). New law reforming NY state central registry will provide justice and relief to families. *Rise.* Retrieved May 2, 2022, from www.risemagazine.org/2020/04/scr-reforms/

Fricker, M. (2007). *Epistemic injustice: Power and the ethics of knowing.* Oxford: Oxford University Press.

Gadamer, H.-G. (1986). *The relevance of the beautiful and other essays.* New York: Cambridge University Press.

Gade, C. B. N. (2017). *A discourse on African philosophy: A new perspective on Ubuntu and transitional justice in South Africa.* Lanham: Lexington Books.

Galli, T. (2016). *Die Schwere der Schuld.* Berlin: Das Neue Berlin.

Galli, T. (2017). *Die Gefährlichkeit des Täters.* Berlin: Das Neue Berlin.

Galván, N. Q. (2021). Editor's note: Growth in unprecedented times. *Columbia Journal of Race and Law*, *11*(3): 421–426.

García, M. N. (2007). Jorge Luis Borges's 'The lottery of Babylon' as allegory for the criminal justice system. In M. Nagel, & S. Asumah (Eds.), *Prisons and punishment: Reconsidering global penalty* (pp. 125–135). Trenton: Africa World Press.

Garza, L. M., & Williams, T. (April 13, 2016). Teenager who used 'affluenza' defense is sentenced to jail. *The New York Times*. Retrieved April 24, 2022, from www.nytimes.com/2016/04/14/us/teenager-who-used-affluenza-defense-is-sentenced-to-jail.html

GBD (2021). Fatal police violence by race and state in the USA, 1980–2019: A network meta-regression. *The Lancet*, *398*(10307): 1239–1255.

Gbowee, L., & Mithers, C. (2013). *How sisterhood, prayer, and sex changed a nation at war*. New York: Beast Books.

Geraghty, M. A. (2016). *Genocide ideology, nation-building, counter-revolution: Specters of the Rwandan Nation-State* [Doctoral dissertation]. University of Chicago.

Geraghty, M. A. (2020). Gacaca, genocide, genocide Ideology: The violent aftermaths of transitional justice in the New Rwanda. *Comparative Studies in Society and History*, *62*(3): 588–618.

German, M. (June 26, 2020). The FBI targets a new generation of black activists. *The Brennan Center*. Retrieved March 14, 2022, from www.brennancenter.org/our-work/analysis-opinion/fbi-targets-new-generation-black-activists

Gershoff, E. T. (2016). Spanking and child outcomes: Old controversies and new meta-analyses. *Journal of Family Psychology*, *30*(4): 453–469.

Gibson, J. A. (1992). *Concerning the league: The Iroquois league tradition as dictated in Onondaga by John Arthur Gibson*. In H. Woodby, R. Henry, & H. Webster (Eds., Trans.), *Based on A.A. Goldenweiser's manuscript, 1912*. Winnipeg: Algonquian and Iroquoian Linguistics.

Gibson, S. (February 22, 2018). Industrial fishing occupies a third of the planet. *National Geographic*. Retrieved from www.nationalgeog raphic.com/science/article/global-industrial-fishing-footprint-spd

Gibson, T. (1989). Symbolic representations of tranquility and aggression among the Buid. In S. Howell, & R. Willis (Eds.), *Societies at peace: Anthropological perspectives* (pp. 60–78). New York: Routledge.

Gil, E. (2017). *Posttraumatic play in children: What clinicians need to know*. New York: The Guildford Press.

Gilligan, J. (1996). *Violence: Our deadly epidemic and its causes*. New York: Grossett Putnam Books.

Gilligan, J. (2003). Shame, guilt, and violence. *Social Research*, *70*(4) (Winter): 1149–1180.

Gilmore, R. (2007). *Golden gulag: Prisons, surplus, crisis and opposition in globalizing California*. Berkeley: University of California Press.

Gilmore, R. W. (2021). *Change everything: Racial capitalism and the case for abolition*. Chicago: Haymarket Books.

Gladwell, M. (2008). *Outliers: The story of success*. New York: Little, Brown and Company.

Gleissner, J. D. (2013). Prison overcrowding cure: Judicial corporal punishment of adults. *Criminal Law Bulletin, Summer*, *49*(4): 711–55.

Gobodo-Madikizela, P. (2003). *A human being died that night: A South African story of forgiveness*. Boston: Houghton-Mifflin.

Gobodo-Madikizela, P. (2008). Working through the past: Some thoughts on forgiveness in cultural context. In P. Gobodo-Madikizela, & C. Van Der Merwe (Eds.), *Memory, narrative and forgiveness: Perspectives on the unfinished journeys of the past*. Newcastle upon Tyne: Cambridge Scholars Press.

Goldberg, M. (September 30, 2015). Has child protective services gone too far? *The Nation*. Retrieved November 26, 2016, from https://lockerdome.com/thenation.com/8078031935782164

Gottschalk, M. (2015a). *Caught: The prison state and the lockdown of American politics*. Princeton: Princeton University Press.

Gottschalk, M. (2015b). Bring it on: The future of penal reform, the carceral state, and American politics. *Ohio State Journal of Criminal Law, 12*: 559–603.

Graness, A. (2016). Der Ubuntu-Diskurs in Südafrika und sein Beitrag zur Gerechtigkeitsdebatte. In S. Dhouib (Ed.), *Gerechtigkeit in transkultureller Perspektive* (pp. 145–167). Weilerswist: Fellbrück Wissenschaft.

Greaves, W. (Dir.). (1989). *Ida B. Wells-Barnett: A passion for justice*. IMDb.

Greene, J., & Cohen, J. (2004). For the law, neuroscience changes nothing and everything. *Philosophical Transactions B 359*(1451): 1775–1785.

Groetzinger, K. (March 26, 2019). Civil rights activists push lawmakers to confront Texas' dark history of convict leasing. *Texas Observer*. Retrieved February 8, 2020, from www.texasobserver.org/civil-rights-activists-push-lawmakers-to-confront-texas-dark-history-of-convict-leasing/

Guggenheim, M. (2005). *What's wrong with children's rights*. Cambridge: Harvard University Press.

Guggenheim, M. (2015). General overview of child protection laws in the United States. In M. Guggenheim, & V. S. Sankaran (Eds.), *Representing parents in child welfare cases: Advice and guidance for family defenders* (pp. 1–18). Chicago: American Bar Association.

Guggenheim, M., & Sankaran, V. S. (Eds.). (2015). *Representing parents in child welfare cases: Advice and guidance for family defenders*. Chicago: American Bar Association.

Gunn Allen, P. (1986). Who is your mother? The red roots of white feminism. *History is a Weapon*. Retrieved from www.historyisaweapon.com/defcon1/allenredrootsofwhitefeminism.html

Hall Fitz-Gibbon, J. (2017). *Corporal punishment, religion, and United States public schools*. Cham: Palgrave.

Hamber, B. (2000). Repairing the irreparable: Dealing with the double-binds of making reparations for crimes of the past. *Ethnicity and Health, 5*(3–4): 215–226.

Hamber, B. (2015). There is a crack in everything: Problematising masculinities, peacebuilding and transitional justice. *Human Rights Review, 17*(1): 9–34.

Hamber, B. and Wilson, R. A. (2002). Symbolic closure through memory, reparation and revenge in post-conflict societies. *Journal of Human Rights, 1*(1): 35–53.

Hands off Assata! Campaign. (n.d.). *Assata: Exile since 1979*. Retrieved March 12, 2022, from www.assatashakur.com

Hannah-Jones, N. (2018). The 1619 project. *The New York Times*. Retrieved April 25, 2022, from www.nytimes.com/interactive/2019/08/14/magazine/1619-america-slavery.html

Hare, T. (1999). *ReMembering Osiris: Number, gender, and the word in ancient Egyptian representational systems*. Stanford: Stanford University Press.

Harris, K. (2007). Transformative justice: The transformation of restorative justice. In D. Sullivan and Tift (eds.), *Handbook of restorative justice: Global perspectives* (pp. 555–566). London: Routledge.

Harris, L. (2002). Insurrectionist ethics: Advocacy, moral psychology, and pragmatism. In J. Howie (Ed.), *Ethical issues for a new millennium* (pp. 192–210). Carbondale: Southern Illinois University Press.

Hauser, C., & Fortin, J. (August 31, 2017). "We only kill black people," Police officer says during traffic stop. *The New York Times*. Retrieved April 28, 2022, from www.nytimes.com/2017/08/31/us/black-kill-police-georgia.html

Hernandez, J. (December 14, 2021). An ex-NFL player who killed 6 people and then himself had CTE, doctors say. *National Public Radio*. Retrieved August 6, 2022, from https://www.npr.org/2021/12/14/1064130612/phillip-adams-nfl-player-killed-6-people-cte

Hill Collins, P. (2000). *Black feminist thought: Knowledge, consciousness, and the politics of empowerment*. New York: Routledge.

HIP. (2017). Keeping kids and parents together. *Human Impact Organization*. Retrieved from www.prisonpolicy.org/scans/hip/keeping_ma_kids_and_parents_together_2017.pdf

Ho, S., & Burke, G. (April 29, 2022). An algorithm that screens for child neglect raises concerns. *AP News*. Retrieved May 2, 2022, from https://apnews.com/article/child-welfare-algorithm-investigation-9497ee937e0053ad4144a86c68241ef1

Hobbes, T. (1985). *Leviathan*. New York: Penguin.

Hoffman, J. (March 3, 2022). Sacklers and Purdue reach new deal with states over Opiods. *The New York Times*. Retrieved May 8, 2022, from www.nytimes.com/2022/03/03/health/sacklers-purdue-oxycontin-settlement.html

Holmes, C., & Hunt, S. (2017). *Indigenous communities and family violence: Changing the conversation*. Prince George: National Collaborating Centre for Aboriginal Health.

Horovitz, S. (2016). International criminal courts in action: The ICTR's effect on death penalty and reconciliation in Rwanda. *The George Washington International Law Review*, *48*: 505–547.

Howard, K., Martin, A., Berlin, L. J., & Brooks-Gunn, J. (2011). Early mother-child separation, parenting, and child well-being in early head start families. *Attachment and Human Development*, *13*(1): 5–26.

Hudson, M. (2021). Battle of Tenochtitlán. *Encyclopedia Britannica*. Retrieved from www.britannica.com/event/Battle-of-Tenochtitlan

Human Rights Watch. (May 31, 2011). *Justice compromised: The legacy of Rwanda's community-based Gacaca Courts*. Retrieved from December 22, 2016, www.hrw.org/report/2011/05/31/justice-compromised/legacy-rwandas-community-based-gacaca-courts

Hund, W. D. (2011). "It must come from Europe": The racisms of Immanuel Kant. In W. D. Hund, C. Koller, & M. Zimmermann (Eds.), *Racisms made in Germany* (pp. 69–98). Münster: LIT Verlag.

Hunter, T. W. (2019). When slaveowners got reparations. *The New York Times*. Retrieved May 1, 2020, from, www.nytimes.com/2019/04/16/opinion/when-slaveowners-got-reparations.html

ICPR. (2020). *World prison brief: Rwanda*. Retrieved February 27, 2022, from www.prisonstudies.org/country/rwanda

INCITE! Women of Color Against Violence (Eds.). (2006). *The color of violence: The INCITE! anthology*. Boston: South End Press.

Indigenous Services Canada. (January 4, 2022). Agreements-in-principle reached on compensation and long-term reform of First Nations child and family services and Jordan's principle. *Government of Canada*. Retrieved from www.canada.ca/en/indigenous-services-canada/news/2022/01/agreements-in-principle-reached-on-compensation-and-long-term-reform-of-first-nations-child-and-family-services-and-jordans-principle.html

Ingelaere, B., & Verpoorten, M. (2016). *Inter-ethnic trust in the aftermath of mass violence: Insights from large-n life histories*. Working Papers 3. Antwerpen: Institute of Development Policy and Management.

Issifu, A. K. (2015). Exploring indigenous approaches to peacebuilding: The case of ubuntu in South Africa. *Peace Studies Journal, 8*(2): 59–72.

Itkowitz, C. (October 1, 2016). Her son shot their daughters 10 years ago. Then, these Amish families embraced her as a friend. *Washington Post*. Retrieved from www.washingtonpost.com/news/inspired-life/wp/2016/10/01/10-years-ago-her-son-killed-amish-children-their-families-immediately-accepted-her-into-their-lives/

Jackson, V. C. (2004). Constitutional dialogue and human dignity: States and transnational constitutional discourse. *Montana Law Review, 65*, 15–40.

James, J. (Ed.). (2005a). *The new abolitionists*. Albany, NY: SUNY Press.

James, J. (2005b). Introduction: Democracy and captivity. In J. James (Ed.), *The new abolitionists: (Neo)slave narratives and contemporary prison writings* (pp. xxi–xlii). Albany: SUNY Press.

Julien, I. (Dir.). (1995). *Frantz Fanon: Black skin, white masks*. IMDbPro

Kaba, M. (May 8, 2017). Free us all: Participatory defense campaigns as abolitionist organizing. *New Inquiry*. Retrieved February 9, 2020, from https://thenewinquiry.com/free-us-all/

Kaba, M. (2021). *We do this 'til we free us: Abolitionist organizing and transforming justice*. Chicago: Haymarket Books.

Kaba, M., & Schulte, B. (December 6, 2017). Not a cardboard cutout: Cyntoia Brown and the framing of a victim. *The Appeal*. Retrieved April 4, 2022, from https://theappeal.org/not-a-cardboard-cut-out-cyntoia-brown-and-the-framing-of-a-victim-aa61f80f9cbb/

Kant, I. (2019). Observations on the feeling of the beautiful and sublime. In R. R. Clewis (Ed.), *The sublime reader* (pp. 105–112). New York: Bloomsbury Publishing.

Kaplan, M. J. (Dir.). (2005). *Between Joyce and remembrance*. Oley: Bullfrog Films.

Karakatsanis, A. (2019). *The complicity of lawyers in the criminal injustice system*. New York: The New Press.

Kawaharada, D. (2006). *Hawaiian fishing traditions*. Honolulu: Kalamku Press.

Kennedy, E. J. (2019). "We charge genocide!" Still, no justice. *MinnPost*. Retrieved March, 2014, from www.minnpost.com/community-voices/2019/09/we-charge-genocide-still-no-justice/

Kennington, K. (2019). "To favor the side of freedom": Judicial opinions and the law of slavery. *Slavery & Abolition, 40*(2), 225–139.

Kershnar, S. (2012). *For torture: A rights-based defense*. Lanham: Lexington Books.

Khulumani Support Group. (2005). *"Yes to redress" campaign*. Retrieved July 30, 2018, from www.khulumani.net

Kilgore, J. (2022). *Understanding e-carceration: Electronic monitoring, the surveillance state, and the future of mass incarceration*. New York: The New Press.

Kim, M. E. (2018). From carceral feminism to transformative justice: Women-of-color feminism and alternatives to incarceration. *Journal of Ethnic & Cultural Diversity in Social Work*, *27*(3): 219–233.

King, M. L. (1965). "The American dream." Sermon delivered at Ebenezer Baptist Church in Atlanta, Georgia. *King Institute*. Retrieved from kinginstitute.stanford.edu/king-papers/documents/

King, M. L., & Washington, J. M. (1986). *A testament of hope: The essential writings and speeches of Martin Luther King, Jr*. New York: Harper & Row.

Kirchheimer, O. (1929/2017). 50 Jahre Deutsches Reichsgericht (1929). *WestEnd: Neue Zeitschrift für Sozialordnung*, *2*: 185–188.

Knopp, F., et al. (1976). *Instead of prisons: A handbook for abolitionists*. Syracuse: REAP. Retrieved from www.prisonpolicy.org/scans/instead_of_prisons/

Kone, K. (1997). *Bamana verbal art: An ethnographic study of proverbs* [Ph. D. Dissertation]. Indiana University.

Kone, K. (forthcoming 2023). The "Sunjata *Fasa*" and the Mali epic tradition. In P. J. Lothspeich (Ed.), *The epic world*. New York: Routledge.

Kramer, H., & Sprenger, J. (2016). *Malleus maleficarum: The witches' hammer*. Pantianos Classics.

Kraybill, D. B. (1989). *The riddle of Amish culture*. Baltimore: Johns Hopkins Press.

Kraybill, D. B., Nolt, S. M., & Weaver-Zercher, D. L. (2010). *Amish grace: How forgiveness transcended tragedy*. San Francisco: Jossey-Bass.

Kübler-Ross, E. (1969). *On death and dying*. New York: Simon & Schuster.

Kuradusenge, C. (2016). Denied victimhood and contested narratives: The case of Hutu diaspora. *Genocide Studies and Prevention: An International Journal*, *10*(2), 59–75. http://doi.org/10.5038/1911-9933.10.2.1352

Law, V. (2021). *"Prisons make us safer" and 20 other myths about mass incarceration*. Boston: Beacon Press.

Lebrón Ortiz, P. (2020). Resisting (meta) physical catastrophes through acts of marronage. *Radical Philosophy Review*, *23*(1): 35–57.

Le Mon, C. J. (2007). Rwanda's troubled gacaca courts. *Human Rights Brief*, *14*(2): 16–20. Retrieved March 6, 2022, from https://digitalcommons.wcl.american.edu/hrbrief/vol14/iss2/4/

Lesage de la Haye, J. (2021). *The abolition of prison*. Chico: AK Press.

Levenson, J., Willis, G., & Prescott, D. (2016). Adverse childhood experiences in the lives of male sex offenders: Implications for trauma-informed care. *Sexual Abuse: Journal of Research and Treatment*, *28*(4): 340–359.

Levenson, J., Willis, G., & Prescott, D. (2017). *Trauma-informed care: Transforming treatment for people who have sexually abused*. Brandon Vt.: Safer Society Press.

Levin, S. (April 7, 2022). California cities spent huge share of federal Covid relief funds on police. *The Guardian*. Retrieved April 11, 2022, from www.theguardian.com/us-news/2022/apr/07/covid-relief-funds-california-cities-police

L'Indicateur du Renouveau. (September 27, 2017). Justice: Scandale a la prison centrale de Bamako. *Maliweb*. Retrieved April 2, 2022, from www.maliweb.net/societe/justice-scandale-a-prison-centrale-de-bamako-2554372.html

Lindner, E. (2022). *From humiliation to dignity: For a future of global solidarity*. Lake Oswego: World Dignity University Press.
Lionni, L. (1967). *Frederick*. New York: Knopf.
Lipsitz, G. (2011). *How racism takes place*. Philadelphia: Temple University Press.
Lipsitz, G. (2006). *The possessive investment in whiteness: How white people benefit from identity politics*. Philadelphia: Temple University Press.
Loick, D. (2012). Strafe muss nicht sein. Zur Kritik des Strafrechts auf nationaler and internationaler Ebene. *Zeitschrift für Menschenrechte, 1*: 30–43.
Loick, D. (2015). "Expression of contempt": Hegel's critique of legal freedom. *Law and Critique, 26*: 189–206.
Loick, D. (2018). Law without violence. In C. Menke (Ed.), *Law and violence. Christoph Menke in dialogue* (pp. 96–111). Manchester: Manchester University Press.
Loick, D. (2019). *A critique of sovereignty*. London: Rowman & Littlefield International.
Lombardo, L. (1995). The 'pen' and the pendulum: Alternative futures for incarceration in the year 2010. In J. Klofas, & S. Stojkovic (Eds.), *Crime and justice in the year 2010* (pp. 185–204). Monterrey: Brooks/Cole Publishing.
Lombardo, L. (2018). Existence and imprisonment: Denial and pain in public policy. Presented at Institute on Violence and Trauma, San Diego, CA, September 6–9.
Lopez, G. (2017). Federal report: Violent crime rose in 2016. Other federal report: eh, maybe not. *Vox*. Retrieved April 23, 2022, from www.vox.com/policy-and-politics/2017/12/7/16746966/violent-crime-2016
Louw, D. J. (1998). Ubuntu: An African assessment of the religious other. *Paideia*. Retrieved from www.bu.edu/wcp/Papers/Afri/AfriLouw.htm
Love, B. (2019). *We want to do more than to survive: Abolitionist teaching and the pursuit of educational freedom*. Boston: Beacon Press.
Ludwig, T., & Barton, P. (2013). *The invisible boy*. New York: Knopf.
Luft, A. (2015). Toward a dynamic theory of action at the micro level of genocide: Killing, desistance, and saving in 1994 Rwanda. *Sociological Theory, 33*(2): 148–172.
Lyons, B. (1997). Between Nuremburg and amnesia: The truth and reconciliation commission of South Africa. *Monthly Review, September*: 5–22.
Mack, M. (2021). The white supremacy hydra: How the Family First Prevention Services Act reifies pathology, control, and punishment in the family regulation system. *Columbia Journal of Race and Law, 11*(3): 768–809.
Magnani, L., & Wray, H. (2006). *Beyond prisons: A new interfaith paradigm for our failed prison system*. Minneapolis: Fortress Press.
Mama, C. (2019). *Forgiveness redefined: A young woman's journey towards forgiving the apartheid assassin who brutally murdered her father*. Bryanston: Tracey McDonald Publishers.
Marinoff, L. (1999). *Plato, not Prozac!: Applying philosophy to everyday problems*. New York: HarperCollins.
Marshall, J. (2001). *The Lakota way: Stories and lessons for living*. New York: Viking Compass.
Martin, W., & Kurti, Z. (November 16, 2018). Cuomo's "carceral humanism." *Just Talk blog*. Retrieved from www.justtalk.blog/index.php/2018/11/
Martin, W. G. (2007). The prison industrial complex goes to Africa and beyond: Branch plant or apartheid plant? In M. Nagel, & S. N. Asumah (Eds.), *Prisons and punishment: Reconsidering global penality* (pp. 169–183). Trenton: Africa World Press.

Martin, W. G. (July 1, 2020). How police reforms fund the police. *Just Talk blog*. Retrieved from www.justtalk.blog/index.php/2020/07/01/how-police-reforms-fund-the-police/

Marya, R., & Patel, R. (2021). *Inflamed: Deep medicine and the anatomy of injustice*. New York: Farrar, Straus and Giroux.

Maslen, H. (2015). *Remorse, penal theory and sentencing*. Oxford: Hart Publishing.

Mathieson, T. (2014). *The politics of abolition revisited*. New York: Routledge.

Mauer, M. (2000). Plenary session, ICOPA conference, Toronto.

Mbiti, J. S. (2010). "Never break the pot that keeps you together": Peace and reconciliation in African religion. *Dialogue & Alliance – a journal of the Universal Peace Federation, 24*(1), pp. 4-21. Spring/Summer issue.

McBride, L. A. (2020). *A philosophy born of struggle: The Leonard Harris reader*. New York: Bloombury.

McConnell, G. (2020). Indigenous people and sentencing in Canada. *Library of Parliament*. Retrieved April 27, 2022, from https://lop.parl.ca/sites/PublicWebsite/default/en_CA/ResearchPublications/202046E

McCullough, M. (2008). *Beyond revenge: The evolution of the forgiveness instincts*. Hoboken: John Wiley.

McQuade, B. (2019). *Pacifying the homeland: Intelligence fusion and mass supervision*. Berkeley: University of California Press.

Meer, F. (2001). *Prison diary. One hundred and thirteen days, 1976*, Cape Town: Kwela Books.

Meiring, P. (1999). *Chronicle of the truth commission: A journey through the past and present – Into the future of South Africa*, Vanderbijlpark: Carpe Diem.

Menakem, R. (n.d.). *What somatic abolitionism is*. Retrieved from www.resmaa.com/movement

Metz, T. (2007). Toward an African moral theory. *Journal of Political Philosophy*, *15*(3): 321–341.

Metz, T. (2010). The reach of amnesty for political crimes: Which burdens on the guilty does national reconciliation permit? *Constitutional Court Review*, *3*: 243–270.

Metz, T. (2019). Reconciliation as the aim of a criminal trial: Ubuntu's implications for sentencing. *Constitutional Court Review*, *9*: 113–134.

Metz, T. (2022). *A relational moral theory: African ethics in and beyond the continent*. Oxford: Oxford University Press.

Meyer, M. (2018). *White lives matter most: And other "little" white lies*. Oakland: PM Press.

MFP. (2019). *Movement for Family Power*. Retrieved April 29, 2022, from www.movementforfamilypower.org/

Michaelson, V. E., & Durant, J. (2020). *Decolonizing discipline: Children, corporal punishment, Christian theologies, and reconciliation*. Winnipeg: Manitoba University Press.

Miller, L. (1995). *From the heart: Voices of the American Indian*. New York: Knopf

Miller, P. (2021). Brief of the American Professional Society on the abuse of children as amicus curiae in support of the appellants. *Supreme Court of Ohio*. Retrieved March 25, 2022, from www.supremecourt.ohio.gov/pdf_viewer/pdf_viewer.aspx?pdf=899089.pdf

Mills, C. (1997). *The racial contract*. Ithaca: Cornell University Press.

Mitchell, S. (Ed., Trans.). (2004). *Tao te ching: A new English version*. New York: Harper.

Moellendorf, D. (1997). Amnesty, truth and justice: AZAPO. *South African Journal on Human Rights, 13*(2): 283–291.

Mogul, J. L., Ritchie, A. J., & Whitlock, K. (2011). *Queer (in)justice: The criminalization of LGBT people in the United States.* Boston: Beacon Press.

Mokgoro, Y. (1998). Ubuntu and the law in South Africa. *Buffalo Human Rights Law Review, 4*: 15–25.

MonicoABHS. (July 30, 2018). *Long night's journey into day: The Amy Biehl story.* Retrieved from www.youtube.com/watch?v=IyQ10zMmYY8

Monture-Angus, P. (1995). *Thunder in my soul: A Mohawk woman speaks.* Halifax: Fernwood.

Mooney, J. (1902/2014). *Myths of the Cherokee.* Project Gutenberg EBook. https://www.gutenberg.org/ebooks/45634

Moore, J. I. (2015), Reforming the system. In M. Guggenheim, & V. S. Sankaran (Eds.), *Representing parents in child welfare cases: Advice and guidance for family defenders* (pp. 403–426). Chicago: American Bar Association.

Moran, L. (May 30, 2020). Trevor Noah: 'Police in America are looting black bodies.' *Huffington Post.* Retrieved March 8, 2022, from www.huffpost.com/entry/trevor-noah-george-floyd-protests_n_5ed21a1ec5b61d107a259936

Morris, R. (2000). *Stories of transformative justice.* Toronto: Canadian Scholars.

Motsei, M. (2007). *The kanga and the kangaroo court.* North Geelong: Spinifex Press.

Muhammad, G. (2020). *Cultivating genius: An equity framework for culturally and historically responsive literacy.* New York: Scholastic Teaching Resources.

Muhammad, K. G. (2010). *The condemnation of blackness: Race, crime, and the making of modern urban America.* Cambridge: Harvard University Press.

Murakawa, N. (2017). Weaponized empathy: Emotion and the limits of racial reconciliation in policing. In C. J. Ogletree, & A. Sarat (Eds.), *Beyond law and rights* (pp. 89–112). New York: New York University Press.

Murakawa, N. (2021). Ida B. Wells on racial criminalization. In M. Rogers, & J. Turner (Eds.), *African American political thought: A collected history* (pp. 212–234). Chicago: University of Chicago Press.

Murithi, T. (2006a) Practical peacemaking wisdom from Africa. *Journal of Pan African Studies, 1*(4). Retrieved from www.jpanafrican.com/archive_issues/june2006vol1no4.htm

Murithi, T. (2006b). African approaches to building peace and social solidarity. *African Journal on Conflict Resolution, 6*(2): 9–34.

Muthu, S. (2003). *Enlightenment against empire.* Princeton: Princeton University Press.

Nader. L. (1990). *Harmony ideology: Justice and control in a Zapotec mountain village.* Stanford: Stanford University Press.

Nagarajan, C. (2012). An appraisal of Rwanda's response to survivors who experienced sexual violence in 1994. *Wagadu, 10*: 108–131.

Nagel, M. (1998). Play in culture and the jargon of primordiality: A critique of Huizinga's *Homo ludens.* In M. Duncan, G. Chick, & A. Aycock (Eds.), *Play and culture studies: Diversions and divergences in fields of play* (pp. 19–30). London: Ablex.

Nagel, M. (2002). *Masking the abject: A genealogy of play.* Lantham: Lexington Books.

Nagel, M. (2007). Gender, incarceration and peacemaking: Lessons from Germany and Mali. In M. Nagel, & S. N. Asumah (Eds.), *Prisons and punishment: Reconsidering global penality* (pp. 43–51). Trenton: Africa World Press.

Nagel, M. (2013). An Ubuntu ethic of punishment. In M. Nagel, & A. Nocella (Eds.), *The end of prisons: Voices from the decarceration movement* (pp. 177–186). Amsterdam: Rodopi.

Nagel, M. (2014). Beyond the pale: Reflections on the vulnerability of black life in the U.S. In S. Asumah, & M. Nagel (Eds.), *Diversity, social justice, and inclusive excellence: Transdisciplinary and global perspectives* (pp. 69–91). Albany: SUNY Press.

Nagel, M. (2015a). Trafficking with abolitionism: An examination of anti-slavery discourses. *Champ Pénal/Penal Field, 12*: 1–17.

Nagel, M. (2015b). Angela Y Davis and Assata Shakur as women outlaws: Resisting U.S. state violence. *Wagadu, 13*: 43–78.

Nagel, M. (2016). Gender and the law. *Journal of Research in Gender Studies, 6*(2): 107–119.

Nagel, M., & Nocella, A. (Eds.). (2013). *The end of prisons: Voices from the decarceration movement*. Amsterdam: Rodopi.

Narvaez, D. F. (December 20, 2021). Putting childraising back on track: Childraising in the western world is off the rails, *Psychology Today*. Retrieved from www.psychologytoday.com/us/blog/moral-landscapes/202112/putting-childraising-back-track

National Advisory Commission on Criminal Justice Standards and Goals (NAC). (1973). Corrections. *US Department of Justice*. Retrieved March 29, 2022, from www.ojp.gov/pdffiles1/Digitization/10865NCJRS.pdf

National No Hit Zone Committee. (2022). *NHZ Toolkit*. Retrieved March 25, 2022, from https://nohitzone.com/toolkit/

Naydler, J. (1996). *Temple of the cosmos: The ancient Egyptian experience of the sacred*. Rochester: Inner Traditions International.

Neergard, L. (February 18, 2017). Talk to babies and let them babble. *The Associated Press*. Retrieved February 25, 2017, from https://apnews.com/647ba5b170b94d6f896b9e0728c04a4f/Talk-to-babies-and-let-them-babble-back-to-bridge-word-gap

NEPM Documentaries. (2014). *Big ideas for little kids*. Retrieved from https://video.nepm.org/video/wgby-documentaries-big-ideas-little-kids/

Neusteter, R., & O'Toole, M. (2019). Every three seconds: Unlocking police data on arrests. *Vera*. Retrieved March 18, 2022, from www.vera.org/publications/arrest-trends-every-three-seconds-landing/arrest-trends-every-three-seconds/overview

Nietzsche, F. (1993). *Thus spake Zarathustra*. Amherst: Prometheus Press.

Nietzsche, F. (1996). *On the genealogy of morals*. Oxford: Oxford University Press.

Nyseth Brehm, H., Uggen, C., & Gasanabo J.-D. (2014). Genocide, justice, and Rwanda's gacaca courts. *Journal of Contemporary Criminal Justice, 30*(3): 333–352.

OCR. (August 27, 2013). Amy Biehl legacy: Reconciliation that spans generations. *The Orange County Register*. Retrieved from www.ocregister.com/articles/biehl-522733-amy-linda.html?page=3

Office of Children and Family Services (OCFS). (2015). *Administrative directive: Supporting normative experiences for children, youth, and young adults in foster care: Applying a reasonable and prudent parent standard*. Rensselaer: OCFS.

Oglala Sioux Tribe v. Van Hunnik, Dist. Court, D. South Dakota (March, 2015), No. Civ. 13-5020-JLV.

O'Harrow, R., Ba Tran, A., & Hawkins, D. (April 12, 2021). The rise of domestic extremism in America. *The Washington Post*. Retrieved April 25, 2022, from www.washingtonpost.com/investigations/interactive/2021/domestic-terrorism-data/

OJP. (April, 1999). State police review team regarding allegations of racial profiling: Interim Report. *US Department of Justice, Office of Justice Programs*. Retrieved March 17, 2022, from www.ojp.gov/ncjrs/virtual-library/abstracts/state-police-review-team-regarding-allegations-racial-profiling

Oleson, J. C. (2002). The punitive coma. *California Law Review, 90*(30): 829–901.

Oruka, H. O. (1976). *Punishment and terrorism in Africa*. Nairobi: East African Literature Bureau.

Oshinsky, D. (1996). *Worse than slavery: Parchman Farm and the ordeal of Jim Crow justice*. New York: Simon and Schuster.

Ossenbrink, L. (June 1, 2021). Namibia's Ovaherero, Nama slam exclusion from Germany deal. *Aljazeera*. Retrieved from www.aljazeera.com/news/2021/6/1/ovaherero-nama-descendants-criticise-germanys-reconciliation

Pager, D. (2007). *Marked: Race, crime, and finding work in an era of mass incarceration*. Chicago: University of Chicago Press.

Paley, V. G. (1993). *You can't say you can't play*. Cambridge: Harvard University Press.

Palmater, P. (2020). Indigenous knowledge and abolition: Criminalization, decolonization and lessons from indigenous justice systems. *Criminalization and Punishment Education Project*. Retrieved from https://cp-ep.org/indigenous-knowledge-and-abolition-live-webinar-april-30-7pm-9pm/

PBS Newshour. (August 23, 2016). *Assessing whether corporal punishment helps students, or hurts them*. Retrieved November 24, 2016, from www.pbs.org/newshour/bb/assessing-whether-corporal-punishment-helps-students-hurts/

Pedicelli, G. (1998). *When police kill: Police use of force in Montreal and Toronto*. Québec: Véhicule Press.

Peltier, L. (2000). *Prison writings: My life is my sun dance*. New York: St. Martin's Press.

Pepinsky, H. (2006). *Peacemaking: Reflections of a radical criminologist*. Ottawa: Ottawa University Press.

Pepinsky, H., & Quinney, R. (1991). *Criminology as peacemaking. Bloomington*, IN: Indiana University Press.

Piliavsky, A., & Sbriccoli, T. (2016). The ethics of efficacy in North India's goonda raj (rule of toughs). *Journal of the Royal Anthropological Institute, 22*: n/a-n/a. 10.1111/1467-9655.12404.

Pinker, S. (2011). *The better angels of our nature: Why violence has declined*. New York: Penguin.

Plessy v. Ferguson, 163 U.S. 537.

Porges, S. W. (2017). *The pocket guide to the polyvagal theory: The transformative power of feeling safe*. New York: Norton.

Powell, K. (2015). *The education of Kevin Powell*. New York: Simon & Schuster.

Prescott, J. (1997). Breastfeeding: Brain nutrients in brain development for human love and peace. *The origins of peace and violence*. Retrieved from www.violence.de/prescott/ttf/article.html

Price, J. M. (2015a). *Prison and social death*. Rutgers: Rutgers University Press.

Price, J. M. (2015b). Serving two masters? Reentry task forces and justice disinvestment. In W. G. Martin, & J. M. Price (Eds.), *After prisons? Freedom, decarceration, justice disinvestment* (pp. 77–98). Lanham: Lexington Books.

Prison Policy Initiative. (2017). *Following the money of mass incarceration*. Retrieved April 5, 2022, from www.prisonpolicy.org/reports/money.html

Project NIA. (2013). *Transformative justice: A curriculum guide*. Retrieved from https://niastories.files.wordpress.com/2013/08/tjcurriculum_design_small-finalrev.pdf

Proulx, C. (2003). *Reclaiming aboriginal justice, identity, and community*. Saskatoon: Pourich Publishing.

Quandt, K. R., & Altshule, A. (March 22, 2022). COVID fueled solitary confinement still plagues prisons and jails. *Solitary Watch*. Retrieved May 7, 2022, from https://solitarywatch.org/2022/03/22/covid-fueled-solitary-confinement-still-plagues-prisons-and-jails/

Raemisch. (February 20, 2014). My night in solitary. *The New York Times*. Retrieved April 23, 2022, from www.nytimes.com/2014/02/21/opinion/my-night-in-solitary.html

Ramose, M. B. (2003). The philosophy of ubuntu and ubuntu as a philosophy. In P. H. Coetzee, & A. P. J. Roux (Eds.), *The African philosophy reader: A text with readings* (2nd ed., pp. 230–238). New York: Routledge.

Ramose, M. B. (2022). *African philosophy through ubuntu* (rev. ed.). Harare: Mond Books.

Ramsey, M. (2009). The lived experience of receiving empathy and forgiveness for six South African perpetrators. In P. Gobodo-Madikizela, & C. van der Merwe (Eds.), *Memory, narrative and forgiveness: Perspectives on the unfinished journeys of the past* (pp. 130–147). Newcastle upon Tyne: Cambridge Scholars.

Rautenbach, C. (2015). Legal reform of traditional courts in South Africa: Exploring the links between *ubuntu*, restorative justice and therapeutic jurisprudence. *Journal of International and Comparative Law*, *2*(2): 275–304.

Redleaf, D. L. (2015). The impact of abuse and neglect findings beyond the juvenile courthouse: Understanding the child abuse register system and ways to challenge administrative child abuse register determinations. In M. Guggenheim, & V. S. Sankaran (Eds.), *Representing parents in child welfare cases: Advice and guidance for family defenders* (pp. 389–401). Chicago: American Bar Association.

Reznik, R. (2019). Retributive abolitionism. *Berkeley Journal of Criminal Law*, *24*(2): 123–194.

Reticker, G. (Dir.). (2008). *Pray the devil back to hell*. Passion River Films.

Rhodes, L. (2004). *Total confinement: Madness and reason in the maximum security prison*. Berkeley: University of California Press.

Rice, J. D., & Smith, C. (2019). Justice in America, Episode 19. What justice could look like. *The Appeal*. Retrieved from https://theappeal.org/justice-in-america-episode-19-what-justice-could-look-like/

Riggs, M. (Dir.). (1986). *Ethnic notions: Black people in white minds*. California Newsreel.

Roberts, D. E. (2002). *Shattered bonds: The color of welfare*. New York: Basic Books.

Roberts, D. E. (2018). Abolish family policing, too. *Dissent Magazine*. Retrieved March 22, 2022, from www.dissentmagazine.org/article/abolish-family-policing-too?

Roberts, D. E. (2021). Keynote. Strengthened bonds: Abolishing the child welfare system and re-envisioning child well-being. How I became a family policing abolitionist. *Columbia Journal of Race and Law*, *11*(3): 454–469.

Roberts, D. E. (2022). *Torn apart: How the child welfare system destroys black families–and how abolition can build a safer world*. New York: The New Press.

Rodríguez, L. J. (2001). *Hearts and hands: Creating community in violent times*. New York: Seven Story Press.

Rodriguez, S. M. (2021). Queer abolitionist alternatives to criminalising hate violence. In M. J. Coyle, & D. Scott (Eds.), *The Routledge international handbook on penal abolitionism* (pp. 190–200). London: Routledge.

Rodriguez, S. M. (2022). Queers against corrective development: LGBTSTGNC anti-violence organizing in gentrifying times. *GLQ: A Journal of Lesbian and Gay Studies, 28*(2): 165–184.

Rodriguez, S. M., & Clark, B. (2022). Not behind bars: The rippling of carceral habitus and corrective violence on the family and community life of prison guards. In M. J. Coyle, & M. Nagel (Eds.), *Contesting carceral logic: Towards abolitionist futures* (pp. 50–64). New York: Routledge.

Roesch, S. W. (1992). The Iroquois influence on women's rights. In J. Barreiro (Ed.), *Indian roots of American democracy* (pp. 115–134). Ithaca: Akwe:Kon Press.

Roodt, D. (Dir.). (2011). *Winnie Mandela.* IMDb.

Rosga, A. (1999). Policing the state. *The Georgetown Journal of Gender and the Law, Summer*: 145–171.

Ross, R. (1996). *Returning to the teachings: Exploring aboriginal justice*. New York: Penguin.

Ross, R. (2014). *Indigenous healing: Exploring traditional paths*. New York: Penguin.

Roth-Arriaza, N. (2004). Reparations in the aftermath of repression and mass violence. In E. Stover, & H. Weinstein (Eds.), *My neighbor, my enemy: Justice and community in the aftermath of mass atrocity* (pp. 12–140). Cambridge: Cambridge University Press.

Russell-Brown, K. (2008). *The color of crime: Racial hoaxes, white fear, black protectionism, police harassment and other macroaggressions* (2nd ed.). New York: New York University Press.

Rwanda Preamble to the Organic Law No 40/2000. (January 26, 2001). Fundamental Law. Republic of Rwanda.

Sachs, A. (2009). *The strange alchemy of life and law*. Oxford: Oxford University Press.

Sachs, A. (2014). *The soft vengeance of a freedom fighter* (2nd ed.). Oakland: University of California Press.

Sack, F. (May 16, 2018). Zur Aktualität des Staates für die Kriminologie. Presentation at Kritische Kriminologie und Soziale Arbeit im Dialog, Hochschule für Angewandte Wissenschaften Hamburg.

Sadhguru. (January 23, 2020). I don't forgive anybody, because .... *OnePath.* Retrieved from www.youtube.com/watch?v=uoL2AM7IVQ

Safe OUTSide the System. (n.d.). *Tools and resources*. Retrieved from https://alp.org/programs/sos

Salah-El, T. A. (2006). *Autobiography of Tiyo Attallah Salah-El.* New York: iUniverse.

Salah-El. T. A. (2007). A call for the abolition of prisons. In M. Nagel, & S. Asumah (Eds.), *Prisons and punishment: Reconsidering global penality* (pp. 201–205). Trenton, NJ: African World Press.

Salah-El, T. A. (2020). *Pen pal: Prison letters from a free spirit on slow death row.* New York: OR Books.

Saleh-Hanna, V. (Ed.). (2008a). *Colonial systems of control: Criminal justice in Nigeria.* Ottawa: University of Ottawa Press.

Saleh-Hanna, V. (2008b). Penal coloniality. In V. Saleh Hanna (Ed.), *Colonial systems of control: Criminal justice in Nigeria* (pp. 17–54). Ottawa: Ottawa University Press.

Saleh-Hanna, V. (2017). An abolitionist theory on crime: Ending the abusive relationship with Racist-Imperialist-Patriarchy [R.I.P.]. *Contemporary Justice Review, 20*(4): 419–441.

Salles, F, Curtis, Z., Sharpe, A., & Barber, J. (2022). *Tiyo's songs of life*. Bailey: Tapestry Records.

Saul, Q. (Ed.). (2018). *Maroon comix: Origins and destinies*. Oakland: PM Press.

Schaefer, C. (2006). *Grandmothers counsel the world: Women elders offer their vision for our planet*. Boston: Trumpeter Books.

Scheler, M. (2010). *Ressentiment*. Milwaukee: Marquette University Press.

Schept, J. (2015). *Progressive punishment: Job loss, jail growth, and the neoliberal logic of carceral expansion*. New York: New York University Press.

Schoenfeld, H. (2010). Mass incarceration and the paradox of prison litigation. *Law and Society Review*, *44*(3/4): 731–768.

Scott, D. (2018). *Against imprisonment: An anthology of abolitionist essays*. Sherfield Gables: Waterside Press.

Scott, D. (2020). *For abolition: Essays on prisons and socialist ethics*. Sherfield Gables: Waterside Press.

Scott, J. C. (2010). *The art of not being governed*. New Haven: Yale University Press.

Second Face, & Museum of Cultural Masks. (n.d.). *The Apache Ga'an Dance*. Retrieved March 12, 2022, from www.maskmuseum.org/apache-gaan-post/

Sentencing Project. (n.d.). One third of Black men have felony convictions. *Race and Justice News*. Retrieved from www.sentencingproject.org/news/5593/

Sered, D. (2018). *Until we reckon: Mass incarceration and a road to repair*. New York: The New Press.

Shakur, A. (1987). *Assata: An autobiography*. Chicago: Lawrence Hill Books.

Sinha, M. (2016). *The slave's cause: A history of abolition*. New Haven: Yale University Press.

Sjöö, M., & Mor, B. (1987). *The great cosmic mother: Rediscovering the religion of the earth*. San Francisco: Harper & Row.

Smith, D. (2015). South African death squad leader Eugene de Kock to be freed from jail. *The Guardian*. Retrieved March 25, 2015, from www.theguardian.com/world/2015/jan/30/south-africa-eugene-de-kock-released-prime-evil

Smith, J. E. H. (2015). "There is blood, a lot of blood, very red blood": The death penalty in crisis. *The Chronicle of Higher Education*. Retrieved April 28, 2022, from www.chronicle.com/article/there-is-blood-a-lot-of-blood-very-red-blood/

Smith Ledesma, S. (2015). The Vanishing of the African-American family: "Reasonable efforts" and its connection to the disproportionality of the child welfare system. *NACC Law Manual*, 280–308. Retrieved November 25, 2016, from https://c.ymcdn.com/sites/www.naccchildlaw.org/resource/resmgr/2015_Conference/Children's_Law_Manual_2015.pdf

Somé, M. P. (1997). *Ritual: Power, healing, and community*. New York: Penguin.

Somjeen, S. (October 23, 2018). Decolonizing reconciliation: Changing the narrative to the indigenous museums of peace in Kenya and South Sudan. *Public lecture: Florida International University, Miami*. Retrieved from http://dpanther.fiu.edu/sobek/content/FI/KH/00/00/17/00001/2018%20October%2023rd%20Public%20Lecture%20FIU.pdf

Soyinka, W. (1972). *The man died*. Toronto: Collins Publishers.

Spade, D. (2015). *Normal life: Administrative violence, critical trans politics and the limits of law*. Durham: Duke University Law.

Staas, C., & Ullrich, V. (March 5, 2015). Verbrechen der Wehrmacht. *Die Zeit*: 10, 18–19.

Staples, W. G. (2014). *Everyday surveillance: Vigilance and visibility in everyday life* (2nd ed). Lanham, MD: Rowman & Littlefield.

Startz, D. (2016). Schools, black children, and corporal punishment. *Huffington Post.* Retrieved July 17, 2017, from www.huffingtonpost.com/entry/black-children-corporal-punishment_us_56a975e7e4b0d82286d4eb61

Steinhoff, U. (2013). *On the ethics of torture.* Albany: SUNY Press.

Stelloh, T. (December 17, 2018). Michigan appeals court to review judge's sentencing of Larry Nassar. *NBC News.* Retrieved April 11, 2022, from www.nbcnews.com/storyline/sexual-misconduct/michigan-appeals-court-review-judge-s-sentencing-larry-nassar-n949126

Stevens, J. P. (2010). On the death sentence. *The New York Review of Books.* Retrieved April 28, 2022, from www.nybooks.com/articles/2010/12/23/death-sentence/

Stevenson, B. (2019). *Just mercy: A story of justice and redemption,* New York: Spiegel and Grau.

Stiftung Gewaltfreie Kindheit. (May 21, 2021). *Wilhelm Buntz – Der Bibelraucher.* Retrieved from www.youtube.com/watch?v=yU5RjvAQnZQ

Stroud, A. M. (March 30, 2015). Lead prosecutor apologizes for role in sending man to death row. *Shreveport Times.* Retrieved April 28, 2022, from www.shreveporttimes.com/story/opinion/readers/2015/03/20/lead-prosecutor-offers-apology-in-the-case-of-exonerated-death-row-inmate-glenn-ford/25049063/

Struthers Montford, K., & Taylor, C. (2022). *Building abolition: Decarceration and social justice.* New York: Routledge.

Sudbury, J. (Ed.), (2005). *Global lockdown: Race, gender, and the prison-industrial complex.* New York: Routledge.

Sudbury, J. (2009). Maroon abolitionists: Black gender-oppressed activists in the anti-prison movement in the U.S. and Canada. *Meridians: Feminism, Race, Transnationalism, 9*(1): 1–29.

Takaki, R. (2008). *A different mirror: A history of multicultural America.* New York: Little, Brown and Company.

Teleki, M., & Kamga, D. K. (2020). Recognizing the value of the African indigenous knowledge system: The case of ubuntu and restorative justice. In S. O. Oloruntoba, A. Afolayan, & O. Yacob-Haliso (Eds.) *Indigenous knowledge systems and development in Africa* (pp. 303–327). New York: Palgrave Macmillan.

The Forgiveness Project. (March 12, 2021). *Linda Biehl and Easy Nofemela.* Retrieved from www.theforgivenessproject.com/stories/linda-biehl-easy-nofemela/

The Movement for Black Lives. *Policy platforms.* Retrieved from https://m4bl.org/policy-platforms/

The Rwandan Lawyer. (May 16, 2021). Rwanda: Failure of Gacaca Court objectives. *The Rwandan.* Retrieved February 28, 2022, from www.therwandan.com/rwanda-failure-of-gacaca-courts-objectives/

The Sentencing Project. (March, 2018). *Report of the Sentencing Project to the United Nations Special Rapporteur on contemporary forms of racism, racial discrimination, xenophobia and related intolerance.* Retrieved March 29, 2022, from www.sentencingproject.org/wp-content/uploads/2018/04/UN-Report-on-Racial-Disparities.pdf

Thomas, H. (2006). *The shame response to rejection,* 2nd ed. New York: Albanel.

Thomas Suh, R. (Dir.). (2016). *Reject.* IMDb.

Thompson, T., & Copeland, L. (1987). Rural justice: Ex-convicts as cheap labor; an old habit that dies hard. *The Atlanta Journal,* A/1.

Thompson, V. E. (2022). "There is no justice, there is just us!" Towards a postcolonial feminist critique of policing using the example of racial profiling in Europe. In M.

J. Coyle, & M. Nagel (Eds.), *Contesting carceral logic: Towards abolitionist futures* (pp. 90–104). New York: Routledge.

Thuma. (2019). *All our trials: Prisons, policing, and the feminist fight to end violence*. Urbana: University of Illinois Press.

Tobin, B. (2014). *Indigenous peoples, customary law and human rights – why living law matters*. New York: Routledge.

Tom, P. (2006). The Acholi traditional approach to justice in Northern Uganda. *Beyond Intractability*. Retrieved from www.beyondintractability.org/casestudy/tom-acholi

Tonry, M. (Ed.), *Why punish? How much? A reader on punishment* (pp. 337–352). New York: Oxford University Press.

Tossounian, J. (2016). *The human kennel: Journals written inside a provincial jail for women*. Rockland: Ankle Bone Books.

Towner, E. (2013). Documenting genocide: The "record of confession, guilty plea, repentance and apology" in Rwanda's gacaca trials. *Technical Communication Quarterly*, *22*, 285–303. https://doi.org/10.1080/10572252.2013.780963

Tutu, D. (1999). *No future without forgiveness*. New York: Doubleday Books.

Tutu, D. (2016). Pray for the person who holds a weapon. *Huffington Post*. Retrieved February 27, 2022, from www.huffpost.com/entry/pray-for-the-person-who-holds-the-weapon_b_8168102

Ure, M. (2020). Resentment/ressentiment. *Constellations*, *22*(4): 599–613.

US Department of Justice Civil Rights Division. (2015). Investigation of the Ferguson Police Department. *US Department of Justice*. Retrieved April 15, 2015, from www.justice.gov/sites/default/files/opa/press – releases/attachments/2015/03/04/ferguson_police_department_report.pdf

van Schilfgaarde, L., & Shelton, B. L. (2021). Using peacemaking circles to indigenize tribal child welfare. *Columbia Journal of Race and Law, 11*(3): 687–709.

Van Tuinen, S. (2021). Authentic ressentiment? The polemics of Jean Améry. *Philosophy Today*, *65*(4): 807–827.

Vasquez, J. (2016). On the verge of hell. In J. Ridgeway, & J. Casella (Eds.), *Hell is a very small place: Voices from solitary confinement* (pp. 55–60). New York: The New Press.

Vasquez, J. (January 11, 2021). Voices from solitary: Flashes from hell. *Solitary Watch*. Retrieved April 25, 2022, from https://solitarywatch.org/2021/01/11/voices-from-solitary-flashes-from-hell/

Vielle, S. (2011). *Rethinking justice in transitional justice: An examination of the Māori conception and customary mechanism of justice*. Ph.D. Dissertation. The University of Western Ontario. London, Ontario.

Villa, C. F. (2016). Living in the SHU. In J. Ridgeway, & J. Casella (Eds.), *Hell is a very small place: Voices from solitary confinement* (pp. 35–42). New York: The New Press.

Vitale, A. (2017). *The end of policing*. New York: Verso.

Waldorf, L. (2009). Remnants and remains: Narratives of suffering in post-genocide Rwanda's gacaca courts. In R. A. Wilson, & R. D. Brown (Eds.), *Humanitarianism and suffering: The mobilization of empathy* (pp. 285–305). New York: Cambridge University Press.

Walker, D. (1830). An appeal to the colored citizens of the world. *David Walker Memorial Organization*. Retrieved February 2, 2020, from www.davidwalkermemorial.org/appeal

Walters, R. D. (2013). The thirteenth amendment "exception" to the state action doctrine: An originalist reappraisal. *George Mason University Civil Rights Law Journal, 23*(2): 283–331.

Wa Thiong'o, N. (1982). *Devil on the cross*. London: Heinemann.

Wa Thiong'o, N. (1986). *Petals of blood*. Oxford: Heinemann.

Watts, D., Adams, W., & Dixon, B. V. (2014). *I can't breathe (Eric Garner)*. Retrieved May 8, 2022, from https://vimeo.com/102204410

Wa Wamwere, K. (2002). *I refuse to die: My journey for freedom*. New York: Seven Stories Press.

Wells-Barnett, I. B. (1892/2005). Southern horrors: Lynch law in all its phases. *Project Gutenberg*. Retrieved February 3, 2020, from www.gutenberg.org/files/14975/14975-h/14975-h.htm

Wells-Barnett, I. B. (1895/2005). A red record: Tabulated statistics and alleged causes of lynchings in the United States. *Project Gutenberg*. Retrieved February 3, 2020, from https://archive.org/stream/theredrecord14977gut/14977.txt

Whewell, T. (April 14, 2016). Norway's Barnevernet: They took our four children... Then the baby. *BBC News*. Retrieved October 8, 2016, from www.bbc.com/news/magazine-36026458

Whitlock, K., & Heitzeg, N. A. (2021). *Carceral con: The deceptive terrain of criminal justice reform*. Berkeley: University of California Press.

Wilde, O. (1896). The ballad of Reading Gaol. Retrieved October 31, 2014, from www.gutenberg.org/files/301/301-h/301-h.htm

Wilkins, B. (June 22, 2021). "The Zapatistas have invaded": Indigenous activists sail from Mexico to Spain. *Common Dreams*. Retrieved from www.commondreams.org/news/2021/06/22/zapatistas-have-invaded-indigenous-activists-sail-mexico-spain

Willett, C. (2014). *Interspecies ethics*. New York: Columbia University Press.

Wilson, R. A. (2000). Reconciliation and revenge in post-apartheid South Africa. *Current Anthropology, 41*(1): 75–98.

Woolman, J. (2015). Special considerations representing clients involved with the criminal justice system. In M. Guggenheim, & V. S. Sankaran (Eds.), *Representing parents in child welfare cases: Advice and guidance for family defenders* (pp. 51–64). Chicago: American Bar Association.

Yamamoto, E. K., & Ayabe, S. D. (2011). Courts in the "age of reconciliation": *Office of Hawaiian Affairs v. HCDCH. University of Hawai'i Law Review, 33*(2): 502–535.

Young, I. M. (1997). House and home: Feminist variations on a theme. In I. M. Young (Ed.), *Intersecting voices: Dilemmas of gender, political philosophy, and policy* (pp. 134–164). Princeton: Princeton University Press.

Zehr, H. (2011). Restorative or transformative justice? *Zehr Institute for Restorative Justice*. Retrieved from https://emu.edu/now/restorative-justice/2011/03/10/restorative-or-transformative-justice/

Zeleza, T. (1983). African history: The rise and decline of academic tourism. *Ufahamu, 15*(1): 9–42.

Zimmerman, M. J. (2011). *The immorality of punishment*. Peterborough: Broadview Press.

Zinn, H. (1980). *A people's history of the United States*. New York: HarperCollins.

Index

abolition: *vs.* 'abolitionism' 39, 56; of family regulation system 74; democracy 107–8, 137, 193; lessons of 127–9; penal 13, 133, 153; in the postcolony 27; and prisons as healing centers 30; retributivist 137, 150; somatic 152; of nation-state 163; teaching 168; and TJ Curriculum Kit 175
Abu-Jamal, M. 14, 34, 58, 107
accountability 7, 144–8; accessibility of 143; community 137; critique of community 150; healing beyond 133; and justice game 21; necessity of 133
Achebe, C. 8
Acholi 19; and Mato Oput 151, 186–7
Agbakoba, J. 8–9
Agozino, B. 4, 23
Alexander, M. 29
Améry, J. 122, 139, 181
Apache Spirit Dancer 1; and Ga'an Dance 11
Ashforth, A. 51–2
Azanian People's Organization 36, 121

Baldwin, J. 182
Bazant, M. 155–7
Ben-Moshe, L. 137
Bernstein, E. 28, 78
Bernstein, N. 89, 105
Black Lives Matter 14, 33, 56, 89, 97–9, 149, 172; and Kantian racism; and love (*agape*) 149
Black Panther's Ten Point Action Program 191
Braithwaite, J. 6–7, 113, 148
Bread and Puppet Theater 62
Brendtro, L., Brokenleg, M., & Van Bockern, S. 10, 136, 165
Bronx Defenders 82
Brown, M. 11, 100
Brown, R. P. 1–2
Brown, W. 161
Buntz, W. 179–81
Butler, P. 15, 47, 101, 105

Cherokee 10; Trail of Tears 93
Chigumadzi, P. 192
Chun, M. N. 159–61
Combahee River Collective 106
Cornell, D. 4, 8, 42
Cover, R. 27
Coyle, M. J. 23, 39, 137

Davis, A. 89–90, 99, 101–3, 107, 137, 178
Deloria, V. 131
Dhawan, N. 42–5
Dierckxsens, G. 50–1
Diné 161; court 170–1
Dotson, K. 68
Douglass, F. 95–6, 99
Du Bois, W. E. B. 137
Dübgen, F. 23

Equal Justice Initiative 99
Erbrich, E. 182

Floyd, G. 14, 101
Foucault, M. 61
Frankl, V. 139, 182
Frazier, D. 100
Fricker, M. 67

Galli, T. 29, 177, 181, 189
Geraghty, M. 112, 115–18
Gilligan, J. 125
Gobodo-Madikizela, P. 6, 119, 123, 125–6, 139, 183
Guggenheim, M. 75–6, 78

Hall Fitz-Gibbon, J. 47, 70, 76–7
Hands off Assata! 103
Harris, L. 15, 89, 100
Hawai'i 93; Aloha Spirit law 160; and Ho'oponopono 136, 151, 158–61
Hobbes, T. 26, 41, 47, 88, 91–2, 108, 135, 144, 174

INCITE! Collective 150
Indigenous world view: and African reconciliation practices 136; assault on 13; and beyond forgiveness 183–5; Black feminist hauntology 44; and forgiveness rituals 19, 158–61; and healing 16; and healing circles 168–71; and healing-informed care 153; Inkundla/Lekgotla 160; and *jeliws* 138; joking relations 19; and Kgotla courts 53; nested care 8, 10, 17, 26, 51, 77, 83; and peaceful societies 174; and peacemaking 16, 135; and recovery of law 163
International Conference on Penal Abolition (ICOPA) 63
Iroquois: Council of Matrons 187; Great Law of Peace 162; oldest democracy 187; role of women 187

James, J. 34
Jim Crow 12, 56, 88, 98; and anti-Black racism 12, 190; death dance in New Jim Crow era 12–13, 133; looting of Black bodies 15
justice: and African jurisprudence 119; in alternative courts 48–9; ambiguity in 49–51; Bamana 19; colonial 41, 51–64; as correctional ethos 28; and collective responsibility 125–7; and criminalization of Black women 74; and criminal legal system 39–41; "cripping TJ" 141; and death row 12, 33, 58–9; and decriminalization 151; as deterrence 57–8; and epistemic injustice 67–8; and family court 66–87; healing circles 10; Hip-Hop theory 15; implicit bias in 46; insurrectionist 15; 99–107; as judicial ethos 28; and juridical pathologies 55; just-desert 11; and kangaroo trial 14, 52–3; Kantian 42–5; as nullification of Indigenous law 93; as peacemaking 16–18; and racist sentencing 53; and racist war on drugs 29, 39, 133; reforming 133–4; as reintegrative shaming 15; relational 19; restorative 15, 118; 135, 144–8; as retribution 57–9; 2 senses of 30–7; socio-centric *vs.* ego-centric 161–4; and testimonial injustice 182; therapeutic 118; Tikanga 170; transformative 10, 16, 130–93; transformative *vs.* restorative 142–3; as vengeance 25–65
Justitia *see* Lady Justice

Kaba, M. 57, 63, 103, 144, 175
Kalief's Law 29–30
King, R. 100
King, M. L. K. 149
Kondile, C. 119
Kone, K. 138, 159
Khulumani Support Group 120
Knopp, F. 154

Lady Justice 4, 11, 17, 55–6; and ego-centric worldview 12, 30–1; and retributive justice 17
Lakota 10; accountability 181, 186; circle of courage 20, 164–7; circle of life 151, 172; class action law suit 77; healing circles 136; Iktomi 167; medicine wheel 10, 185; sociocentric cosmology 162; women 162
Lao-tzu 170, 184
Loguen, J. W. 96–7
Loick, D. 54–5, 169
Lombardo, L. 26, 138
ludic Ubuntu 3; as agonistic game 32; 55; battles in; and masking reciprocity 60–2; and circle of life 167–8; constructivist xiv; game of separation *vs.* carefree playfulness 185; and interspecies ethics 136; masks of personhood 54–5; and moral outrage 21; peace practices 187; 5 phases 9–23; play therapy and healing 176; and pretend play 189; role of laughter and forgiveness 177–84; and scapegoat 151, 156–7, 160; spiritual dimension in 173–5; and trauma informed care *vs.* healing-informed care 151–4; through performance art 154–8; and tricksters 137; and win-win games 131

Maafa 13, 90
Ma'at 11, 17, 169; and heart-based justice 11, 17, 30–1

Mack, M. 68–72
Madikizela-Mandela, W. 33
Malcolm X 152
Mama, C. 19, 126, 139–41, 181
Mandela, N. 30, 60, 111, 119–20
Marshall, J. 131, 164–7, 181, 184–5
Menakem, R. 152
Metz, T. 4–5, 44, 118, 125
Miller, L. 89–90, 93
Mills, C. 92
Moagi, L. 36
Mokgoro, Y. 5–6
Morris, R. 23, 151
Motsei, M. 53
MOVE organization 49
Movement for Black Lives 15, 189
Movement for Family Power 74, 82
Mtimkulu, S. 123

Narvaez, D. 51, 77, 144
National United Black United Front 104
Nietzsche, F. 9, 28, 122, 169, 181
Noah, T. 90, 100

Onondaga xv
Oruka, H. O. 7, 27

Pamunkey 96
Patuxent 91
Peltier, L. 28, 33, 171–2, 188
Pepinsky, H. 73, 170
Piepzna-Samarasinha, L. L. 141–3
policing: and ASFA 76–9; Black children 131; and Child Protective Services 66–87; and chokehold 48; defunding 15; and family regulation system 68; homophobia and transphobia in 106; and invisible criminalization and surveillance 66–87; and killings of civilians 39, 46, 101; and medical brutality 39; misogyny in 21; mothers 74; racism in 14
Porges, S. 176–7
prison: Abu Ghraib 28, 93; Black Consciousness activism at Robben Island 30, 36; and children 81; as 'civil confinement' 154; colonial 32; and Covid pandemic 36, 176; devolution 23; gender-responsive 37–8; Guantánomo 28; and incarceration rates 13, 63; 113, 152, 190; Malian 8, 25, 32; and persistent traumatic stress disorder 23; and post-traumatic incarceration syndrome 176; and pregnancy 19–20; Pretoria 36; Prison Industrial Complex 4; psychic effects of 27; PTSD in 19, 29–30; and recidivism 31; reform 31; silent system and separate system of 33; and slow death row 59–60, 117; and social death 32; and solitary confinement 29, 33–7, 117; and Stanford experiment 8; Taodénit 32; transphobia in 38
Prostitutes Union of Massachusetts 106
Pukui, M. K. 160
Punishment: and carceral ethics 32; and carceral humanism 13, 83, 99–107; desert 19; and Kantian ethics 42–5; as revenge 27–9; and ruse of objectivity 31; in schools 47; rethinking need for 132–3; retributivist 50, 113

Ramose, M. 4, 7, 10, 170
reparations 13, 191–3; for colonial family regulation system 13, 136; as restitution 135–6
Respons Kollektiv 150
Reznik, R. 150
Ricœur, P. 49–51
Roberts, D. 28, 72–3
Rodríguez, L. J. 175
Rodriguez, S.M. 18, 153
Ross, L. 104
Rwanda: Gacaca court 15, 110–12; genocide 16; and genocide ideology 116, 127; International Criminal Court of 111; National Unity and Reconciliation Commission 110; Organic Law No. 40/2000; and survivors of sexual assault 115; and transitional justice 16

Sachs, A. 18, 182–3
Safe OUTside the System of the Audre Lorde Project 18, 141, 153
Salah-El, T. 30, 137
Saleh-Hanna, V. 4, 23, 27, 44, 56–7, 89
Sangaré, S. 32
Scott, D. 23
Scott, J. 169
Sered, D. 144–8
settler colonialism 13, 39; and carceral structures 61–2; corporal punishment of children 77; and genocide 13, 60, 163; and legacy of chattel slavery 56; 94–9; and marooned freedom fighters

87–109; and misogyny 188; and natal alienation 80; and outlaw nation, and racist codes 88; and outlaw nation-building 15, 89–107; and penal democracy 34, 60–2; and proceduralist justice as terror 17; and racial contract 92; and residential/boarding schools 13, 47, 56, 93, 136; state violence and white supremacy 47–8; 88–107; and unnested care 20, 163; unnested care and toxic masculinity 132; Shakur, A. 19, 90, 101–5
shame 11, 22; and feelings of rejection 15; and humiliation 124, 174; and moral shaming 121; and resentment 22, 121–5; *ressentiment* 110, 121–5, 139
Somé, M. P. 153
Somjee, S. 186–7
Soyinka, W. 27
Stand Watie 90, 99
Stevenson, B. 99
Sudbury, J. 38, 108

Thomas, H. 15, 52, 177
Thuma, E. 104–6
Truth and Reconciliation Commission (TRC) of South Africa 3, 110–11, 119–29, 139; and Amy Biehl family 121, 124–5, 178–9; and just deserts 120; as symbolic judgment 15–16; as therapeutic 119
Tutu, D. 3, 5, 111, 117, 119–20, 122, 174, 192

Ubuntu: authentic 110; dance of interrelatedness 10; dignity 42–5, 94–109, 111, 162, 187; ethic of solidarity 10; and forgiveness 110; forward-looking relational ethics 5–9, 26; negative 15, 51–4, 110; politics of recognition and solidarity 10, 136; positive 15; or Utu 187
uprising, popular: Attica 103; Ferguson, Missouri 14; Haitian Revolution 96, 173; 1959 Hutu revolution 112

Villa, C. F. 35

Wa Thiong'o, N. 8, 27, 171
Wa Wamwere, K. 36
Walker, D. 90, 95–6, 99, 103
Wells-Barnett, I. 90, 98–9, 103
Wiccomiss 91
Willett, C. 2, 10, 18, 136
witnessing dance 6–8, 11, 192

Yazzie, R. 170

Zapatistas 191–2
Zimbardo, P. 8
Zinn, H. 77, 89–96
Zomnians 193

For Product Safety Concerns and Information please contact our EU representative GPSR@taylorandfrancis.com Taylor & Francis Verlag GmbH, Kaufingerstraße 24, 80331 München, Germany